MW01277612

GIFTS FROM THE
UNKNOWN

Louis E. LaGrand
Author of MESSAGES AND MIRACLES:
Extraordinary Experiences of the Bereaved

GIFTS FROM THE UNKNOWN

USING EXTRAORDINARY EXPERIENCES TO COPE WITH LOSS & CHANGE

Louis E. LaGrand, Ph.D.

Authors Choice Press
San Jose New York Lincoln Shanghai

Gifts from the Unknown
Using Extraordinary Experiences to Cope with Loss & Change

All Rights Reserved © 2001 by Louis E. LaGrand

No part of this book may be reproduced or transmitted in any form or by any means, graphic, electronic, or mechanical, including photocopying, recording, taping, or by any information storage or retrieval system, without the permission in writing from the publisher.

Authors Choice Press
an imprint of iUniverse.com, Inc.

For information address:
iUniverse.com, Inc.
5220 S 16th, Ste. 200
Lincoln, NE 68512
www.iuniverse.com

ISBN: 0-595-17869-3

Printed in the United States of America

Praise for GIFTS FROM THE UNKNOWN

If you are a human being, you will experience the death of friends and loved ones. Such experiences will be the greatest hurts – and, if worked with properly, the greatest catalyst to becoming a wiser and more loving person that you will ever have. The fundamentalist scientism and blind materialism of modern times places major obstacles in our path of living and growing here, but GIFTS FROM THE UNKNOWN is a big help in reclaiming the depth of our humanity and spirituality, with its practical advice on understanding and working with the real human experiences, such as ADC's (After Death Communications), that can open our hearts and minds. Whether you are grieving a loss, thinking about your own eventual death, or just curious about the Great Mystery of death, LaGrand's book is must reading.

> Charles T. Tart, Ph.D.
> Professor, Core Faculty, Institute of Transpersonal
> Psychology, Professor Emeritus, University of
> California at Davis, Senior Fellow at the Institute of
> Noetic Sciences, and author of the classics *Altered
> States of Consciousness* and *Transpersonal Psychologies*.

Drawing on a variety of sources and a thorough reframing of the "extraordinary," LaGrand has pioneered examination of yet another (see Messages and Miracles) little regarded, yet widely reported phenomena of bereavement experience. GIFTS FROM THE UNKNOWN is an exceptional and intriguing coping resource for mourners and their helpers everywhere.

> J. Eugene Knott, Ph.D., ABPP
> Associate Professor, Human Development & Family
> Studies, University of Rhode Island

This book is a valuable resource, which explains the great impact ADCs can have, and gives detailed methods for using them to help the bereaved. As a hospice nurse, grief counselor, and one who has experienced several ADCs, I strongly recommend this book to counselors and hospice personnel so they can understand and assist those who are concerned and/or are puzzled by their extraordinary experience.

> Shirley Scott, RN, MS, Vitas Healthcare
> Corporation

GIFTS FROM THE UNKNOWN provides an extraordinary tool for all those working with the bereaved as well as for the bereaved themselves. LaGrand's work helps validate the experiences of many bereaved individuals. His work suggests ways to use these special experiences that individuals have, to assist them in coping with loss. The professionals have too long ignored this area. The bereaved have been afraid to share some of these experiences lest someone think they are just imagining things. At last we have a book that provides meaning to these experiences, comfort to those having them, and understanding to the professional working with them.

> Dana G. Cable, Ph.D., Psychologist
> The GPT Group, Adolescent & Adult
> Psychotherapy & Counseling

To Deb and Bob

Contents

Acknowledgments

I must begin by thanking all of the people who have written or spoken to me about their extraordinary experiences (EE's). It is because of their openness and honesty that this book came into existence. I am especially grateful to those who were willing to answer questions that caused them to state their beliefs and in doing so expose themselves to the critics. However, I am confident their contributions far outweigh the risks, since they will help many others who are coping with the deaths of loved ones and experience the extraordinary.

My profound thanks to all those who read various parts of the manuscript, especially Shirley Scott, whose little green pencil brought many fine additions and some needed deletions. Also, Professor Jan Londraville, whose insightful comments have helped widen my perception of alternative interpretations of extraordinary experiences. And to Chris LaGrand, who reminded me often how important it is not to tire the reader, I extend my thanks for your persistence.

I also must thank my colleagues for their support in dealing with a topic which stirs much controversy within the counseling profession. Last but not least my heart felt thanks to my wife Barbara who allows me to spend so much time on the word processor and continues to support my efforts to bring a sense of normalcy to one of the mysteries of life.

Introduction

It is certain one soul can influence another soul at a distance…
—Camille Flammarion, French astronomer

Sheila Wedegis, an accomplished artist, had not written to her favorite aunt, even after learning that Aunt Peg wasn't feeling well and was depressed. For not writing, Sheila felt guilty, especially when she learned that her aunt had a stroke. Two weeks later, on passing a darkened window at 6:20 in the morning, she glanced at the window pane and saw her Aunt Peg, dressed in a lovely black dress with a white collar. She was wearing her favorite broach, and on her face was a big smile. Pleased at this reminder of her aunt, Sheila went on into the kitchen. "I was calm," said Sheila later, "because Aunt Peg was someone I loved very much and was someone who loved me very much."

That evening on returning from work Sheila received a phone call from her mother to tell her that Aunt Peg had died that morning at 6:20—the very moment when Sheila had glimpsed the image of her aunt in the window. At once Sheila realized that her aunt had appeared before her at the moment of her death in order to give her peace and to release her from her guilt for not writing.

This was Sheila's Gift from the Unknown, one bestowed upon her by her loving Aunt Peg (and some believe by a Higher Authority). Not infrequently, millions of people have received a similar gift of peace and comfort confident that their loved ones live on, death is not the end of life, and there will be a reunion some day. Others who have received the gift report no fear of death, comfort in knowing the loved one is whole and healthy again, and an awareness that the deceased still cares.

No matter how we speculate about these nonlocal (mind acting outside of the body) events, it is abundantly clear they do not conform to the known laws of physics. When carefully scrutinized, however, the Unknown and the unknowable is perhaps the most important part of reality and yet, paradoxically, it is hardly recognized for its contributions in living with life's changing scenes. In particular, dreams, along with near-death experiences (NDE's) and the phenomena of after-death communication (ADC's), are dimensions of reality which many people have learned not to accept as sources of wisdom and meaning.* Nevertheless, though pushed into obscurity by our hi-tech society, there is ample evidence to show that such scientifically unexplainable phenomena has had a significant impact on people around the world. This book will add to the storehouse of evidence showing that information coming from outside the sensory boundaries we are all familiar with makes major contributions to the individual who is coping with loss.

There is a tendency to forget that subjective human experience like Sheila's (commonly referred to as a crisis experience) has always been an inherent part of life, a valuable resource for decision making. It should never be trivialized simply because it does not coincide with current logic or reason. Reason becomes a tyrant when it excludes that which it is unable to readily define. Historically, yesterday's supposed illusions have a way of turning into tomorrow's new discoveries. And for the bereaved, this neglected dimension of the Unknown must never

---

* An ADC is the research term for experiences *occurring to the bereaved* involving the belief that they have received a spontaneous contact from a deceased loved one or a Higher Power. Since initial use of the term began several years ago, others have lumped a number of different experiences under the same heading confusing its meaning. Therefore, in the interests of clarity and to focus specifically on the point of view of the bereaved, in this book I will substitute the term extraordinary experience (EE) for ADC in most instances, although I will include ADC when a mourner uses it in reporting her experience.

be ignored, because the price of ignoring inevitably means unnecessary emotional and physical pain.

GETTING THE MOST FROM THIS BOOK

The book is written for those who are mourning and have experienced the gift of the extraordinary *and* for helpers—those family members, friends, and volunteers—who are giving support to a mourner who shares an extraordinary experience (EE) with them. Helper and mourner alike will be able to work together in using the book in the process of adapting to tragic loss. Both will learn to trust what cannot be proven by the scientific method, as millions of others have, and collaborate in utilizing the experience as a major resource. *Gifts from the Unknown* is also readily adaptable for use in reading and discussion groups. This is a book to be read, absorbed, and mulled over. Some ideas will "hit" you squarely the second time around.

Although the first two chapters are designed primarily for those helping someone who is mourning, the mourner will also obtain useful information from reading them. These chapters present background on grief, loss, and extraordinary experiences as well as guidelines for using the extraordinary. Chapters 3-10 provide authentic examples of extraordinary experiences of survivors who were coping with the death of a loved one and unexpectedly received information convincing them they could accept and integrate their loss into life. Following each example is a series of questions you can ask yourself, if you are mourning the death of a loved one (or you can ask the mourner if you are a family member or friend). They are designed to help the reader better understand and determine how to tailor a specific extraordinary experience to the process of adaptation and to stimulate thinking that will shed light on further use of the EE.

At the conclusion of reading each story you may think that the questions I present are moot because the subjects who tell their stories always insist that the experience has helped them, thus there is no need for probing questions. In reality, they have only begun to reap the rewards of their experiences. Further thought and consideration will surely uncover benefits that will influence their lives for years to come. The questions I propose set the stage for plumbing the depths of the experience and extracting insights and understandings far beyond the overall message obtained. Or look at it this way: If you were hungry and found a piece of your favorite fresh fruit when scavenging through your refrigerator, you would get the immediate flash that this is something that meets your immediate need. But it is not until you bite into it that the texture, exquisite feel, and sweet taste are freed to entice and fully satisfy. So too with the extraordinary experience: The initial message is only an outside covering for deeper treasures that lie within. It is not until the answers to many questions are considered that the full potential, the true meaning and range of use of the experience, is made known. Then the gold mine for relearning the world is found.

At the close of each chapter you will find a list of additional concepts to explore and develop in conjunction with the questions that follow each EE. If you want to edge closer to confronting your loss or need practical ideas to help someone else, go immediately to the sections near the close of each chapter, beginning with Chapter 3, that start with the heading CONCEPTS TO EXPLORE. Although these recommendations for coping with loss are based in part on the content of the examples that precede them, you can pick and choose whatever ideas seem to meet your specific needs or combine them with your original ideas.

If you are interested in learning how to use an extraordinary experience in order to effect a specific change (like create a ritual or finish unfinished business), go directly to the appropriate chapter after finishing this Introduction. Each chapter does not have to be read in order. On the other hand, rereading the account of an experience can bring additional ideas for using it and for developing your ability to find creative ways to implement those ideas.

It is my intention to urge anyone who is mourning or who provides support to the bereaved to become more aware of the wide range of unexpected but helpful events that constantly occur. At the same time, it is my hope that you will be alerted to the tempest of mystery in the universe and review your own history of the extraordinary. Perhaps you will begin to notice and pay more attention to the synchronicities in life, those small gifts of the Unknown that consistently present opportunity for growth, and train yourself to recognize and use these unifying events. In this way, you will be more accepting and better equipped to cope with loss or assist the bereaved in meeting the changes and challenges imposed by their losses. In cultivating the Unknown you will create a mind-set most conducive to expanding the options at your disposal for dealing with life's ongoing cycle of losses.

Let's set the stage for using EE's by first examining the types of experiences reported and one context in which they frequently occur: the grief process.

1

The Role Of The Extraordinary
In The Grief Process

There is no such thing as chance; and what to us seems merest accident, springs from the deepest source of destiny.

-Friedrich von Schiller, German playright

The Extraordinary Is Ordinary

I feel so blessed to have been chosen as the recipient for my brother's visits. He knew for a long time that I was a strong believer in after death communication so I guess he figured I would be the best candidate for his visits. He knew that I would not freak out, and that I would know the visits were genuine and real.

> —Janice S.
> On her EE's after the death of her brother

∞   ∞   ∞   ∞   ∞

"My wife passed from cancer on December 16th in

Wisconsin," said Gerald Zwolinski, a business man from Eagle River, Wisconsin. "She had so looked forward to spending Christmas in Florida as we had just bought the house on the lake. She had only been in it six weeks before we had to return to Wisconsin where I still have a business. Normally, we would spend six months in Florida and six months in Wisconsin."

"Before she died, she asked me to have her ashes in Florida for Christmas, which I did. I put them right where she wanted them. That night I was sitting on the closed-in porch overlooking the lake and really feeling down. I was talking out loud to her, asking her for some kind of sign, and crying at the same time. Time passed, and still crying and asking, out of the corner of my left eye I saw a ball of light about one foot in diameter. It wasn't like a man made light. It floated right through the concrete block wall and into another part of the house. This did not scare me at all. It was like—I knew it was her."

This plaintive description of separation of husband and wife, accompanied by a convincing sign of reassurance (light is commonly associated with transcendence and the divine), are two unfamiliar faces in the unavoidable story of separation not commonly told.

However, separation, loss, and change are never-ending processes—conditions of existence. Thus death and numerous other loss experiences occur simply as part of the human condition, not as some sinister cosmic plot unleashed as punishment or retribution. There is no choice here; death is not optional. Everyone throughout life must address, both directly and indirectly, the task of adapting to massive life-changes, especially those imposed by the death of a loved one. And it follows, each in their own way have to toil with the grief of separation.

In this regard, it is difficult for all of us to confront a most basic fact of life: All relationships end in separation and grief temporarily reigns supreme. Marriages, families, friendships of every kind, eventually come to an end. It would seem that the reality of that lifelong condition would suggest the need to prepare for the inevitable, to learn about how to deal with the aftermath of massive change. Yet little formal education is addressed to such an important repetitive process, especially at an early age when critical beliefs are formed. Nonetheless, loss and change remain as perpetual invitations to learn about the awesome features of life, mystery, and the universe. And it is the extraordinary experience that frequently accompanies the grief process, which often shatters old worldviews and ushers in a new domain of consciousness. That consciousness involves seeing the world in a more realistic way. I have visibly experienced this shift in consciousness on the death of my daughter and whenever I am with a dying person in a hospice setting.

THE EXTRAORDINARY EXPERIENCE: PERPETUAL GIFT

As sure as no one is exempt from pain and suffering accompanying the death of a loved one, no one goes through life without encountering the gifts of the Unknown in an hour of need. Everyone experiences the unexpected in some form, sometimes when mourning, at other times in vexing circumstances when least expected. *Everyone.*

Let me emphasize that those grieving other losses—divorce, miscarriage, loss of a home by fire, incarceration of a family member and so on—also experience unexpected and extraordinary events that assist in adjusting to the mortal realities of life. Like EE's associated with those mourning the death of a loved one, they can be subtle indeed: A phone call at the right time that unexplainably lifts one's depression. An unexpected visit from a friend offering temporary shelter or a new job. An inspirational reading that brings new insight to a problem. The list is endless. The point is that the unexpected and the extraordinary—Gifts from the Unknown—are pervasive in loss events just as they are in other confrontations with life. But they are commonly relegated to the bin of illusions. The invitation is often rejected in the confusion of change.

Once more, our narrow view of life minimizes the role of the unusual and the unseen and such experiences are commonly labeled with words of camouflage—like random event, happenstance, odd coincidence, chance occurrences, or synchronicities (a step up from coincidence). Others suggest they are nothing but wishful thinking, a form of self-deception, or hallucinations, and are swept aside. There is more: sophisticated terms like anomalies, aberrations, and spontaneous remissions litter the research landscape in a desperate attempt to do away with the unexplainable.

This curious discarding of subjective experience occurs because we live in a culture dominated by physical reality and scientific material-ism. When secular wisdom reigns supreme, the philosophical and the spiritual become a turn-off for many, and so too is the extraordinary experience because we are directly taught not to recognize the validity of realities that cannot be proven by the seeing-is-believing ethic. We forget that sense experience alone is not the true test of reality; our senses are inadequate for the job of understanding the full picture, even though we are told to rely on them exclusively. Nevertheless, the consis-tent appearance of the extraordinary and the unexpected, especially when one is in need, is a puzzling hallmark of life.

TYPES OF EXTRAORDINARY EXPERIENCES

Among other things, this book is designed to assist anyone in understanding the frequency and variety of unusual phenomena which are experienced by many who are mourning the death of a loved one or other traumatic losses. If you are a friend, helper or caregiver of someone who is mourning and are unaware of the perva-siveness of extraordinary experiences and their unlimited potential to aid mourners in their chaotic period of transition, you will miss a golden opportunity to bring meaning and peace of mind.

For twenty years I have interviewed, spoken to, counseled, and written about numerous individual mourners who have experienced the extraordinary. They have used it to deal with their tragic losses, reduce suffering, and live again. The study of this hidden dimension of reality is one that leads to the conclusion that it clearly helps the mourner in changing her* perception of loss and her ability to cope with it. When it occurs after the death of a loved one, it is routinely dismissed by skeptics (I use that word with reverence, not in a negative way) as the "hoped for return of the deceased" or as an indication that the mourner's thinking is clouded and disorganized. However, when carefully examined, the phenomena continues to present itself as an authentic and powerful healing tool, despite little or no encouragement from those in the support system of the mourner.

Briefly, here is a review of the extraordinary experiences of the bereaved according to eleven basic categories I have developed over the years. Let me preface my remarks by reemphasizing that they are not called up by the mourner or self-generated. They occur spontaneously and their origin is an outside source, although it will always be an issue of great debate whether they come from within or outside the mourner. One thing is clear: it is generally not an issue for the person who has the experience. But there is no incontrovertible proof in either direction, and proof is not the issue. Given this condition, I encourage you to utilize the experience to lighten the mourner's grief work.

1. The sense of presence or the intuitive experience.

Arguably, the most common experience on record, the intu-

---

* I have chosen to randomly use "he" or "she" and "his" or "her" throughout the book. Either usage includes both genders and no insensitivity is intended.

itive or sense of presence, involves the conviction that the spirit of the deceased loved one is with the mourner, who can feel the energy or sense the presence. Several people may sense it at the same time or only a selective few. Others report the sense of presence at or near the moment of death *before* they have been officially notified of the death. The intuitive experience has also been reported when a person finds herself in a dangerous or depressing situation and receives strength from the presence to deal with the situation. Here are two examples of comforting intuitive EE"s that consoled and eased the guilt of the mourner.

"I DO FEEL THEY ARE SIGNS SAYING THEY'RE OKAY"

My parents died this past year, my Mother on October 26 and my Dad November 1, just six days later. Needless to say I was very distraught. We moved to Florida last July and I was alone. Roger was working in Tampa, only coming home on weekends. I had been praying desperately for a sign that they were okay. One day, I was cleaning my mother's jewelry and I felt such a calm come over me and felt her beside me. Then, after we sold the family home in Boston, I bought a car. Feeling a little guilty, I have since felt my Dad next to me in the car, and I chat away. I do feel they are signs saying they're okay—I'm okay.

The sense of presence also occurs in conjunction with an auditory or olfactory EE.

2. The visual or apparitional experience.

Seeing the deceased loved one in whole or in part is one of the more dramatic and convincing experiences for the mourner. This can take place at the moment of death (Recall the visual experience of Sheila in the Introduction.) or any time after the death. Sometimes it occurs many years later. The deceased loved one may speak, smile, say nothing, or there may be a conversation between the deceased and the mourner. There is a long history of visual experiences in which the deceased rescues, gives guidance, prevents harm, or provides comfort to the bereaved.

Bob Rushford's four-year old son Tommy, was rushed to the emergency room in Baraboo, Wisconsin when they were on a family vacation where he died unexpectedly. A few days later he had the following experience.

THE VISION

I opened the drawer that contained the crucifix, which had been in my father's coffin at his wake, and placed it on my headboard that night before going to bed. As I started to doze off, I sensed this awesome presence like a mountain or ocean in front of me. I opened my eyes and was startled to see TOMMY off to my left. My father, who had been dead fourteen years at the time, was standing at the foot of our bed. Even though Tommy was beaming with happiness, I was frightened. So I sat up and turned on the bed light. I thought to myself, "When you and Susie {Tommy's sister} were frightened, I always tried to put you at ease, so take it easy on your old man." Then I instantly felt a little more relaxed and less panicked.

*Tommy was there to tell us he was **very** happy—and that he understood everything. Now how, one might wonder, could a just turned four-year old understand why he had to die? Then it came to me. If a little four-year old heard some commotion on the other side of the wall, and went around the corner to see what it was, he could say, "Oh that's what's making that noise."*

Then my attention was drawn to my father. He said, "I understand your impatience with mother, Bob, but remember how much she loves you. It's okay about Mr. Arvidson" (the man my mother married after my father died). Then I asked my father, "Is that on the level about Rosemary Brown?" (Rosemary Brown wrote a book in which she claimed that long dead famous composers supposedly composed music through her.) My father answered, "We're not here for that purpose."

Then back to Tommy. With a gasp, I said to my wife Peggy, "He wants us to have another child."

At first, I thought we should be careful who we told this to. They might think I was cracking up. We could tell Peggy's father, but we better not tell her mother or Aunt Jerry. We could tell my mother etc. etc. But then I decided to tell everybody because it really happened. Let them deal with it as they may.

Although extremely dramatic in its effects, the visual experience is not rare in occurrence.

3. The auditory experience.

Hearing the voice of the deceased or other sounds related exclusively to the loved one is also a fairly common event. It often occurs as a single experience or in combination with the sense of presence or the olfactory experiences. Sometimes the voice is heard as in a normal conversation, at other times it comes through as a mind to mind or telepathic communication. The latter is what happened to Kathy, whose brother succumbed to a sudden heart attack while alone in his home.

She had also been forewarned and experienced her brother in a tactile EE at the time of his death.

"HE IS ALWAYS A THOUGHT AWAY"

I had a crisis ADC when my brother Harvey died on October 26, 1997, although until reading your book I was unable to put a name to it. I have read a lot on loss and grief since my brother died and I hope being able to put a name to my experience will help me to move on.

I had been keeping a journal of my dreams the year that he died so I was alert and aware when I awoke on that Sunday that some-

one had been patting me on my left shoulder through the early morning. I was not certain who it was but I knew it was a male and I knew as the day progressed I would learn who it was. I got the call around 7:00 p.m. that evening that Harvey had dropped dead of a heart attack alone in his house. (He was recovering from the flu.) I instinctively knew it was him in my dream. He had died sometime during the early morning as his son found him in the early evening when he was in full rigor mortis.

Anyway, I had another instance of contact two days later at 2:00 p.m. when I went to say my "Good-byes" at the funeral home before he was to be cremated. He spoke to me telepathically in the room and it was the most spiritual event so far in my life. I could feel his energy all around me even though his corpse was lying on a table. He, the corpse, was no longer the brother but just the flesh that had housed his spirit. He told me that it wasn't bad at all and that he would be helping my sister and me a lot through the pain.

I am still grieving the loss and do not feel alone since his death. When he was alive he often answered my thoughts in a very peculiar way. Like I would be thinking something and he would usually "say" it. As far as I know, I am the only one of the siblings to have experienced this spiritual connection with him.

4. The olfactory or sense of smell experience.

Odors associated with the loved one may range from the perfume or after-shave lotion used to flowers or smoking tobacco. They normally appear to be present at times when there is no available source to account for the odor being experienced. The experience is commonly reported, sometimes in conjunction with a tactile or intuitive EE.

In June of 2000, in Nikiski, Alaska, Kelley Borgen's fifteen year-old son Robert, was killed in an accident when the bicycle he was riding collided with a truck. She had several experiences following his death, among them an olfactory EE that was shared by two other people.

"I NEVER IN MY LIFE EXPERIENCED ANYTHING LIKE THIS"

The night of his service we got home and my husband walked into the bathroom. The door had been shut and the fan was on (it vents outside). My husband called me into the bathroom because he could smell our son's cologne. My sister and I went in and also smelled the cologne. It was strange because the cologne we could smell was the cologne that was on my son's dresser in his room. With the fan venting outside, we shouldn't have had any odors in the bathroom. Since that evening, I've smelled his cologne on five other occasions. Three times I smelled it walking down our driveway, once at a movie theater (there wasn't anyone sitting within a twenty-foot radius of us), and another time when I was sitting in a chair in the livingroom.

Since my son has passed on, our family has experienced some interesting things. I have never in my life experienced anything like this. I didn't experience it when I lost my parents. Now I wonder if I just wasn't paying attention. I don't think I've gone off the deep end. Maybe I'll find out different at the end of the month. I've felt at times an unbelievable sense of peace.

Having since checked in again with Kelley, she told me that she has no doubts about the authenticity of these events in her life.

Roberta Allen and her brother experienced the following after the death of her father.

Several weeks after my father's death, I smelled the strong aroma of cigars, an aroma I always associated with him. I could not find any external source. This incident took place around 3:00 p.m. Later in the evening, my brother who lives in St. Charles phoned to say he had smelled a strong aroma like the talcum powder my father used. He associated this aroma with my father more strongly than cigars. This took place around 5:00 p.m. Given the two hour time difference between us, these events occurred simultaneously.

5. The tactile or sense of touch experience.

A number of mourners have reported the sensation of being touched, kissed, or embraced by the loved one. Sometimes the sense of touch is reported as being of divine origin. In any event, the experience is always thought to be real, whether in a dream visit or while the mourner is awake, because of the deep love that human touch communicates.

The first report I came across involving a tactile experience was twenty years ago. It occurred in combination with an auditory EE. A young college student shared it with me. She had returned home from her father's funeral and with all of the confusion of invited guests, decided to take a break and went upstairs to her bedroom. As she closed the door, she felt her father's hand on her shoulder, and she heard him say, "Take care of your mother."

Here is another example from Pat L., whose mother had been misdiagnosed, and eventually died from cancer after a long hospital stay.

"IF YOU ARE HERE, PROVE IT"

I have had two tactile experiences, one that I am sure was my mother. In the first, I was lying in bed, having spent a sleepless night when someone suddenly hugged me. In the second, I again was lying in bed, and this time in my mind someone was saying something but I could not understand the words. I said out loud, "It can't be you, Mom, you've been dead for years." Then I heard, "It doesn't seem that long." I repeated, "If you are here, prove it." Immediately, someone gave me a whack on the side of the head. I felt it, but it did not hurt. That was all, but I was awake.

6. Dream visitations.

The dream visit by the deceased is among the most common yet deeply comforting experience that often has a dramatic effect on the mourner. Problems have been solved, love given and received, and unfinished business taken care of. Dream visits commonly give reassurance that the loved one is whole, happy and in a beautiful place. A dream may also be part of a series of EE's that involve a vision as in the following report.

"WHEN I SEEMED TO BE AT MY LOWEST, MY HUSBAND WOULD COME TO ME IN A DREAM"

My father passed away when I was 35 years old. He died of cancer of the throat that had spread to his brain. He had lost a lot of weight and looked like a concentration camp victim. When he was lying in bed dying, he would put his hand up as if someone was holding it, but no one was there. I always felt as though one of his parents or his brother, who had all passed on, was there to comfort him.

I was very close to my father and after he died I could feel his presence time and again by this overwhelming feeling of love that would bring tears to my eyes. I also had this same feeling when my first husband passed on from three heart attacks in one day. Right after my father died, I had my mother over to my house and we were sitting talking when my dog, who was lying on the floor, picked his head up and held it just as if someone was patting him. I said to my mother Dad is here. Another time, I was lying on the couch and started to doze off when I saw my father bend over and kiss me. He was all dressed up and looked great. It was a full-bodied apparition.

Strange things began to happen after my father's death. When one of my sisters and I were little, my father would leave a dime for each of us on the bookcase in the living room. After he died we were always finding dimes. When my mother and I were in the house alone, right after he died, a dime fell on the hassock where my mother's sweater was and then fell onto the floor. When I was going to get married, the day before the wedding a hurricane hit and I was very upset because we had planned the wedding and made arrangements a year ahead. I thought no one would be able to come as the power was out. I was walking to the store to get something and I looked down and there was a dime on the sidewalk just before the entrance to the store. I thought it was my father telling me it was going to be all right—and it was.

My first husband passed away when I was 38 years old. He woke up one morning and complained of a tight band across his chest and he had a cold sweat on his forehead. I thought he must be having a heart attack so I drove him to the hospital which was only two miles away. Before we left my husband spent time patting the dog and talking to him. I was thinking, "What is he doing? We've got to get going." When I got him to the emergency room they immediately hooked him up to a electrocardiogram machine. As they watched the machine, the doctor turned to me and said he is having a coronary and then he told the nurse to take me out of the room. As I was sitting outside the room, I heard them yell code 99 and people came flying from everywhere. There were two emergency rooms and my husband was in the one off to the left and I was facing the one right in front of me. I could see part of the room and a paper towel dispenser. All of a sudden I saw a caricature of my father, just like the one someone painted of him that was in the Elk's lounge that was named after him. I thought, "Dad are you trying to tell me my husband is going to die?" My husband had two other heart attacks that day which ended his life. I always felt my father came to prepare me for his death that came later in the day.

When I returned home from the hospital that night with my husband's clothes, I was talking to my dog Lucky. I used to play a game with the dog where I would tell him to go find Papa. The dog would then run throughout the house looking for my husband. That night when I asked the dog to go find Papa, he looked at me like I was crazy. He didn't go look and he never did again. I swear the dog knew he was gone. One more thing about the dog. After the funeral I got several sympathy cards. One day I was sitting on the couch reading the sympathy cards when I started to cry. The dog was lying on the floor when he got up, came over to me and sat as close to me as he could and put his paw on my thigh. It was just like a person would put their hand on your thigh and pat you and say everything is going to be all right. It was very comforting. It was just the dog and I as I have no children and that dog was like my child. Unfortunately, I lost the dog to a brain tumor two months after my husband died.

{The following paragraph is an excellent description of the experience of grief through the eyes of a mourner, the importance of education about loss, and the need for family and friends to be so much more aware of how they can help the mourner by their presence, not by what they say. It also exemplifies that knowledge is power and that most mourners need basic information about grief when dealing with their losses. This presupposes that family and friends need that same basic information if they are to be most helpful in normalizing the grief experience.}

I had a hard time getting over my husband's death. It seemed I felt everyone thought I should be over it in a couple weeks. I thought something was wrong with me and I was going crazy. It seemed I would take two steps forward and three back. I wasn't sleeping well—only about three or four hours a night. I would find myself crying when I would hear certain songs on the radio. Things I normally would be able to do I couldn't seem to handle. I felt a part of me had died and was buried in the grave with my husband. For the first three or four months I kept thinking why doesn't he come home. I knew he was dead and wouldn't be coming home but I guess it was my brain's way of handling it. I kept thinking something must be wrong with me when one Sunday I got the paper and there was an article in there about widows and grief and how you have to go through the stages of grief and each person progresses at their own pace. After that article, I felt so much better and realized what was happening to me was normal. I learned I had to go at my own pace. I felt people did not give me the support and understanding I needed. They thought I should be over it fast. Just at the time I needed people the most they stayed away. It was as though I had a disease and they didn't want to catch it. Maybe its because people don't know what to say or they don't want to bother you, but that is the time you need someone the most. Even if it is just to sit and be there with you, it is help. Thank God for that article.

When I seemed to be at my lowest, my husband would come to me in a dream. The first one I had of him he was still in his pajamas and he said he couldn't stay long. The second one I had of him he was all dressed up and he looked like he did in his prime. He put his arms around me and said, "Remember how we used to dance?" and we danced. When he was alive, he would tell me that if something happened to him he wanted me to find someone. He didn't want me to be alone. It took me a long time to think of going out with someone else. I was only 38 years old when he died and I didn't want to spend the rest of my life alone. After a year and 8 months I did meet another man. We fell in love and got married after going together for two years. One night, I had a dream and my fiancée and I were in my bedroom lying on the bed when my father came to the doorway and looked in and nodded his head yes and winked at me. I felt my father was giving me his blessing to marry this man. All of these things (ADC's) seem to say that we do not die and our loved ones are watching out for us and know what is going on in our lives.

7. Symbolic experiences involving objects or nature.

A wide variety of objects—flowers, stones, clocks, trains, radios, pagers, TV's—to name a few, may be involved in a symbolic experience. Unusual happenings such as a tv coming on by itself, a clock starting that has long been in need of repair, a doorbell ringing and no one being there, or finding an object closely associated with the deceased, are often interpreted as meaningful signs. It may also be a rainbow appearing at an unusual time or an abrupt and unexpected change in the weather that coincides perfectly with a ritual or cemetery service. Sometimes it involves the manipulation of electricity as reported by Joanne Rossi after the death of her father due to cancer.

"I HAD NO DOUBT MY FATHER WAS COMMUNICATING TO US"

We had him laid out in his tuxedo, a handsome and charismatic man, even in his coffin. It is on our way to the first viewing at the funeral home that I say to my husband and sons, "Watch my father do something with electricity." My father's nickname on Wall Street was "Polish Lightning." As the wake commences, perhaps for about fifteen minutes or so, we begin to hear people discussing the sudden power outage. Shortly thereafter, the funeral director comes into our viewing room to ask if the electricity is functioning properly. We tell him everything is fine. He then explains to us that a car had hit a pole in front of the funeral home knocking out all the electricity on the block, including the church and school. Our electricity and the rest of the funeral home remained intact. I had no doubt my father was communicating to us, nor did the rest of my family and friends.

8. Experiences involving birds and animals or insects.

The unusual behavior of birds, animals, and insects are commonly accepted by mourners as symbols of communication that the loved one is okay. For example, doves, black birds, dogs, and butterflies have been observed in behavior that provides comfort and solace to the bereaved. The bird or animal may have been a favorite of the deceased or the appearance a sign that all is well and life can and must go on. I have heard of several EE's involving Cardinals that were the favorite bird of the deceased. They appeared in unusually large numbers in an area familiar to the deceased, but where they had never appeared before.

Here is an example of the return of deer to the home of the deceased from Debra Oryzysyn, who through the years has had several unusual contacts from her aunt, maternal grandparents, and from her mother.

"...IT GIVES ME A POWERFUL SPIRITUAL SENSE OF LIFE AND EXISTENCE, OF THE CONTINUITY OF ALL THINGS"

I have had a few "visits" from animals that made me feel a connection to my Mom. We had been staying at her house when she died, and we stayed on for a while after. We drove back out there from New York City one night, and pulled into her driveway. Her sensor lights were already on, and we saw a family of deer standing there in the snow. They were beautiful, and rather than running in fear, they stood where they were and stared at us in our car, unafraid. It was a sacred moment. There had always been deer running through my Mom's yard, and she made a point, especially in the winter, of putting out food for them to make sure they had something. She loved to watch them, and admired their graceful beauty. To this day, I believe that these deer came to her home to pay their respects to her and her family after her death.

To summarize my feeling about all of these experiences through the years, I would have to say that it gives me a powerful spiritual sense of life and existence, of the continuity of all things. I do not fear death for myself or for others (of course, I am sorry for their pain and suffering while they are sick, and I miss them when they are gone). I believe there is so much more out there if we open up to it. Also, I have achieved much resolve with people, even after they are gone.

Margaret Allwine's son took his own life. Her connection to her son through a Mockingbird is of special interest and gives insight into the wide variety of ways comfort can be found.

"DON'T GRIEVE FOR ME, JUST FINISH WHAT I STARTED"

My son always fed the birds. There was one Mockingbird he fed regularly. How did he recognize it? I don't know. But he told the story that he was on a job and there was the Mockingbird. He said, "What are you doing here? You're supposed to be at home." He said when he came home after work, there was the Mockingbird. Now I feed the birds and squirrels. Yes, there is a Mockingbird. The reason I do this is because of something I read—"Don't grieve for me, just finish what I started."

9. Third-party experiences.

A number of extraordinary experiences occur to people who are not primary mourners, and in some cases do not know the deceased, but the message received is to be relayed to the grief-stricken. Sometimes the message comes through a dream, a vision, an apparition, or an auditory experience and then is shared with the mourner. These EE's are among the most intriguing, as it is a mystery why certain people are chosen to be the bearer of such a gift. Take for example, the case of Maria Pinto (all names in this EE have been changed to protect the anonymity of those involved).

"MY FATHER USED YOU TO ALLOW ME TO RECEIVE THIS MESSAGE"

I just remember I was in bed in my nightshirt when the man showed up at the door of my bedroom. Was I dreaming? At the beginning, I was frightened a bit but then, because of his peaceful attitude, I was relieved. "Are you Maria Pinto?" he asked. "Yes," I answered, "I'm Maria Pinto." Then he said, "If it won't bother you, I would like to ask you a favor." I remained silent, waiting for his request. He continued, "Tell Leanne Bero that I forgive her," and all of a sudden he disappeared as quickly as he had come.

I woke up filled with anxiety and could not go back to sleep out of fear of meeting this man again. He did not return. Perhaps it was a nightmare. I got up, had a glass of water and tried to go back to sleep again, which was difficult to do.

All during the next day, I kept thinking about this episode because I knew Leanne Bero. We were just two teachers from the same school that see each other once a week at the teacher's lounge. And the worst part of it is that she was not really a pleasant person to be around. She used to come to the lounge with anger written on her face, greet us coldly, and go about correcting papers or preparing notes for her classes. She seemed to ignore everyone in the room. I tried a couple of times to start a conversation but she was always putting a wall between us. Because of that, it was difficult for me to face her and tell her what had happened to me.

Not many people know me as well as my sister, Sarah. After two days of holding my experience within, she was wondering what was making me sad. She thought that perhaps I was sick, since I was silent and not willing to say much. Finally, I knew I had to tell her. She did not doubt me for a second and recommended that I go tell Leanne, if I was to find relief. If it was important or not, it would then be up to Leanne to use it or let it go.

I mustered up the courage, and at the first opportunity, I faced her directly. "Pardon me," I said. "You know who I am don't you?" Surprised, she answered, "Yes, you're one of my sister's teachers here in school." "Yes, I am but what I need to tell you doesn't have anything to do with school. It's a very delicate subject that I don't want to upset you with, but I feel I have to tell you as I can no longer keep it inside." Somewhat annoyed, she said "Say what you need to say."

"The other night in a dream, a man appeared and asked me to give you a message. He said, 'Tell Leanne Bero that I forgive her." Her expression changed as she asked me what the man looked like. "He was a tall man with dark hair, moustache, and very pale eyes," I said. "He was wearing a uniform, maybe from the Marines." She handed me a photo from her purse and asked me, "Did he look like this?" I recognized him immediately and said, "Yes, he's the one."

She started crying loudly, almost shouting. I closed windows and doors in order to keep others from hearing what was going on. I rushed to the water fountain and returned with a drink of water, which she immediately accepted.

As I tried to calm her down, without asking, she began to confess to me. "I know I have a bad temper. I always have had it, and one of my victims was my father, who I never forgave a thing. One morning, I stormed out of the house, furious over some little problem. My father tried to stop me to have breakfast with the family, but I declined and rudely left slamming the door. That same day, in the afternoon, they looked for me at school to tell me that my father had suddenly died. I have lived with that pain to this day, without peace in my life. Although it is difficult to explain what has happened, I must admit that my father used you to allow me to receive this message. Thank you, thank you very much Maria, and I am sorry for not treating you as you deserve. May God bless you for this huge gift you just gave me."

From that day on, not only our relationship changed, but also her attitude to face life took a dramatic turn for the better.

10. Fourth-party experiences.

One of the most intriguing experiences that occurs involves a fourth-party. That is, one person receives a message (often it is a person with highly intuitive abilities) who is twice removed from the person who is grieving. This person tells a close friend, relative, or counselor who then contacts the mourner. This experience needs to be carefully studied by the scientific community. Sometimes it involves individuals who, in some cases, do not personally know the mourner or the deceased, yet they become a source for conveying a life changing message of hope. It may also occur within a family or among relatives.

The first fourth-party EE I uncovered was written about in *Messages and Miracles.* I repeat it here in an abbreviated form because of its thought provoking implications. It involves a mother, daughter, a bereavement counselor, and a friend of the counselor who had a very special intuitive gift. The counselor had helped the husband and father throughout his illness and up to the time of his death. Many months after his death, the counselor was celebrating her fortieth birthday, and decided to have friends over to her home for a birthday party. Among the invited guests was her highly intuitive friend, who she had not spoken with or seen for eight months. Upon her arrival, she immediately asked her host if they could be alone as she had something she had to say to her. Away from the noise of the party, she told her host that on the way over to her home she had received some unexpected information that just came to her from someone who had died awhile ago, but that she had never known. As she began to relay the nature of the information, the counselor immediately recognized that her friend was describing the very man she had counseled a long time ago. At the same time, with paper and pencil in hand, she took two pages of notes about their conversation.

Back to the party they went. The next day the counselor is at a loss as to what to do with the two pages of information from her friend. Should she tell the mother and daughter what she had heard, and from someone who had no previous knowledge of their loved one? She was in a bind. After holding the information for two weeks, she finally decided to call the deceased's daughter. They met for lunch and with trepidation the counselor told all. The daughter was ecstatic and convinced that the information was from her father for one reason: Her father had said, "Tell Ann that I approve of the man she is going to marry." Significantly, neither Ann nor her boyfriend had announced to anyone their intentions to marry, and certainly not to the gifted intuitive who they had never met. Mysteriously, the message came from the father, through an intuitive friend, who passed it on to a counselor and from the counselor to his daughter and eventually his wife.

11. Out-of-body experiences.

The OOB involves the classic encounter associated with the near-death experience (NDE), but in this instance the mourner is able to speak with or see the deceased and does not experience the conventional barrier (where they are told to go back) and other characteristics. In some instances the mourner is not sure if the experience was part of a dream or was an actual out-of body experience. Here is an out-of-body experience as described by Peggy Caine of Sylacauga, Alabama and the dramatic changes that occurred in her worldview.

"I KNOW WHEN THE TIME IS RIGHT I WILL JOIN ALL THOSE PEOPLE THAT I LOVE"

My father died in an accident when I was only five years old. That was many, many years ago. I do not remember him and I have not dreamed of him in any way. There has been no connection in any way.

Recently, my mother called me from Texas asking me if I had some papers pertaining to my father that she needed for some official reason—like the death certificate. She needed some dates: my mother is old now and gets things mixed up at times. I did not have the death certificate but I have some papers with dates on them that she needed so I told her I would get them out. I have a metal safety box where for many years I have kept important papers. That has never changed and the papers would be in that box. I went through it several times but the papers I was looking for could not be found. I looked in other places, again nothing was found. This went on for a few days. I could not think of where else they could be.

On a Monday I took off from work. I had been sick with some bronchial problems. I laid down to take a nap in the afternoon. As I laid there I felt very relaxed and began to just drift—this is not unusual for me. I could feel myself drifting and floating and very relaxed—sort of in that in-between stage of half awake and half asleep. I remember it all clearly. I was floating and it was as if I was no longer lying on the bed. I could see the universe, millions and millions of stars against a dark sky and I remember thinking how beautiful it was, so clear. (No, I was not on any medicine.) I was so relaxed and felt as though I was drifting through the universe. It was so peaceful and clear.

Then the mood changed. Things became misty-like, foggy-like. The mist began to clear and I could see people standing everywhere. Lots of people, a large group. They stood separate from each other; it was like a group of people had gathered together for some purpose, like a reunion of some sort. As I got closer, I recognized an old friend who had died suddenly in 1991. She came up to me smiling, wearing a beautiful pink dress and I started talking to her. I was saying, "Frankie, Frankie, I have missed you so much." She continued smiling and put out her hands to me. She never said a word but we were happy to see each other after all of this time. Then I turned and I could see others standing all around. Frankie stepped back. She looked so pretty, so young, like twenty years ago. She smiled as she stepped back.

I walked toward the others. As I did the group parted so I could walk between them. I looked at this one and that one and I knew them all. They were all smiling and happy looking. They were my aunts, uncles, both sets of grandparents, my sister and friends that I loved—all who are now dead, passed away through the years. I recognized them all. I remember being happy to see them and surprised at the same time. I even remember wondering what were they all doing there. One of my aunts kept trying to come up to me (Aunt Ella) to tell me something. Then she would step back. However, she seemed anxious to talk to me.

I kept walking and as I did the group moved back. There at the very end of the group was my father. I knew it was him even though I did not remember what he looked like as a child. He put his arms around me. I was so happy to see him—like a child. Then he said to me, "I have something to tell you. You have some old pictures of yourself given to you by your mother and your aunt. They are baby pictures. Remember the leather pouch where you have loose photos? There is also a small chest there. With those baby pictures you will find the papers you are looking for." Then he said, "I want you to meet someone." He turned to his right and there was a bright light, rays of light, soft and yet bright. In that light was a form of a person. It was Jesus! Although I did not see him clearly as

I had the others, I knew it was Him. It was beautiful. He said nothing to me: I just remember the wonder and glory of it all. Things began to fade and I was moving backwards. Once again my Aunt Ella came up to me a and this time she said, "Peggy, it is time to plant the tulips." My Aunt Ella lived on a farm all her life and she had flowers all over the yard all of the time. I had tulip bulbs in the refrigerator stored away to be planted later. Then I woke up.

When I awoke I lay there for a short time thinking of everything. I remembered all the details as I do now. I immediately began to think of what my father said about the papers and pictures. Then I remembered the small chest. I got up and I found that large leather pouch full of loose pictures. There was nothing else in it. I looked in the second drawer. Nothing! I began to think I was nuts. Then I looked in the bottom drawer. It was full of magazines and newspaper articles I had stuck there for whatever reason. I started to close the drawer and just forget the entire experience when I stuck my hand in the bottom. Way in the back, all covered up by magazines and junk, was an old photo album that I had long ago forgotten. I pulled it out. There in the front of it where the pictures of me when I was about 2-4 years old. Along with them were the papers I was looking for and all the dates that my mother needed. I called her immediately and gave her the dates.

I have not told her yet how I came about them. I had told her the week before I could not find them. But it was all there together, just as my father said it would be—in the exact place. I never would have looked in that chest: it never dawned on me to look there. I still do not remember putting them there or why I would put something of that importance there and not in the metal safety box. That is unusual for me because I am an organized-type of person. Everything has its place and most of the time everything is in its place.

This all happened a month ago. Yet it is all still as sharp and clear as if it happened just moments ago. Why I was given the opportunity to visit with all of the people I have known and loved that have passed on I do not know. One or two would not be unusual but everyone??? As I have said, it was like a big reunion, all gathered together to greet me. My friend Frankie loved the color pink and she often wore that color. I have gotten the tulips planted now. I did it that following weekend. I wish there were words to tell you to describe it all as it truly was—so beautiful, calming, and overpowering in ways. It was as real as me sitting in front of this word processor writing to you. I was given the opportunity to visit the after-world or whatever you want to call it. I have had experiences of someone visiting me—especially through dreams. However, I have never had an experience of me going to someone who has passed on—and certainly not everyone at the same time. They all looked happy and peaceful and there was joy among them. It was like a big homecoming party. The most important thing was my visiting my father: he has always been like a dream, no connection because I was so young when he died so suddenly. Yet, the most beautiful part was knowing that Christ was there. It was like He was sitting in the center at the head table and I knew without a doubt that He had put it all together. And the peace He radiated with love is beyond words to tell you.

I know that when the time is right I will join all those people that I love whom are no longer in the physical and it will be like a big reunion. And no fear! However, I also know what is important now is life and living it the best way we know how. It was a wonderful and beautiful experience for me and I am very thankful that I was allowed to be a part of it all and to be able to remember it well—and to be given the information of where the papers were for my mother.

Learning more about these phenomena, particularly the many variations or combinations of experiences that occur, will give you better understanding of why they have such a penetrating impact on the mourner. For example, part of Peggy's OOBE provided information that led to her finding important papers. (There are many evidential EE's where information previously unknown is made known to the recipient.) You will also become aware of a surprisingly large number of people who have had several extraordinary experiences that have brought them through their tragic losses. It is estimated that 70 million people have experienced the extraordinary when grieving. Increasing your knowledge about the variety of EE's that occur will help prevent prejudging a person who shares her experience(s) with you, thereby cutting off an important source of strength to be used in the process of grieving.

THE PURPOSE OF THE EXTRAORDINARY

Clearly, despite its shadowy unpredictability, *the extraordinary is goal oriented*—to assist, to prod, to guide, to love, to give advice, to heal, to care. *And most importantly, to give meaning to existence.* There is an organizing principle at work. Most intriguing is that the extraordinary promotes an unexpected trend toward growth and development of the individual, toward tapping into the innate wisdom of the person.

Many call the extraordinary a gift because it gives the person motivation to take a new road in life just as it causes mystery and nonphysical reality to surface and be recognized. The extraordinary, by its very nature, initiates deep introspection and an internal review of thoughts about the universe, the nature of humanity, and the meaning of life. The whole of existence is obviously more than science is capable of proving. The lessons of the extraordinary, by whatever name it is currently labeled—coincidence, illusion, or whatever—are deeply intuitive, deeply personal, non-rational to western thinking.

Extraordinary experiences (EE's) work as well, and in some cases better, than the most sophisticated treatment protocols devised by grief therapists. Just ask the mourners who have had the experience. But EE's are not either/or phenomena, either you use them or you rely on the traditional tried and true approaches of grief support. Both can and should be used.

In your pursuit of knowledge about the extraordinary, be sure to include information on the complexity of grief; it can be brief or prolonged, strong or weak, instant or delayed, seducing or distancing, chronic or revisiting, and more. Most important of all, if you are helping another, know that grief is not predictable in a stage-like fashion. There are no timetables. Yes, there are grief models showing stages of progression, but they are used primarily to study a complex human process, not to predict behavior. Like all human relationships, each mourning process is unlike any other, because we each have our own unique relationship with the deceased loved one.

SECONDARY LOSSES AND THE EXTRAORDINARY EXPERIENCE

All major losses, where there is deep emotional investment in the deceased, result in what counselors call secondary or associated losses. One not only suffers the loss of the person; many other losses are involved depending on the nature of the relationship and some of these can be as painful as the death of the loved one. They include, but are not limited to, such things as having to move to another location, loss of family income, loss of a companion, loss of transportation, loss of parental guidance and encouragement, loss of a confidant with whom to share thoughts and feelings, loss of a sexual partner, and loss of a source of inspiration. A common secondary loss, one that is often overlooked by all, is the loss of dreams for the future with the person who died (to see him graduate from college or to have gone on an extended vacation or to have built a retirement home in a favorite location). These losses need to be recognized, talked about, *and* mourned. They are a significant part of grief work.

Any friend or family member can make a critical contribution by encouraging the mourner to talk about the deceased in order to uncover as many secondary losses as possible, recognize that they need to be mourned either publicly or privately, and bring them to the attention of the mourner. It cannot be done on a single occasion; it will take many conversations to talk about and discover secondary losses. Some may not surface until months later. And the EE can be a vehicle for uncovering many of them.

Some secondary losses will not be recognized until a particular time of the year when a tradition is no longer carried out the same way or the loss is made clear because of something that used to be done with the deceased at that particular time.

As part of the mourning of secondary losses the extraordinary experience may be used to free the mourner from holding on to the implications and the pain of those losses. Here is an example from Carrie Mertes who had what she called a "semi-conscious dream" visit from her father who had died unexpectedly at age fifty.

"HE SAID HE LOVED ME"

I had come back home to visit for the first time after Dad's death and felt a little eerie going to bed. I laid awake for several hours before falling into a fitful sleep. It was during that sleep that I had my first conversation with Dad since his death. I'll call my experience a "semi-conscious dream," although it was nothing like a dream, that was clear!

In this dream I was sitting at the dining room table when I heard my Dad's car pull into the driveway. No one else was home when my father walked in the door. I knew immediately that he shouldn't be there, after all he was dead. But this was no ghost, no vision—it was him. As he walked towards me, I could make out the stubble on his chin, the crooked tooth that was visible when he smiled (a trait I had forgotten about!), and the few wisps of hair that fell to his face when he needed a haircut.

My first reaction to seeing him was fear, and I started to cry. He walked up to me and asked me to stop. Then he wiped my tears away with his big, callused hands. I spewed out a string of questions, my voice getting louder and my tears getting bigger. I told him to get away and I backed myself into a corner, sobbing. He persisted, in his gentle way, to ask me to listen. He said to me, "Carrie, its me. Its Dad." And he took my hand to his face. "Go ahead touch me, feel my whiskers, and listen to what I have to say." He continued to talk and I began to calm down. He told he had come to me because I was the "logical choice." Mom had too many unresolved feelings and was mad at him for leaving (She was!). Chris, my brother, wouldn't have wanted to believe it. Laura, the younger sister, would've run off crying the other way.

He said he needed to tell me he was okay, in a good place, and happy. He made no reference to his accident or hospital stay, except to say he was proud of the way we conducted ourselves through everything. He said he loved me, he could watch our lives unfold from where he was, and that he'd always be with us. I woke up from that experience crying. For days, I could think of little else.

Were you able to find nine messages from Carrie's father? If not, you may want to go back and reread the account. Examining the messages she has received will give hints about her secondary losses. For example, a helper can begin with asking what she misses most about her Dad. Is it his gentleness, touch, counsel, companionship, love, silent support, conversations, vacation trips, family holidays, or the confidence he showed in her? Over time, these and other losses can be recognized, talked about, and mourned.

IMPORTANT THOUGHTS

In dealing with secondary losses, a helper could expand on several of the messages that Carrie's experience presented. For example, the statements "Carrie its me. It's Dad" and "He could watch our lives unfold from where he was" might be explored for the confidence and reassurance they provide. The comments could also be tapped for their sense of long-term caring and the implications they have for inspiring her to deal with her secondary losses when they are recognized. The same could be said for his expression of love for Carrie. What has her dad taught her about coping with hardships (and those secondary losses)? How would he want her to go on with her life? Deal with the loss of his guidance? What will she do in the future when she deeply misses him at a key time in her life, like when she gets married or when she would expect him to be there for her, which are critical secondary losses?

A helper might also explore the way various family members conducted themselves through the early stages of the loss. What were the useful things they did and how could some of those same responses be used in recognizing and coping with secondary losses. The information that her father is happy, is in a good place, and everything is okay can be used as a way to confront his absence and the losses it continues to entail. If she believes he is happy, she has a good start in working on adjusting to his absence.

ENCOURAGING THE ARRIVAL OF AN EE

Many times I have been asked, "What can I do to receive a contact from my loved one?" Keeping in mind that at root the EE is an unpredictable experience, one that comes without prior warning, there is no surefire way it can be invoked. However, here are four approaches that may influence the possibility of a contact, as you will see from some of the stories in the pages ahead.

First, you can ask your deceased loved one to send you a sign, if it is possible for her or him to do so. Speak silently or out loud with your request. Some people ask before they go to sleep, others during the day at a particular time when they are alone and meditating. No one knows why some deceased loved ones make contact with survivors and others do not, although many have a pet theory to explain the difference. Second, take the time to lift your level of awareness of the ways that you may receive a sign. Not infrequently, unexpected or unexplainable events occur that are overlooked or dismissed due to inner preoccupation with sadness, anger, and emptiness that limit awareness. Or you may have been conditioned to believe that your EE is simply a part of the "craziness of grieving." Practice higher awareness by starting to notice the things that occur which bring release from suffering, give flash insights, and a sense of awe about the world

Third, many mourners have prayed to God as they know Him for a sign that their loved one is safe and in good hands. I recall a well-known writer who prayed for the simple sign of a white bird as an indication that her son was okay. About a month later, as she was sitting in his room reading, she looked out at the evergreen tree—and there was a white bird. It gave her much comfort. Some people think it is misleading to suggest that a mourner pray for a sign that the deceased is okay. But prayer is something the vast majority of Americans engage in (actually surveys show that some 80-90% of Americans pray regularly). Suggesting prayer is as normal, and in most cases as essential, as encouraging the expression of emotion over the loss. Besides there is much evidence that prayer works. Here is a prayer that you may wish to consider in praying for a sign.

Prayer For Discernment
Dear Lord, I am sad and broken at this moment
as I face the loss of _____. In my sorrow, I
humbly ask that you allow him/her to send me a
sign that he/she is okay and safe with you. O Lord,
please strengthen my faith, and instill in me the hope
and wisdom to recognize and understand your answer

in whatever form it may come. Strengthen me to be
patient in the days ahead. Your will, not mine, be
done. Amen

Last but not least, review your life for the unexpected events that
have occurred and helped you in a particular way. Try changing your
worldview to include the extraordinary as an integral part of life available to all. By doing so, you will be developing the mind-set that is conducive to replacing the ingrained cultural ethic that seeing is believing
with *believing is seeing* (think about this phrase carefully). You will be
surprised at the gifts from the Unknown that have already come your
way and will continue to unfold and brighten your days.

TO ALL HELPERS

As we close this chapter, let me remind you that if you are a helper
your education about extraordinary experiences and the grief process
will be a milestone in your commitment to your friend or relative. It
will be part of your on the job training. The more you can learn about
both subjects the more you will see them as normal human experiences
and relay that critical message in your demeanor as you interact with
the person who is mourning. That in itself will be a major contribution.

How will you respond to the call of your friend or loved one when
needed? What insights can you develop and take with you as you provide support? How can you decide what to do once you have been
trusted with the story? And what questions should you ask? We turn to
these and other concerns to expand insight into the potential of the
extraordinary experience to become a significant factor in dealing with
the long period of adjustment following major loss.

2

Guidelines For Using Extraordinary Experiences And Helping Mourners

The only gift is a portion of thyself.
-Ralph Waldo Emerson-

The Reality of the EE

*I could not have made this up. Anyone who knows me and knows both my faith **and** my mind, my theology, my love of and belief in practical logic knows that I **wouldn't** make this up.*

—Ken G.
On his EE after the death of his stepson

∞   ∞   ∞   ∞   ∞   ∞

"My father and I were always very close," said Australian native Olivia Olsen.

"Four years before he died he had a severe stroke which left him partly paralyzed, but worst of all took his speech completely. So he came to live with me bringing a few treasured possessions which included an 8-day wind-up clock that we installed on the wall opposite his bed. He loved to hear it ticking, would get quite agitated when it stopped, then would relax when I wound it up."

"However, a week before he died, this clock stopped and wouldn't go no matter what we tried. I could see it worried Dad so I went to the local store and bought him an alarm clock just so he could hear the ticking. A few days later he was hospitalized and died. Now here's the strange part. The hospital rang to say that he had died quite peacefully. I went into his room, sat on his bed, thinking about him and crying—when the clock that we couldn't get to work started ticking loudly. At the same—I find this hard to describe—I experienced the wonderful warm feeling of knowing he was there and telling me he was fine, and not to cry. I remember standing up and crying out, 'Oh Dad there is something after death.' It was so comforting and I never grieved after that, just felt happy when I thought about him."

"The clock continued to tick for another week and the atmosphere in his room was so beautiful that it wasn't only me but all the family felt it. We continued to go into his room to feel close to him. The clock stopped after a week and we have never managed to get it going again. But I will never throw it out. It is a reminder of a much-loved Dad, who although he couldn't speak, communicated after he died to tell me he was happy."

Death coincidences (DC's), two coinciding events that do not happen by chance, often involve clocks, TV's, lights, pagers, door bells or other electronic equipment that are somehow affected at the moment of a person's death. They defy scientific explanation. This death coincidence for Olivia and her family is a rich source of healthy life-affirming imagery and healing messages. This imagery will largely determine her reality with regard to her father, his life, and her relationship with him. Her experiences can be used not only in the immediate future to cope with the loss of her father, but like most extraordinary experiences can be a source of joy and family history lasting a lifetime. Consider, for example, the symbolic meaning of the 8-day wind-up clock in the years ahead and how it will provide comfort and fond memories. In addition, think of the implications of Olivia's interpretation of the event, that her father was telling her he was happy. There is much substance to her interpretation of the experience to form the basis for discussing far reaching matters of how she will live her life in the future.

Before examining guidelines for using EE's like Olivia's and providing support to those who are mourning, it is necessary to address the importance of being skeptical in our work, yet always allowing the mourner to be in charge of her grief work.

GOOD SKEPTICISM

So what's the major problem with using the unexplainable (from the scientific viewpoint) and the unseen to cope with the death of a loved one? To begin with, if you are a friend who is intent on helping a friend, you may be challenged to consider making a major paradigm shift. Or at the very least, it will be necessary to temporarily suspend your beliefs about unexplainable phenomena in the best interests of the person you are helping. Obviously, this is easier said than done. You are likely to hear some stories that border on the incredible, but for the mourner they will be as real as the sunrise. Most likely, the vast majority of mourners who share their extraordinary experience with you will be rather composed, given all they have been going through. In fact, most will be far from the stereotypical and inaccurately portrayed mourner filled with confusion, despair, and doubt as they spill out their story.

It is necessary to be cognizant of the fact that anyone who helps the bereaved is essentially a product of a culture by which they have been strongly conditioned. Contemporary society, particularly with regard to exposure to science and the scientific method, does not openly embrace nonphysical reality or consider unverifiable phenomena as real or useable. It would be an exception to the rule if some of that thinking did not influence you to second-guess a mourner who trusts you with an extraordinary experience. In some instances, your background and/or training may itself have suffered from the same lack of openness to alternative explanations (as mine did) that spawns hard core skepticism and has built a subtle prejudice against the unexplainable. But don't think for a moment that I am advocating you abandon your scientific skepticism: it is essential to keep from falling victim to superstition, magic, or the belief that we have the final word on the seen and the unseen.

But your willingness to allow the mourner to have her experience and not dismiss it as irrelevant is equally important, if you are to help her use it as another tool to adapt to the absence of the deceased. You can train yourself to accomplish this by keeping in mind that the grief process you are witnessing belongs to the mourner. And the EE is part of that grief process for many. It is not yours to distort or change based on your belief system. If you do not, you will be a major participant in the oldest form of disenfranchised grief. (Disenfranchised grief is defined as grief that is experienced where the loss "is not or cannot be openly acknowledged, publicly mourned, or socially supported.") In short, you are dictating that the mourner follow society's "grieving rules," not hers. The mourner and her convictions are and always should be the top priority. Let her grief process naturally unfold. Make every effort not to allow your intellectual needs to take precedence over her emotional needs. It is easy to lose sight of the bigger picture and quickly eliminate a major adaptive resource.

Certainly it would be helpful to keep in mind your original intention for being in the present circumstances: to provide comfort in time of sorrow. Or look at it this way. If you immediately invalidate the legitimate experience as presented by the mourner you run the risk of damaging, if not destroying, the helping relationship. After all, the mourner believes you can be trusted or she wouldn't have shared her experience with you. Therefore, be especially sensitive to how you receive what your friend or relative is sharing with you. Lapses of intensionality may occur when you become too challenged or engrossed by a particular experience. Simply try to refer to your purpose for choosing to share the pain of the mourner, and then do what is best for her. It might be good for you to hold your opinion and ask yourself the question: "What is my ultimate goal?"

In this regard, it may be helpful to know that there are numerous explanations for extraordinary experiences. They range from the supernatural—including angels, demons, spirit guides, and a Supreme Being—to scientific materialism—including illusions, hallucinations, natural causes, coincidences, and synchronicities. Naturalism would suggest EE's are an inherent part of our natural abilities. Throw in individual biased thinking, which we are all prone to regardless of philosophical persuasion, and confusion easily reigns.

One can argue that every extraordinary experience reported by a mourner has a natural scientifically rational cause. It can be likewise argued that each has a supernatural origin. For example, when a mourner says she has had a vision or seen an apparition of her deceased loved one, the common scientific response is to say it was a hallucination. Those who have the experience and believe it has a spiritual or other origin would respond with, "Phooey, I know what I saw. And by the way how does your science prove a hallucination? You are using one unproveable to explain away another."

Or they might be much more pointed as were the remarks of a 37 year-old airline captain who wrote me the following: "Like most in my profession, I would consider myself to be a straight forward, matter-of-fact individual. I do not hold any strong religious beliefs. While I have had dreams regarding my deceased parents, I have dismissed them as being products of my subconscious. In short, show me the facts…However, do ghosts and apparitions exist? Of course they do—I have seen them. Beyond that everything else is pure speculation." Acausal (undetermined origin) factors unquestionably affect the way even the most disciplined among us live our lives. It's all in the interpretative eye and feel of the beholder. We need to be guided by those who have the EE not by those who have not, yet claim to know what someone else has experienced.

Finally, if you are a caregiver or helper providing support to a loved one, consider the following: Mourners, especially those who have had an EE, are our benefactors because they give us pause to see existence in a much more awe-inspiring and life-affirming way. They provide us with opportunities to give and to grow. In many instances, they show us the meaning of courage in facing fear and pain. We discover who we in working with those who are mourning and have EE's.

How then can those providing support help a mourner achieve the lofty goals that affect quality of life? We will explore some answers in this chapter as we suggest directions and guidelines to consider in tapping the full potential of the extraordinary to assuage the sting of grief. So for just a moment, let's review some of the tasks the mourner faces that you will be able to assist with.

WHAT IS THE WORK OF MOURNING?

As British psychiatrist Colin Murray Parks and American philosopher Tom Attig so insightfully suggest, the work of the individual mourner after the death of a loved one, and I would add after a divorce and other major losses, is to relearn the world. That is, one must learn new life routines, break old habits, unlearn that which is no longer viable because of the death of the beloved, develop new skills, and look at the Self through new lenses. (I capitalize *Self* to indicate unique individual wholeness, according to Jung, and to delineate it from the ego or "small self".) In short, the mourner has to learn to live in a different world. Others have referred to all of this as "doing one's grief work" or "the work of mourning." And hard work it is. This relearning cuts across physical, emotional, cognitive, behavioral, and spiritual paths after a loved one dies. For example, Gerald, (who you met in Chapter 1) now living alone, will have to learn to cook and shop for himself, deal with loneliness, and strengthen his social ties with friends and family as a single person. These are not easy tasks for widow or widower.

Additionally important is the fact that no one can do this relearning for the mourner. You and I can be special assistants in the journey of relocation, but in the final analysis, the mourner alone makes the decisions to reach out, take on new responsibilities, and meet the daily challenges of facing the world without the requisite skills.

And while many psychiatrists and psychologists tend to promote letting go or ending the relationship with the deceased—a no win task—in reality few mourners let go. Instead they establish a healthy new relationship with their loved one, sometimes a hidden relationship, as they go about reconstructing their lives. This is a major task. They remember and cherish critical memories to sustain the relationship. Is there anyone who really can let go or forget someone they loved for so many years? The strength to go on, to work through the transition, though demanding, with a little help is within reach.

WHERE DO WE DRAW STRENGTH WHEN MAJOR LOSS OCCURS?

There is a tendency to forget that when confronted with major loss we do not turn to the scientific method, proven hypotheses, or recent discoveries to assuage the hurt and heal the heart. The "scientific facts" are farthest from our minds. On the contrary, most people consistently rely on those aspects of their human and spiritual natures that are infinitely more difficult to measure: courage, ideals, faith, perseverance, love, hope, inner strength. In short, we turn to nonphysical reality. What is most difficult to quantify and predict is at the very heart of coping well with adversity. Our scientific age has all but excluded those human traits that cannot be conveniently placed under the microscope. The result is that these imponderables are relegated to a lesser role in the scheme of coping and adapting throughout life when they should be standing at the forefront of interest in dealing with traumatic change.

Nevertheless, self-confidence and fear, hope and doubt, enthusiasm and despair, security and worry are some of the many variables that make the difference in how we deal with the trials of life. The nonphysical in all of its manifestations is just as important as physical reality is to life in general when dealing with massive change. Why? Because when a loved one dies the major part of adapting to his absence is taking an external oriented relationship and reconstructing it into an internal bond. There are many roads along which the internal reconstruction can travel: memorials, inner pictures, prayer, rituals, poignant memories, dreams, and self-talk to name a few. One source that is overlooked is through the gift of the extraordinary.

The extraordinary experience is a special opportunity to give meaning to death and *begin the construction of the internal relationship with the deceased to replace the old one.* As Carl Jung suggested many years ago, "Meaning makes a great many things endurable—perhaps everything." We underestimate the importance of meaning thinking it is some ivy tower nicety when it actually gives sanctuary and is often the difference in endless suffering or deeper appreciation for every breath we take. Let me emphasize, however, the extraordinary experience will not take away the pain of loss. A bewildering array of decisions still has to be made. The legal and financial pressures of resolving medical, housing, and property issues will still exist. The adjustment to role changes in the family, to a new environment, and finding peace-giving pursuits will still be demanded. But the extraordinary will help provide a firm base for inner strength, dialogue and stability—critical factors in dealing with all of the changing scenes of life.

Where then should you begin with the mourner who shares her EE? Begin by determining her perception of the experience and its influence or effect. What does she believe has occurred and is she happy with it? Then look for the message or messages she has received. That is, what insights she has gained. Her take should be your initial focus to better understand the impact it is having on her emotional state. In particular, the message the mourner draws from her experience is the basis for how she will later respond and use her experience to cope with the transitions that lie ahead. Teach yourself to allow the mourner to accept and present her experience by showing interest through eye contact and by asking questions. Therefore, as a primary helper, you do not need to believe in the extraordinary experience as reported by the mourner— only take advantage of the opportunities it presents.

Your first task is not to judge authenticity but to bring a nonjudgmental attitude to the helping relationship. That attitude is highly influential in the flow of information from the mourner. Later, you may want to question authenticity in the best interests of the mourner, although I have found this to be very rare indeed.

FOUR PIVOTAL FACTORS

There are four factors to be considered in using the extraordinary experience as a coping resource. These factors will shape your efforts to help the mourner in her search to find meaning in the death, integrate it into her life and find healthy ways to celebrate the life of the deceased loved one. For if the mourner finds meaning in death, it follows that she will then find meaning in life and more easily confront the specter of change.

1. The nature of the experience.

A complete presentation of the experience should be elicited from the mourner once she has chosen to share it with you. Remember, by choosing to reveal her experience to you, by telling her story, she is in fact honoring you. You are a special person in her life at this time. So make every effort to fully understand *her point of view,* especially her beliefs, values, and interpretations attached to the experience. Seeking first to understand is sound thinking in the formation of any strong interpersonal relationship, and it takes a special commitment to do so in this instance.

Study her *nonverbal communication* as she tells her story to determine, in so far as possible, the impact the experience has had and the extent of validation from you that is required. Some who have the experience, though convinced of its authenticity, have a lingering doubt that in hearing their secret the helping friend or relative may think less of them. Or worse, think that there is something wrong with them. Your initial response has to be an intuitive one, once you assess all the cues. Other people will be exceedingly clear on the meaning and message of their experiences and will leave you with no doubt about their beliefs. Of course, your own nonverbal listening behavior will provide feedback to the mourner and whether she should continue with her story or back off and stop sharing. Be encouraging and open to hearing everything that has to be said. The initial negative response to the experience, whether verbal or nonverbal, always reduces communication.

It is certainly common to ask questions such as where did the EE occur, how did it begin, under what conditions, what message or meaning resulted, how did you feel during the experience, and how did it end. Inquire with genuine interest and respect as you would in asking about any other subject being discussed with you by a friend.

The terminology you use in referring to the experience and how you respond initially has great bearing on setting the mourner at ease. It will also provide an atmosphere where she feels free to be open while revealing her deep feelings and insights about what happened. Because these experiences have profound effects on the mourner, you will be hearing very moving expressions of love, concern, and comfort.

How you refer to the story as it unfolds is another intuitive call to be made. ADC, EE, extraordinary experience, the gift, the event, the experience, the visit, the spiritual experience, are all possibilities. My own preference is usually to call it a gift, but that's in line with my belief system and the way I want to come across to the mourner in order to provide security. This is especially true when I am not sure that she is clear about my response. Again, you have to "read" the mourner, take in all the cues of your relationship with her, and choose questions and terminology as you see fit. That's part of a helper's work. In any event, your initial response should reflect great interest, if not enthusiasm, and suggest normalcy of the experience. Trust the mourner and the experience.

2. The person reporting the experience.

Mourners from all walks of life, of all creeds, races, and professions have reported EE's involving deceased loved ones. Teens as well as adults, males as well as females, the elderly as well as the very young, the rich and the poor, and the famous and not so famous, have all experienced help from unexpected sources. While you are listening to the story of any bereaved person you can begin to assess her emotional condition, the strength of her belief in the experience, and the potential it has for helping navigate the period of adjustment. There are, however, some rare potential problems you may encounter.

The first has to do with the mourner who in the past always relied on the deceased loved one when making decisions. This total reliance will probably carry over after death and the mourner will tend to respond to problems based on what the deceased would have recommended. While it is quite common for some mourners to pray for assistance from God or the deceased as part of the decision-making process, it is especially important to beware of total reliance on the deceased. Any time it appears the mourner is actually allowing the deceased to control her life ("He would insist I do this." Or, "I don't think I should do this because I know my husband wouldn't agree."), you must not be a party to this unfortunate, misguided commitment. When it is clear the mourner does very little without consulting the supposed wishes of the deceased before making decisions, it is time to seek professional assistance. **Self-reliance is an essential goal in the process of adapting to the death of a loved one, especially when the mourner has relied too much on the loved one when he or she was alive.** Recognizing this goal and working toward its fulfillment is an important contribution for any helper.

The second potential problem has to do with the obviously emotionally distraught mourner who reports seeing the deceased or having some other type of contact. The mourner who is highly agitated should be treated with great care and her reports of extraordinary phenomena should not be actively pursued until a considerable time after she has worked through this trying time, if at all. If she insists on pursuing the matter—listen. Later, when she is composed and her anxiety level is reduced, there will be plenty of opportunity to discuss the experience. As I have already said, these are rare conditions in which discussion of extraordinary phenomena should be delayed so as not to add to the distress and disorganization of the moment.

The emotional health of the mourner should be taken into account not only at the present time but also, in some situations, before the loss occurred. I am referring here to those who may have schizophrenic or other similar disorders even though they were under control at the time of the loss. Many emotional problems before the death of a loved one occurs can be exacerbated by a specific loss leaving the mourner in such a state that her powers of observation and perception are compromised. This needs to be taken into account when an individual shares an extraordinary experience with you. Needless to say, most of the individuals whom you choose to assist will not be incoherent or show disoriented or confused thinking.

3. The validation of the experience.

"Telling the story" is as old as humanity and is in itself a therapeutic plus for any mourner. It is through story that we learn, grow, create ritual, and pass on traditions throughout life. Accepting and validating experiences in the story of another is a critical relationship builder as well as a source of healing. In almost all instances, validation of the experience should occur when you are responding to the initial telling. The primary reason for this is simply that in most instances the mourner, in telling what happened, is convinced of the reality of the experience beyond a shadow of a doubt, or believes but is looking for your approval that her convictions are sound.

In some situations, you may have to reassure the person there is nothing wrong with her. She is not insane or "going crazy." Indicating it is a well-documented common experience for millions of bereaved people should be part of this normalizing process.

Once you understand the way the mourner perceives her experience you can begin to communicate by reflecting back what you have heard. The way you do this can be most comforting. If the person shares an experience in which she interprets the deceased as being whole again, or healthy and very happy, you can respond with something like, "I'll bet you can picture your Dad in his plaid shirt and khakis walking in a beautiful wooded area like he used to do." Or, "I'll bet you can see your father brimming with energy and having a great time with his parents or your uncle who have welcomed him." As warranted, include reassuring statements like, "This must have brought great feelings of being near your loved one" and "Your experience must bring a sense of relief and a feeling of an ongoing relationship that will never die." With some thought you can create various word pictures to highlight the positive aspects of his new life based on the beliefs of the mourner. This is also a time when a remark like, "What a beautiful memory of love this experience has provided" can later be recalled in using the experience as a coping tool.

Feedback of this type begins the process of validating the experience as well as reinforcing strong memories for later recall and use when the mourner is graphically reminded of the absence of the deceased. Emotional word pictures are potent sources of empowerment as well as motivators for coping with change. You can use them to clarify what the mourner has said about her experience ("You see this beautiful experience as saying your Dad lives on in a pain free existence surrounded by loved ones who have gone before him."). You can use them to point out the power of love ("Even after death your Dad is showing that he loves you very much and deeply cares about how you and your mother are doing."). Or they can be employed to honor the deceased ("Your brother's concern for you and your daughter is much like the parents who are very concerned about their adult children even though they are married and out of the house.")

Allowing the mourner to own and cherish her experience opens the door to the infusion of energy it provides while making it a source of strength to call upon in the years ahead. You are helping her make sense of her experience. Let your heart be your guide in this effort.

4. Choosing to use the EE.

Now that you know the extent of the experience, are convinced of the credibility of the mourner, and if necessary validated the EE, it may be time to discuss how to use the experience to deal with the loss. I say it "may be time" because each situation will be different and you may sense it would be best to discuss this subject after a significant event like the memorial service or a coming anniversary. The next time could be when the mourner brings up the subject or when you sense it is appropriate.

Deciding how to integrate the experience into the coping repertoire of the mourner calls into being the need for a variety of choices with the predominant responsibility always in the hands of the mourner. In fact, the single most important factor in the use of any EE must be the mourner's beliefs about her experience. Most mourners (and helpers) are not aware of the wide array of choices one has in using the unexplainable as a resource for doing grief work. After seeking input from the mourner with regard to how she would like to use the experience, it is appropriate to ask questions that provide additional choices to be considered. (Examples of the types of questions to be asked are found after each EE under the heading QUESTIONS TO BE POSED in the chapters to follow.)

HOW CAN YOU HELP THOSE WHO ARE MOURNING?

The need for support when mourning the death of a loved one, or any other major loss, has never been more critical than it has become in modern times. This is the result of an increase in many more deaths that are sudden and unexpected, leading to a corresponding increase in complicated mourning, in which the normal phases of grieving are compromised or denied legitimate expression. Add the fact that there are numerous survivors who were overdependent on the deceased or are presently overdependent on family members who are poor grief models, and the demand for a patient, persistent, and understanding helper becomes essential. It is also not unusual for us to forget, if not understand, the sense of loss that can be felt by one individual when a loved one dies and the relationship between the two had been one of deep honesty and mutual commitment.

This brings us to a most critical understanding: there is a tendency to downplay how powerful a friend, family member or volunteer can be in the supportive relationship. Our emotions and manner of relating to the bereaved can have a subtle but very influential impact on the mourner. That influence seeps through our exterior, though we are unaware of it, and is felt in full force by the mourner. Our matter-of-fact or loving manner, our trite or gentle responses, will be sensed and carried by the mourner in her journey through grief. In other words, relationships of dominance always hinder the healing process, while relationships of equality foster growth through loss.

Just remember the power to persist and heal that your presence alone brings. Presence is needed at key points throughout the grief process, what C.S. Lewis called "the circular trench." This metaphor is an important learning tool as it highlights a major characteristic of grief: the reappearance of feelings that the mourner thought she had overcome and left behind. It is during this return, this coming back to a place the mourner thought she had passed and left behind, where the helper's presence plays a major role.

Where can one begin the task of providing the care and consistency that assist the bereaved through a critical transition period in life? Arguably, one starts with an awareness that the grief process is not time bound and, therefore, a helping friend or relative has to make a commitment to walk with the mourner at her pace and for the period of time which her individual style of mourning dictates. This is easier stated than accomplished. It could mean many weeks, months, or years of visits and phone calls, something not commonly understood by the general public. Many mourners are abandoned before their major work of adapting ebbs because their support persons tire and believe positive change should occur more rapidly. It cannot be overemphasized that consistency is the secret of serving with effectiveness. Being there for a mourner is the key element in providing support through any loss experience. Deciding when to talk and when to listen, the latter being incredibly more helpful, is a very sensitive issue that has to be constantly monitored. Your presence, your pain tolerance—not your words—says it all.

Or look at it this way, the mourner needs to feel safe in your company since most mourners have feelings of fear fed by emotions they never thought could be so volatile. Consistent unconditional presence and respect meets that basic human need, especially in times of loss. You can help the person find her own truth in the most trying of circumstances.

GROWING THROUGH PAIN

Regardless of your station in life, or your training, there are three things you can do to help any mourner grow through the pain of loss. You do not need a graduate degree to do this. You do not need to have had experience with other mourners in order to provide these important services. You only need to be willing to be yourself, free from all pretense. (1) Talk and listen endlessly about the deceased loved one when the mourner feels like talking. This is time demanding but exceedingly important. (2) Encourage the mourner to allow her emotions to surface by your verbal and nonverbal behavior. (3) Make frequent contact with her according to individual circumstances, yet always respecting her need for privacy. Let's look at these in depth.

1. Talk about the deceased.

While in the presence of the mourner it is critical that you provide opportunities for her to review her life with the deceased and encourage her to talk about him (or her). This life review can be facilitated with simple questions like, "When did you first meet Bill?" or "When did Martha first start feeling ill?" or "Tell me about your Dad." If you were giving support to Gerald after he told you about his EE involving his wife, you might ask him "When was it you and your wife talked about the disposition of her ashes?" If the mourner is ready, and wants to talk to you, the opportunity has been provided. Then you must be willing to bear the discomfort of seeing your friend or relative express her excruciating pain. This will be far more difficult than anything else you have to do, but it will also be the greatest test and a testimony of your love. Be with the pain of your friend. By sharing it you will have helped in its reduction. Teach yourself to be around pain—and this can be done—and you will possess the skill of a lifetime.

Also, be ready for repetition of the painful event, even the retelling of the same stories over and over again. Repetition is critical to reconciliation for the mourner because it allows for the gradual release of deep emotional bonds with the deceased. This release is part of a major task of mourning—accepting the death of a loved one—and you will be giving much more than you realize by listening to the replay of pain.

2. Encourage the expression of emotions.

Not only must you readily accept the repetition of pain that seems never ending, it is incumbent upon you to encourage the expression of tears as emotion surfaces. The word *encourage* means "to inspire with courage." Although tears naturally accompany a discussion of the relationship between the deceased and the survivor, it often takes courage to openly allow them full expression. But it leads to a healthy outcome, one that will eventually result in healing. With this insight you will be able to help the mourner face the inevitable pain of loss, not run or hide from it. In Chapter 4 you will learn how to use an extraordinary experience to initiate life review that often leads to needed emotional expression.

Know that although discussing the relationship with the deceased is a painful process, it is essential to the final acceptance of the loss. Final acceptance does not mean liking the conditions one must live with, it implies not experiencing distress and discomfort when thinking of the loved one. Too often the mourner is influenced to circumvent grief by keeping busy, trying not to think about the loss, or by the subtle remarks, "you're doing so well" or "you're looking good." Such remarks force the mourner to keep her pain inside instead of bringing it out and facing it. Later, much later, as the mourner clearly progresses in her grief work you will have ample opportunity to note her growth with a comment like, "I admire your persistence and strength."

Remember, no matter how many losses you have personally grieved, you cannot know how the mourner feels, even if several of your losses were similar. You can only imagine the depth of sadness, fear, and despair. Most important of all, keep in mind that it is difficult to love when filled with pain. This is where you can make a significant contribution. Through your example, you will remind the mourner of the supreme importance of love. You will be a reminder of goodness that leads to peace. How? By consistently relating to the mourner with gentleness and tenderness. Love is kind. You never fail to convey love to a mourner by what you do. Thus your nonverbal behavior—physical touch, facial expression, gestures—will say so much more about your caring than what you say. For example, a hug at a time of crisis is perhaps the most powerful communicator of caring and will be long remembered by those in mourning. More importantly, it will make strong the emotional lifeline every mourner needs.

3. Make frequent contact.

Talking about the deceased and facilitating the expression of emotion is a beginning but only a beginning. Much work has to be done by the mourner to fit the death into her worldview and change her view of the world. Thus, as stated earlier, by its very nature the helper's support of the mourner must be a long ongoing commitment. This means being aware of the worn conventional view that grief is a two-week job that is quickly assimilated and then the mourner "becomes her old self again." In reality, she will never be her old self again, nor will she be over it in two weeks. This devastating assumption usually causes the abandonment of the mourner when she does not follow the societal script calling for the rapid resolution of grief. Knowledge that the length of the grief process varies with the mourner and is always longer than what the general public is led to believe, is strong motivation to develop a consistent ongoing relationship as a helper.

Your frequent contacts with the mourner will create the feeling that you are dependable and can be trusted. But a far more important contribution will be the safe environment you provide in your relationship. The mourner will need to feel that she can find a haven in your presence without having to be on guard in the way she conducts herself. This will be especially relevant months later when other friends and neighbors have assumed she is doing so well and no longer inquire about how she is doing. Over time, you can gradually try to draw her into a social set-ting to give her respite from her grief, a dinner out, a trip to the mall, or perhaps a movie. Mourners often initially reject these overtures in a misguided belief they would be demeaning the memory of the deceased by engaging in such behavior. Let it go and try again at a later date. In the interim, when the time is right, gently point out that the energy demands of grief are enormous and giving oneself a break from the stress of grief will partially restore needed energy to deal with it.

Your knowledge of the grief process and the fact that it often carries with it pervasive feelings of fear, loneliness, disorganization, and confu-sion—that come and go like the ups and downs of a roller coaster ride—will help sustain you in your attempts to give comfort. Your understanding will be reflected in the attitude you take when a sugges-tion you make is not heeded.

∞   ∞   ∞

TELLING FAMILY MEMBERS AND FRIENDS

Sharing the extraordinary experience with others is another impor-tant step for the mourner. However, it may sometimes lead to conflict resulting in added pain when a listener rejects the experience out of hand. So when should the person tell others, and when should a sup-port person encourage the mourner to do so?

Obviously, the nature of the relationship between the mourner and whomever she wants to share her experience is a key factor in the process. If she enjoys unconditional trust and has shared her intimate thoughts in the past with the person, the odds are good she will not be embarrassed or challenged in a hurtful way. Some individuals have told their husbands, wives, or family members immediately after having the experience with full confidence they were doing the right thing. Others have taken time to decide on the next course of action. Here are some suggestions you can relay to the person who wants to tell others what has happened, yet is fearful of the potential consequences of rejection.

First, if the mourner is distraught or having a bad day, especially down, recommend that she wait until she is composed, able to clearly present the experience, and answer questions and minimize misinterpreting the response of the listener. Second, if the potential listener is also a primary mourner close to the deceased, it is important to be sure that she is not feeling depressed or in a state of mind that would hinder communication.

Thirdly, suggest presenting the experience in a low key, matter of fact way to reduce the possibility of the listener misinterpreting the emotional state of the mourner. For example, "You may think I've lost some of my perspective, but I just feel I have to tell you what happened to me last night." Or suggest beginning from the neutral or third-party point of view with, "I'm sure these things have happened to others who were grieving, and maybe they are figments of the imagination due to the confusion accompanying grief, however, last night…"

Once the experience has been relayed it is entirely appropriate for the mourner to ask the listener to respond by simply saying, "What do you think?" Depending on the answer, particularly if it is noncommittal, the mourner may have to ask the listener if she needs time to think about it. Of course, it can also be interpreted as a polite rejection. In any event, the mourner has the option to invite the listener to ask questions regarding details or meaning of the experience. Through all of this the mourner will be reading the nonverbal communication of the friend or family member. What is important to emphasize here is that finding additional validation is especially useful in dealing with the grief process when one believes the extraordinary experience is indeed a sign or a message. If by some chance that validation and the inherent encouragement it contains is not found within the family, then suggest to the mourner to look for it elsewhere. In addition, make it clear that when anyone says things that differ from the norm, you have to expect there will be dissenters. It strikes a nerve and upsets their narrow view of reality.

ASK THE RIGHT QUESTIONS

A major difference between outstanding helpers, volunteers, caregivers, or friends and family members providing support and the not so outstanding ones is *the ability to ask the right questions*. Those who ask the right questions help mourners find their own answers that can be used in problem solving, answers that the mourner already possesses deep inside, and answers the mourner can live with. Asking the right questions is as much an art as a science and calls everyone in a support position to possess a deep respect for the ability of the mourner to ultimately find her own solutions to implement in adapting to change.

Obviously, questions about extraordinary experiences must be based on a thorough understanding of the particular experience under discussion as well as some insight into the phenomena in general. The way the mourner tells the story, the details or lack of details provided, the apparent parallels to earlier life experiences with the now deceased, and your intuitive creativity all play roles in the formation of questions.

USE LEADING QUESTIONS

In framing questions to ask the bereaved, presuppose she has the inherent ability to cope well. Most individuals are able to adapt, if they have some caring support. Also, focus questions primarily on what can be accomplished and the implications of the extraordinary experience. Help the mourner search for ways to integrate her experience into her coping repertoire. The more you demonstrate through your questions that it is inevitable the mourner will make it though her difficult loss, the more you will help her. This means instead of asking, "Now that you have had this EE, do you think it will help you deal with his death?" try "When will you know you are doing better, now that you have had this experience?" or "How will others know you have begun accepting the death of your mother?"

In the first instance, you are likely to receive either a "yes" or "no" answer. In the second, you are implying the mourner will eventually cope with her loss and you are causing her to do some additional thinking about her progress. This expectation will encourage her to recall and reinforce good feelings and thoughts she already has as an outcome of her extraordinary experience. She can then consider direction—specific behaviors to employ in the process of adapting. Or you may want to pose the following question: "What will you take from your extraordinary experience into your new life to sustain you?" In this instance, by your question, you have introduced the concept that the mourner has to begin a new life without her loved one (a concept not easy to deal with) and get her to think about how the experience will aid in the transition. Based on her answers, you can help her identify needed changes in behavior and alternatives to explore. Once the mourner chooses to share her experience with you, the stage has been set to talk about *anything* relating to the grief process.

Here are some additional standard questions to help the mourner realize she can cope with her loss and deal with the pain of separation. Rephrase them as necessary so you will feel more comfortable in using them.

* "Who will notice that you are more accepting of your son's death now that you have had this experience?"
* "How does your EE convince you that your loved one is no longer in pain?"
* "In what ways will your behavior change for the better because of your extraordinary experience?"
* "How are you more effective in dealing with the lonely evenings as a result of your extraordinary experience?"
* "What will you do to demonstrate your conviction that your father is happy and at peace?"
* "How will your loved one live on in your life?"

As you can see, the above are open-ended questions that demand some thought instead of a quick short response. Develop your skills in asking open-ended questions and you will have a more effective way of helping the mourner discover her inner wisdom.

If you sense that the mourner has been immediately comforted by her extraordinary experience, a common occurrence, ask, "What is better or different since you have had the experience?" The underlying supposition here is: The experience you have had has been useful in adapting to the loss of your loved one. In addition, asking, "What would you like to do with your experience?" implies that it is a resource and gets the mourner thinking about how it can become a further source of comfort. Follow up with, "When will you start to use your experience to help you cope with Joe's death?" This suggests the mourner will cope with her loss, that the EE will be part of the process, and that she is the one who takes action when she so chooses. After her response, you might continue with, "Will you include some of your family or friends in the way you use the experience?" Leading questions provide for breadth and depth of thinking and strengthen the sense of validation in the mourner.

USE OPEN-ENDED QUESTIONS

With minor changes, you can use the questions listed after each EE whenever you encounter a mourner who has shared similar experiences, or you see a particular question as having relevance to enhancing a part of her grief work. It is not necessary to ask the specific questions you find in each chapter; use them only as a guide. Each experience is highly individual and questions must evolve from that particular experience. It is likely you will have to ask more of your own making. Obviously, the experience you are privy to hearing will suggest the creation of many specific questions that will only evolve after you hear the mourner's description of the event. Use your judgment and knowledge of the mourner in fashioning your list. Much depends on the four pivotal factors previously discussed and your ingenuity in assessing the quality of your relationship with the mourner. Then you must decide if it is the appropriate time to pose a specific question.

As a general rule, try to stay away from questions that can be answered with a "yes" or a "no" when your goal is to suggest growth-producing courses of action. I know that is easier said than done, and you will find a number of "yes" and "no" answer type questions in the chapters to come; some are inevitable. But you can gradually develop the skill of asking open-ended questions and in the process stimulate critical thinking. Work on developing the ability by starting with how you address your friends and family members with common questions. Instead of "Did you get a good night's sleep?" try "How was your night?" or "How did your night go?" Instead of "Hi, how ya doing?" substitute "What kind of a day are you having?" or "How is your day going so far?" You not only will get more of an answer, you'll also be showing greater interest by avoiding the expected inquiry, and you'll be developing an important helping skill.

Like the acquisition of any skill, it takes trial and error learning. Be prepared to receive answers to questions that are not expected when you decided on a particular course of action with a mourner. Everyone makes mistakes. That's how we learn. So don't let initial failures get you down.

One final note. Do all mourners need to work on all aspects of the topics in the following chapters? No. Some may have to work on restructuring their identity or finishing unfinished business with the deceased. Others may need to build their memory bank to establish a new relationship with the beloved. Some may only need to use their experience as a warm reminder of the beauty and goodness of their loved one. As time goes on, what is required will begin to emerge. Then the mourner, with your encouragement, can begin to put together an approach to utilize her experience as part of the road to reconciling her loss. This is where you can help in designing a strategy that leads to the acceptance of her loss and the rebuilding of her life at her own pace.

Let Emerson's insight, which opened this chapter, always be your guide, "The only gift is a portion of thyself." Your gifts of empathy and encouragement, entering into the feelings world of the mourner, are needed skills to refine and they will demand humility and perseverance mixed with faith in the mourner. Be assured, they will be the most important visual gifts of love you can deliver. *Every person*, whether mourning or not, needs encouragement as much as they need the basic necessities to sustain life. It is needed in the right dose, at the right time, and delivered in the right way so that it does not sound hackneyed and trite. Encouragement can change the way the mourner functions and the limits of her world. Psychiatrist Rudolph Dreikurs couldn't put it better when he said, "We constantly encourage or discourage those around us and thereby contribute materially to their greater or lesser ability to function."

We turn now to examining the many ways the extraordinary experience can be used in managing traumatic change and learning new behaviors in the quest to adapt to major loss. The focus is on the foundation for successful management and new learning that dictates all coping behaviors: personal beliefs.

3

Using The Extraordinary To Strengthen Beliefs

What does not destroy me, makes me stronger.
-Friedrich Nietzsche-

The Power of Subjective Experience

I was a lifetime skeptic. I did not believe that communication with the deceased was possible. I now believe my son did communicate with us.

—Paul L.
On a series of EE's after the murder of his son

∞   ∞   ∞   ∞   ∞   ∞

"I had been raised born-again Baptist," a Public Defender wrote to me. "At a young age, I gave up religion and proclaimed myself an atheist. I had been reexamining those philosophies prior to Jerry's death, but the ADC's have persuaded me that death is not an end, but a new beginning. I also feared my own mortality. Now, although I have no desire to leave this life because I am nosy, I do not in the least fear death."

"The events that happened shortly after Buddy's death made me even more aware of life after death," said a nurse with fifteen years experience. "They have certainly made my beliefs stronger in the fact. Because I was raised in a loving and caring Christian home and have cared for the needs of dying patients with compassion, I was able to evaluate the "clues" surrounding the curious events shortly after his death. My experiences reassure me that Buddy is still living, although in a different dimension."

A mother whose daughter died unexpectedly wrote, "I never expected any of these experiences and I was so surprised when they happened. I'm very open to the spiritual realm and the reality of it, but this was amazing to me. Without a doubt all of my beliefs have been strengthened beyond my comprehension. For the past few years I've been questioning my basic beliefs, but now I know that if these things happened to me, I can believe that God is capable of anything and is all powerful."

Notice the degree of belief-backed certainty in the above statements, a characteristic of encountering the extraordinary. All of these individuals, having experienced unexpected phenomena in relation to the death of a loved one, underwent profound alterations in beliefs with long-term implications. This happens every day somewhere to someone who is facing the aftermath of loss. Because change is constant and ongoing, everyone has to adapt by taking new paths including reevaluating beliefs about the seen and the unseen. The aftereffects of an extraordinary encounter commonly precipitate shifts in attitude, beliefs, behavior, and the associated changes in routines and lifestyle that ultimately assist in adapting to the death of a loved one.

WHAT DO YOU BELIEVE TO BE TRUE?

Anyone interested in helping others use hard-to-explain experiences as a source from which to draw strength in coping with the death of a loved one—or the changes demanded by loss—must begin by taking a serious look at their own beliefs about the Unknown. Where did they originate? Who or what continues to influence those beliefs? Most of us are born into the beliefs we hold. Consequently, it is inevitable that family members and relatives play a major role in influencing perceptions of extraordinary experiences. How has your family affected your life choices? Were alternative beliefs ever discussed? Or did you just have to accept the party line? Irrespective of the origin of your beliefs, the influence of the Unknown is lifelong, for we all continue to experience mystery and unexplainable phenomena whether we want to or not. These experiences can be discarded, overlooked, deliberately ignored, or ridiculed. Or they can be viewed as an unknown asset to raise consciousness and make inroads on the illusionary beliefs we all live with.

In *Honey from Stone,* science columnist and professor Chet Raymo uses an intriguing metaphor borrowed from a friend to explain the present state of our knowledge about the universe and everything in it. "Knowledge," he says, "is an island in a sea of inexhaustible mystery." The more we find out, the more we discover, the more mystery we encounter. Small wonder that ultimate and complete explanations are hard to come by in science; there is always constant revision. We are engulfed by mystery as we dig for answers. That does not mean we should stop digging. There are no final answers to the big questions about life and the universe that science can stand by with incontrovertible proof. The scientific community constantly revises its position.

This alone is reason enough to challenge our beliefs and be open to the possibilities of other realities that are growth producing. Each of us believes that our perceptions of the world are the way life really is, just as those in other countries have learned and are convinced that their view of the world is the correct one. Should we not say here that there are as many viable realities as there are people? Is not the journey the true destination? The wisdom of the ages tells us again and again: We all have our own unique path of development.

BELIEF CHANGE AND THE EXTRAORDINARY

Let's pause for a moment and look at an EE and the dramatic impact it had on the belief system of a sociology professor when he was able to find validation and share the meaning of his gifts. His beliefs were not only changed but he was able to rid himself of the haunting thought that there was something wrong with him, because he had experienced the extraordinary. This is a good example of the need for being open to these experiences and the influence for good they exert on the bereaved. I insert it here to emphasize how prejudice toward the Unknown can take a damaging toll in unexpected ways.

"THANK YOU FOR REAFFIRMING MY BELIEF THAT LIFE AND LOVE ARE ETERNAL"

*I have just completed reading your book **After Death Communication**. It's one of the most valuable books that I have ever read as it assured me that I have not been slowly losing my mind during the past four years since my girlfriend SHIRLEY passed on to another life due to cancer at the age of 38.*

About a month after SHIRLEY passed on, I stopped to visit her gravesite. As I stood there contemplating the good times we had together, a huge Raven (?) swooped down and slapped me on the shoulder with its wing. After several annoying slaps, I moved away from the grave. The raven didn't bother me. However, as soon as I started to approach the grave again, the Raven swooped down for further slaps. (Birds occasionally do this to protect their eggs or their young but these attacks occurred in August—long past nesting season.) After about a half dozen slaps on my head and shoulders, I heard SHIRLEY'S voice whisper in my ear: "You just don't get it, do you? I'm not here. Go home." I drove home and had my first olfac-

tory ADC—my kitchen was permeated with the smell of garlic—one of SHIRLEY'S favorite cooking ingredients.

Another experience that helped me had to do with one of SHIRLEY'S favorites, the ladybug. In summer, she was constantly surrounded by them. One day, while SHIRLEY was in the hospital, she told me that she would send me ladybugs to let me know that she is thinking of me after she passes away. Since that time, I have received a ladybug on my birthday for the past four years as well as a few other times regardless of whether I'm in the car, the classroom, in a restaurant or outdoors.

My birthday, two years ago, is especially memorable. I was feeling quite depressed and lonely that day so I decided to distract myself from my misery by shopping for some trees and shrubs to plant in my backyard, as I just moved into my new home and the landscaping was not yet complete. I made a list of what I needed and headed out to the tree nursery. I walked around the nursery like a lost puppy wishing that SHIRLEY could be with me to help me select the plants that I needed. She was passionate about horticulture and knew much more about picking out the best trees and shrubs than I did. As I was wandering through the nursery and feeling very sorry for myself, I spotted a ladybug on one of the trees—and then another one. If I had four rosebushes on my shopping list, only four of the rosebushes in the wide selection had ladybugs on them. I needed one apple tree. Only one tree, out of perhaps a dozen to choose from, had a ladybug on it. And so it went for the rest of my list. SHIRLEY came through to assist me after all.

I have also experienced an ADC in the form of a hug similar to the type mentioned in your book. I think of this hug as an "Angel Hug" since that was my pet name for SHIRLEY while we were seeing each other. The euphoric feeling that the hug generated cannot be described in words. Thank you for reaffirming my belief that life and love are eternal.

Everyone needs to be affirmed, and in this case the affirmation has long term implications.

THE POWER OF BELIEF IS ENORMOUS

The great Russian short-story writer, dramatist, and physician Anton Chekhov wrote, "Man is what he believes." Belief is the most powerful force in directing our lives. There is considerable research showing that beliefs make us well or make us sick since they affect every aspect of our emotional and physical well being. Because the power of belief is the bedrock of all coping efforts, it is of critical importance for mourners to find reassurance from others when they experience nonphysical reality and ponder its authenticity in the pull of scientific conditioning. Extraordinary experiences are teeming with possibilities for helping mourners change their perceptions of loss and their beliefs about their ability to deal with it, just as it did with the sociology professor.

Specifically, we can suggest that through the EE they have an opportunity to use a special resource to see them through a painful transition in life. In this vein, be prepared to normalize the experience by pointing out well-known individuals who have used their encounters to find meaning and deal with their losses (Taylor Caldwell, Winston Churchill, Norman Vincent Peale, Charles Dickens, etc.). Also, be prepared to suggest specific books and articles for the mourner to read. In the effort to help validate the occurrence of the EE it is important to recognize its universality.

Beliefs solve innumerable mysteries and ultimately provide meaning to bring a gradual halt to the pain of loss. The affirmation of the professor's experiences brought him much comfort and empowered him with beliefs that changed his view of himself, his inner life, and his relationship with his deceased loved one. Imagine, if you will, the staggering implications of believing that life and love are eternal. Anyone can deliver that same powerful affirmation to another who experiences the Unknown, regardless of the type of EE that presents itself. And additional perceptions and beliefs can be introduced to give structure to a new view of reality. In a practical vein, the professor's experiences have broadened his coping repertoire—which all EE's do—giving him choices he had not previously had in dealing with his suffering. Supporting his belief that life and love are eternal will provide a catalyst in his attempts to bring balance back into his life and deal with future loss experiences.

SHEDDING OLD BELIEFS ABOUT THE EXTRAORDINARY

If the professor's experiences strain your credulity, or the words "psychical" or "paranormal" touch a raw nerve based on the expected conditioning you have been subjected to over the years, tackle that obstacle head-on. Recognize how reductionistic thinking (thinking that reduces everything to measureable physical causes we are all prone to employing) limits awareness that an unexplainable event can have a positive impact on the person who has the experience. What can diffuse the intensity of the scientific pall that covers the Unknown? What can open the possibility for unexplainable phenomena having a place and purpose in the universe? I too have had to deal with the stigma of cultural conditioning, so let me tell you what helped me. It may help you.

Perhaps you can begin to find answers by reading about the variety of scholars and well-known people, past and present, who have left the door open to the possibility that nonphysical reality is as meaningful as anything that can be seen. Study the remarks of William James, physicist David Bohm, Thomas Edison, psychologist Jule Eisenbud, writers Upton Sinclair and Elizabeth Barrett Browning, atronomer Sir Arthur Eddington, biologist Alexis Carrel, Nobel Prize-winning French physiologist Charles Richet, the renowned Mark Twain, and W.B. Yeats. Throw in a few autobiographies of others who have also had direct contact with the scientifically unexplainable or have studied psi phenomena like C.S. Lewis, Carl Jung, and psychiatrist Elisabeth Kubler-Ross. Study the perceptions of those who have been there and done that. This examination will help strip away the negative images which automatically come to mind when the subject of discussion turns to the unseen and unproveable. It will also show you a number of brilliant women and men who believe in the reality of the unexplainable and have successfully resisted the pressure to conform.

There are two sides to every issue and there is a host of material on the subject of nonphysical reality that is virtually unknown to the general public. This anonymity is a result of deliberate distortions, misinformation and concealment by compulsive disbelievers. Revealed truth is always looked at with a jaundiced eye.

PERCEPTIONS AND BELIEFS THAT LEAD TO HEALING

In facilitating the use of an extraordinary experience to cope with loss, we must first consider the nature of beliefs and perceptions that give rise to coping well. In other words, what beliefs most frequently move the bereaved to deal with the fear of change and inspire a commitment to do one's grief work? Let me suggest four recurring beliefs of those who cope well with massive change and that have proved fruitful to many when dealing with the loss of loved ones through death, divorce, or separation. As you will see, each of these beliefs can be reinforced through the use of an extraordinary experience, even though they may not be openly acknowledged.

---

1. **"I can get through this difficult time."** This is arguably the most important belief of all in coping with the death of a loved one or any major loss. Success in the confrontation with change begins with *the will to cope well*. The resulting commitment to adapt, to manage tragic circumstances and not allow them to keep one from embracing life again is of the greatest significance for any mourner. Making the promise and believing "I will make it" creates a crucial portal to hope

for getting through the feelings of injustice, despair, and self-blame that often predominate. Furthermore, the mind set that things will get better is a treasure beyond description since it rejects the cynicism that sometimes creeps into the coping process.

On the other hand, many mourners do not consciously make the commitment to prevail; it is for them an unconscious process emerging from deep in the psyche. How fortunate they are: They somehow "know" that with a little support they will make the impossible possible. That we have the power to overcome the most tragic loss imaginable and to confidently live again is not only a critical belief—it is a truism. It has been demonstrated millions of times in all cultures and ages and with all types of losses.

The opposite beliefs "I will never be happy again" or "I will never love as deeply" puts great obstacles in the path to freedom from constant anxiety. In fact, many mourners maximize their feelings of loneliness by their beliefs that they are not loved or they will always be lonely. Believing one cannot work through the present turmoil and become reconciled to her loss is not only demoralizing, it is tantamount to putting life on hold indefinitely. If she believes she cannot deal with massive change, then her behavior will consistently follow her belief. She will act downtrodden, wounded, and unable to deal with the changes and losses that cycle throughout life. The human psyche is a master at taking any belief, negative or positive, and turning it into a self-fulfilling prophecy. However, the extraordinary, with its inherent uplifting qualities, suggests that the bereaved can and will make it through her ordeal, and she has been given the assist of an EE with that goal in mind. She can turn it around and get through this difficult time.

2. "I have a future." A major task for most bereaved people is to be able to adapt to an environment devoid of the loved one. "I miss her terribly," is not an uncommon message that continuously haunts the bereaved. A companion thought, "What will I do without her?" often drains hope for the future. The initial feeling that there is no future

without the deceased has to give way to a vision that "suffering will end and I can restart my life." This is easier said than done. But purpose can be fashioned via the extraordinary by showing that there is still relationship, caring, and a reason to live. The message of the experience is essentially a message about the future, about hope in things to come.

Believing that life still has something to offer, that you are needed, that you have a special contribution to make, are strong allies on the road to adjustment. The mourner *always* has something to give back to life, to contribute to the greater good, if she will look for it deep within. Finding out what that something is and getting help in the search is the stepping stone for reinvesting in life and refusing to live in the past. Of all the mottoes I have heard over the years few are more appropriate to dealing with grief and making something happen than this one: "If it is to be, its up to me." Eventually, most mourners come to this conclusion.

3. **"I am not alone."** Perceived isolation is a deep wound that grinds the coping process to a halt. But many mourners, especially men, unintentionally isolate themselves from potential sources of comfort. Of course, what is not recognized is that the emotions of anger, depression, fear, cynicism, and guilt are in themselves *isolating emotions*, building a wall between mourner and potential support persons. The mourner who holds on to these emotions cuts himself off from love, the most powerful transforming factor in adapting to loss. To feel loved is to feel secure in the midst of turmoil; it is to be motivated and to feel self-worth. These are the invisible needs of mourners. Love decreases fear and anxiety at any time because love and fear cannot co-exist.

Isolation also manifests itself in the negative belief that no one really cares or the awareness that people are "too busy" or are growing "tired of my grieving." On the other hand, the conviction that people are there for me, that I have someone to turn to when in special need, someone to temporarily lean on, is especially significant in nurturing the belief that one is not alone. In reality, there is always someone out there willing to help. Sometimes, as difficult as it may be, the mourner has to mount a determined search for the right person.

Social interaction has long been associated with maintaining good health and dealing with the various losses that assail everyone. Helpers need to tactfully reinforce the belief that others care and show it through their tireless efforts. This will be a strong factor in adjustment. Give examples to the mourner of specific caring behaviors that others have exhibited in her social group as well as the caring that is a symbol of the extraordinary experience. ("Your loved one cares or he would not be trying to ease your pain.")

Characteristically, mourners must deal with doubt and despair in the course of their grief work. Like an ill blowing wind, these twins of darkness can wreak havoc, especially when mixed with the overwhelming erroneous fear that they are alone in their struggle. Yet someone is *always* there; we are all connected by the cycle of loss. The vast majority of people throughout history have believed in something greater than the Self—a power, a force, an influence. Since the dawn of civilization, such a belief has been a lifeline for millions dealing with the pain of loss and change. If you are mourning, nurture the belief that you are never alone, for that spiritual presence, by whatever name you wish to call it, is always there ready to give a helping hand, day or night. Just ask for it. Begin to ponder this powerful belief for practical use in coping with your loss. Put it into a behavior like talking out loud to a Supreme Being or a Spiritual Force when you feel isolation creep into your thoughts. Believing you will be heard will steer you through the most dangerous passages, around seemingly insurmountable obstacles, to the light of another day. Perhaps it will help to recall the inscription that is carved in stone over the front door of Carl Jung's home in Switzerland: "Called or not called, God will be there."

4. **"I am grateful for what I have."** Obviously, as a helper you are not going to tell a bereaved person she should be grateful for all that she still has. Yet, there are times when a situation arises in which the bereaved

will recognize there is much to be grateful for. I am reminded here of a widow who came to me for counseling and in our sixth session she made it clear that her husband had done much for her. In particular, she pointed out the beautiful home she was still able to live in. In one of our earlier sessions, she had mentioned the values and insights he had impressed her with during their life together. These were important life affirming signs that assisted in helping her deal with her great loss. She was showing a ray of hope and optimism by acknowledging something she was grateful for that needed to be recognized and used in working through her grief. These are golden opportunities to confirm her observations, add to her list of positives, and revisit those times and places as part of her grief work.

Others are often thankful for the answer to their prayer that the loved one not suffer long. They will point out how much worse it could have been and are grateful suffering was shortened. These beliefs should be strengthened by recognition and recall by helpers. The attitude of gratitude is a powerful mindset in the coping process, as it is in any aspect of life. It reduces the focus on the negative results of the loss. The meaning of the EE to the recipient may also result in expressions of gratitude for having been given the experience.

All of the above beliefs can be introduced and expanded upon both directly and indirectly through conversations about extraordinary experiences. Whether you are a mourner or a helper, your job is to frame those beliefs in the most acceptable and meaningful language for use in the process of dealing with change.

EMPOWERING DREAMS AND VISIONS

Dreams have changed the world and concurrently introduced powerful new beliefs. Not infrequently, extraordinary and unexpected dreams have influenced the course of civilizations, wars, politics, psychological theory, beliefs, and medical treatments, as well as choices in coping with personal problems. The Old and New Testaments are filled with dramatic dream scenarios: Abraham was called to leave his land and go to Palestine; Jacob had the famous ladder-to-heaven dream; Joseph, Samuel, and the prophets all had significant dreams, which affected their lives and the lives of others. Wherever we turn—to Buddhism, the Talmud, the prophet Muhammad or to the Chinese or Indian cultures—dreams are implicit sources of wisdom, knowledge, and prophecy. They are not merely electrochemical signals in the brain that focus on present-day concerns of the dreamer.

Dream-inspired music, poetry, art, even movie stories and television plots are part of the creative wisdom of the ages (Coleridge's epic poem Kubla Kahn and Robert Louis Stevenson's Dr. Jekyll and Mr. Hyde, for example). I would be remiss if I failed to mention Freud and Jung who championed the cause of dreams as immense sources of self-under-standing. The historical record in this regard is exceedingly clear. And let's not forget discoveries like the ring structure of benzene, the elec-trochemical nature of the nerve impulse, or the invention of the lock-stitch sewing machine—all in part the result of dreams. (See *Higher Creativity* by Harman and Rheingold for a detailed discussion of these discoveries.) The evidence for the existence of another level of reality could not be stronger.

Emily Bronte, English author of the masterpiece *Wuthering Heights*, once wrote: "I've dreamt in my life dreams that have stayed with me ever after, and changed my ideas; they've gone through and through me, like wine through water, and altered the color of my mind." Of course, Emily Bronte does not stand alone in this experience of transformation. Even though as a culture we tend to scoff at dream knowledge and its wisdom, the dream messenger (the deceased loved one) stays with the mourner and changes her ideas and beliefs.

Since our beliefs create our personal maps of reality that lead to responding to problems in a very individual manner, it is time to con-sider the momentous impact that visitation dreams have in accepting death, bringing comfort, and assuring continued relationship between survivors and their loved ones.

Here are two examples from Jean Smith, of Normal, Illinois, whose 43 year-old sister died from leukemia three weeks after she was diagnosed. Jean was very close to her sister who was the mother of three young daughters.

"OUR CONNECTIONS AS SISTERS CAN NEVER BE TAKEN AWAY OR DIMINISHED"

My sister was pronounced dead at 5:00 a.m. on a Monday morning. However, I know that she actually died at 4:30 that morning. I had refused to leave the hospital that weekend and was trying to sleep in the ICU's waiting room. I had last checked on my sister at about 1:30 a.m. She had been unconscious for about 36 hours. As I tried to sleep, I remember clutching her journal in my hands, desperate to keep some part of her close to me. Eventually, I dozed off and did not awaken until the PA system called for "Dr. Cart" to my sister's room at 4:30 a.m. She had gone into cardiac arrest again. The PA system awoke me from the following dream:

My sister and I were standing in a garden. I wanted her to come with me to this place to my right where a beautiful light glowed. She was hesitant, though, and stayed back, unsure. I was completely calm in the dream. I smiled at her so easily and I said reassuringly, "It's okay. It's right over here." And I held out my hand to her, gesturing for her to come along. She smiled back at me then and reached out and took my hand in hers. Together we walked toward the light.

It was at that moment I was awakened by the PA system. In my disorientation upon awakening, my first thought had been that my sister would be cured. But as I realized that she was again in cardiac arrest, I knew that she would not be cured; she would be **healed.** *The doctors pronounced her dead at 5:00 a.m. but I believe* *my sister truly died at 4:30 a.m. instead; I believe this because I was with her.*

This dream has been an amazing comfort to me in the months since her death. I have never doubted for a moment that my sister is in heaven and is resting in a beautiful place.

The other dream of my sister came to me about a month after she died. I was missing her terribly and had this dream:

I was in the house that she and I had grown up in. Someone knocked on the back door and I pulled aside the door's curtain to see who it was. Debbie stood there on the stoop, smiling. I gasped and fumbled frantically with the locks on the door, trying to unfasten them as quickly as I could. Once unlocked, I flung open the door, pushed open the screen door, and catapulted myself into her arms. As soon as I reached her, I began to sob with an intensity I cannot describe. She wrapped her arms around me in this amazing bear hug, with one hand cradling the back of my head. As I cried, she spoke the same words over and over into my ear: "I love you so much. I love you so much. I love you so much..." I woke from the dream then, still actually crying, and felt an overwhelming sense of gratitude. She had come to comfort me, to reassure me, and to remind me of how much she loved me.

I would like to say that all of the dreams about my sister (I have had others) have been enormously comforting to me. In them Debbie is every bit as real to me as this computer I use to type. Seeing her in these dreams reassures me that our connection as sisters can never be taken away or diminished. The dreams also give me very much the sense that the time will come when she and I will be reunited in the same place—and this helps me to go on with my life here without her. When I am missing her horribly and I feel that I just want to give up and crawl into my bed and stay there, I have the thought, "How can I just stay in bed? If I do that, when I see her again, I won't have any good stories to tell her!" And so I go on. I think my experiences were simply glimpses into another part of life and living of which I am not often aware, but are always present, nonetheless.

A friend of mine who is a psychologist told me that Jung maintained that the dream life is just as real a world as the one we are living in right now. At times I think that my waking mind is too scientific, too rational, to see into this other reality, and that it is only my dreaming mind that can reach past the barriers between my sister and myself. My sister is there, Dr. LaGrand. I am as sure of it as I am of mountains or wind or anything else in this life. She is there. And you're right; she continues to love me as much as I love her.

A comforting reminder of another existence, a suggestion to accept and surrender her sister to a dimension where she is happy and whole again. Visitation dreams are fertile grounds for discussion of dreams in general and how they give information for making choices and taking new directions in life. Our internal dreamscapes have always been meaningful sources for altering beliefs. As a helper, the time will arrive when you may wish to consider asking the mourner if she would be interested in the study of dreams. This could include joining a dream discussion group, reading what the experts say about dreams, and keeping a dream journal as a way to utilize her dreamscape in restructuring her life.

For Jean, her experiences are an immense source of coping power that motivates adaptive behavior necessary for life to be manageable once again, all because of her strong convictions about the reality of her dream visitations. How would you help strengthen her beliefs about her sister's presence, the glimpses into another world, and the love that will always exist between them? What parts of Jean's statements would you pick to explore and expand on that would help her "to go on with my life here without her?" What specific questions could lead into such a dialogue and strengthen the important belief that life is both transient and yet goes on in another dimension? That is the helper's homework.

Here is a sample of questions to consider in creating the needed dialogue highlighting her present beliefs, reinforcing her convictions about heaven, her ability to cope, and that she will see her sister again. Remember that these questions can initiate deep insight and provide meaning far beyond the benefits the mourner currently enjoys. In addition, be alert to and think about how you could integrate into the discussion the *four beliefs that lead to healing* discussed earlier in the chapter. Introducing these concepts during exchanges with the mourner lays the groundwork for helping her find a reason to live in spite of tragedy.

1. What beliefs have helped you cope with your loss thus far?
2. What do you believe is most important in life and living it to the best you know how?
3. Who have you shared your deep beliefs with? What common beliefs do these persons possess that make you feel secure in talking with them?
4. Do you or would you use your EE as part of your prayer life? For example, as a part of meditation or in a daily thanksgiving?
5. Now that you are convinced there is a heaven, does that change the way you will choose to live your life?
6. How does knowing that you will be reunited with Debbie give you strength to go on?
7. Has your compassion toward others changed because of your experiences?
8. Are you more accepting of death and the deaths of your loved ones?
9. Do you see the world and our place in it in a different light as a result of your extraordinary experiences?
10. Do you see any universal beliefs that could unite all people?
11. Has your experience caused you to reject any of your old beliefs?

The Unknown is and always will be able to surprise us. It opens the door to the full realization that although loss is continuous in life, so too is the reemergence of hope. Jean's dreams are not unusual in their information-producing dimensions. In fact, there are a long list of dreams that can be found in the literature on EE's in which directions were given to recover jewelry, money, insurance policies and the like that previously could not be located. Dante's, *The Divine Comedy,* remained incomplete and may have never been published, if he had not appeared to his son Jacopo in a dream to tell him where he had hidden the remainder of the manuscript.

Many EE's can also be the basis for dialogue about practical beliefs concerning an afterlife, the soul, spirituality, or a Universal Intelligence. Obviously, EE's in which one is convinced of the presence of a Superior Being (Allah, God, The Absolute) are especially adaptive to spiritual exploration.

Despite the persistent taboo against talking about EE's as spiritual events (some naturalists claim that to suggest that the EE is a spiritual event is to keep people at a lower developmental level), for many, the strengthening of existing spiritual beliefs and the introduction of new beliefs are important factors in reconciling a particular loss and reinvesting in life. The spiritual landscape becomes an everyday reality, a new awareness, an awakening. Spiritual power is no fantasy; through belief it provides incredible strength that leads to healing and restoration. Later, we will explore how dreams can also be used for other purposes on the road to recovery.

CHILDREN, BELIEFS, AND THE EXTRAORDINARY

The experience of changing the myths and beliefs of earlier years is not exclusively in the domain of the adult. Children, too, can benefit from the impact of an extraordinary experience on their belief system. The wise adult will not dismiss the experience as solely a child's imagination at work, but will use it to expand her awareness of nonphysical reality, mystery and the spiritual life, the importance of giving and receiving, and the belief that relationships are sacred and eternal.

Here is an example from Astrid Sandell, an editor with a major midwest publishing company, who through the years was strengthened in her beliefs about life and death all because of a childhood experience and a mother who taught her well.

"I ALWAYS REMEMBERED THIS PRIVATE GOOD-BYE AS I GREW UP"

My maternal grandfather died in early February, 1978. I was seven years old.

My grandparents lived on a farm in southwestern Minnesota— where my grandmother continues to live. The farmhouse is set about a quarter of a mile off the main road, a gravel driveway leads from the road to the house, passing a thick grove of trees. I'd spent quite of bit of time at the farm in my early childhood and saw my grandparents often.

There wasn't much trauma associated with my grandfather's passing for me, though I was definitely sad. My family didn't shield me from the rituals of death, and I attended everything—the visitation, the funeral, the service at the cemetery, the reception back at the farm. I remember everything vividly even today—situations, conversations, emotions.

One event during those few days, however, did cause me pain. After the funeral, the farmhouse was filled with people laughing and eating and talking. I was very sad following the funeral and graveside service and became extremely angry with all of the people crammed into the living room and kitchen of the house. Shouldn't these people be as sad as me? I ran upstairs crying and refused to come back down. My mother finally came upstairs and explained that these people weren't happy grandpa was dead (which was certainly how it seemed to my young eyes and ears) but that they were celebrating grandpa's life and remembering all the good times they had—it was a special way of saying good-bye. I don't know that I was fully convinced, but I did go back downstairs.

During these days of mourning, I was sleeping in bed with my grandmother, where my grandfather had slept. The night after the funeral, I was in bed and woke up in the middle of the night (my grandmother snores something fierce). I sat up and looked out the window of her first-floor bedroom, which looked down the drive toward the road. Grandpa was walking toward the house. He was wearing coveralls, which was what he nearly always wore around the farm, and seemed not so much bathed in light as being of light. Winter nights in Minnesota glow—especially under the moon on the prairie—but my grandfather was gleaming even brighter. I waved to him. He waved back to me and walked into the grove.

I always remembered this private good-bye as I grew up, but never really talked about it much until the past several years. Lately, I've talked about the experience with other members of my family and have been surprised to hear that several of them have had communication with grandpa, as well.

A private goodbye always carries special meaning to children as well as adults. It is the stuff of lifelong caring memories. We should note that many children who witness the reception that takes place after a funeral are upset by adult behavior they consider frivolous, given the circumstances of death. It is confusing for them to see what is a sad event and yet witness people laughing or talking in a loud or boisterous way. After inquiring about her daughter's behavior, Astrid's mother did a fine job of trying to explain adult behavior.

In discussing her childhood experience, I asked Astrid if the experience had affected her beliefs about life, death, and a Supreme Being. She responded with, "All of the above," meaning that many of her beliefs had been strengthened at the time and through the years. In particular, she singled out the elimination of her fear of death and that her grandfather, by his appearance, was reiterating what her mother had said about the people who were celebrating his life. The behavior of her grandfather's friends and relatives at the reception was then more acceptable. In summing up her experience as she looks back she said, "It's so funny, I'd never thought of the event as particularly extraordinary. I'd mention it to friends and invariably someone would have another story along the same lines. It's amazing how common it is, yet there are always those people who look at you like you're crazy. I hope your work will continue to open the dialogue on this wonderful part of life, death and love."

QUESTIONS TO BE POSED TO ASTRID

If, when Astrid was a child, she came to you as a close relative or friend and shared her EE, what could be done to help strengthen or introduce beliefs that could assist in coping with her loss and integrating the experience into life? To begin with, let any child speak about her experience without interruption. In telling her story, what needs are being expressed? That her grandpa is all right? That she is fearful? That she needs information to understand the behavior of others? Or is she in search of finding a way to say good-bye? To understand her experience? To simply have someone listen and say, "Wow, what a beautiful thing to have happened?" This is a wonderful opportunity to let the child know about the power of love and the way her grandpa and those around her love her. To help Astrid sort out her feelings you might ask the following questions.

1. What have you learned from Grandpa's visit? Were you happy that he came to you?

2. Where do you believe Grandpa is now?

3. What did you like best about seeing your Grandpa? Did it remind you of anything special?

4. Do you think it was Grandma snoring that woke you up or could it have been something else?

5. Why do you think Grandpa decided to visit you? He must have thought you were very special. What motivated you to look out the window after you woke up?

6. Could you tell me how he looked with the light all around him? What was he wearing?

7. Why do you think he waved at you? What was he saying?

8. Was there an expression on his face that you can describe?

9. Why do you think he walked off to the grove after waving to you?

10. Was it hard for you to go back to sleep after you saw Grandpa?

11. What did you tell your Grandma when you woke up in the morning? What did she say to you?

12. Have you told your Mom or Dad about what happened at Grandma's?

13. Who else have you shared your experience with? How have they responded?

14. How do you feel now when you think of Grandpa?

15. Will this experience be a special memory you will always treasure?

16. Is there anything else you would like to tell me about your visit from Grandpa?

With any child who has an extraordinary experience you should consider what you could teach her about life and death. For example, if Astrid was your child, you could introduce many of your philosophical or religious beliefs. Or you could address the reality of an afterlife, the fact that change is part of the natural order, and the EE is often a basic companion of the change process. It would be useful to impress upon her that she will always be loved, something all children need to hear again and again. The importance of thinking of the welfare of others (as Grandpa did with his visit) and being thankful for the things we receive are additional concepts that could be introduced in discussions about the experience. All of this and more could add to a robust emotional life for a child while dispelling any notions of scary ghosts, monsters or other unhealthy interpretations.

After any conversation with a child (or for that matter with an adult mourner), be sure to leave the door open for future conversations. "Any time you want to talk about grandpa or anything, just let me know," is a good way to end your discussion. The child must know she can trust you and come to you with any questions in the future. Keep open the lines of communication at all times, especially because some children will not be able to talk openly with parents if the parents are having great difficulty dealing with the death. You may be the only person the child thinks will listen.

BELIEFS TO THINK ABOUT AND DISCUSS WHEN ONE HAS EXPERIENCED THE EXTRAORDINARY

New beliefs supplant old ones through the application of knowledge gained in the experience of grieving. This is one reason why support groups are effective. It is through suffering that we are often led to wisdom and a new vision. In particular, reading and talking about strategies for adapting, being around other mourners who are positive and hopeful, and learning alternative ways to perceive loss, increases the possibilities of forming beliefs that facilitate healthy mourning.

Helpers and mourners by necessity talk endlessly. The subjects can be far ranging and usually lead back to the deceased loved one. During discussions that result from questions asked in relation to the extraordinary experience, the helper can decide whether the timing is right to introduce beliefs that may be helpful for the mourner to consider in dealing with her loss. Or the mourner may want to share her hidden beliefs with the helper. These beliefs are seeds for action and their implications should be thoroughly studied. Much informative exchange can take place between mourner and helper over the possibilities of adopting a particular belief. Here are fourteen beliefs to stimulate this exchange:

1. Our deceased loved ones can help us much more after death than they could when they were with us on earth. They can look at our current dilemmas in an altogether different way than we do. We can also help them in their spiritual development on the other side by offering prayers of encouragement and specific suggestions based on our relationship with them on earth.

2. Our deceased friends and loved ones care for us, want to help us, and are with us in our times of worry and sorrow. But we have to do our part. We have to take responsibility and be committed to learn about the many faces of grief and the individuality of grief work. They will help, but they cannot do it all.

3. Although grief is a normal human response, we can further express our love by allowing the deceased to go to the other side unencumbered by our grief about his death. This will allow him to embrace his new life knowing that those he has left behind can and will integrate his loss into their lives.

4. Mourners can pray to their loved ones for assistance and intercession with a Supreme Being. Think and send positive thoughts to your loved one and ask for insights in return.

5. The extraordinary experience is an act of love. Believe that there is a great desire for your loved one to add to your learning about love, to see the world anew for the first time. Think of all you have learned through your extraordinary experience so far. How has it resulted in giving and receiving love?

6. If you believe your loved one is with God and God is close to you, then your loved one is also very close to you. This means communion and communication is part of life in both worlds.

7. It is perfectly normal to talk to your deceased loved one and tell him how you feel, that you are trying to cope, and that you miss him. Because of their special place in eternity, our loved ones know us even better now than they ever did before. They understand our motivations and desires.

8. The extraordinary experience suggests a double message: we can both make it though separated. I from where I am, you from where you are. You can be happy again.

9. Our deceased loved ones are not bound by linear time. They are on eternal time and have insight into the past and the future and will help in the transition you face. Ask for ideas on how to deal with a particularly vexing problem you are facing.

10. No one can change the landscape of grief, but everyone can change the position from which they travel through the terrain. The EE puts the traveler in a position of advantage. Make a list of the advantages you hold given the experience you had. How will you plug these advantages into your new life?

11. In eternity the compassion and forgiveness of loved ones for any and all real or imagined transgressions is an automatic result of being surrounded by love. They have let whatever transgression go; you can let it go too.

12. Because there is no distance, no space, and no time in eternity our loved ones can be here with us or there—even though our finite minds cannot fathom this mystery.

13. At the moment of death and often before, loved ones are met by their predeceased relatives and friends, who escort them home. No one dies alone. It is another example that we are all connected.

14. The deceased loved one assumes that there will always be a relationship with those he has left on earth. How will you honor and perpetuate this relationship?

If you are a mourner, some of these beliefs may already be a part of your belief system. Mentioning them to a helper will be a good reminder to initiate a course of action. In any discussion with a helper or contemplation of these beliefs when alone, give careful consideration to short and long term outcomes of adapting a particular belief. Thus the question of how to transfer beliefs into specific behaviors is an important one for you to explore. Decide what will be the initial behavior to employ in dealing with fear, loneliness, guilt, anger, or depression. Use the same strategy for establishing new routines or whatever obstacle has to be confronted. Adapting new beliefs are not effective unless they are translated into clear behaviors with a specific purpose in the conscious pursuit of completing grief work.

CONCEPTS TO EXPLORE AND DEVELOP TO STRENGTHEN BELIEFS

The following concepts may be used to stimulate ideas to use in strengthening existing beliefs or to facilitate changes in beliefs that can be used in doing the work of grief.

1. Beliefs can be changed through modeling the beliefs and behavior of others who have coped well and hold *beliefs you would like to emulate*. There is nothing wrong with adopting beliefs that others espouse about EE's, how to cope with the death of a loved one, or other losses. We model the beliefs of others in all areas of human endeavor from business to athletics. The major task is to find out what those who cope well believe, and then decide if that is the way you want to go. You have grief; it doesn't have you as a prisoner without options. And you can decide how to proceed, even though your burden is heavy.

2. Have you forgotten your strengths? Most of us tend to overlook our strengths and worry about the future. Assess and emphasize your strengths. The analysis of the strengths that have gotten you this far in life will expose critical beliefs and take away the common habit of constant preoccupation with the problems of dealing with change. Ask yourself what strengths you possess, what inner skills you have often relied on, and how you will apply the results of your search to coping with your loss. Ask the person who is helping you in your time of loss where she thinks your strengths are centered. This collaboration will provide much information

for expanding your coping repertoire. It will also give you the sense of control needed in dealing with stress and shore up self-esteem.

3. Break through the limitations that our culture ingrains in all of us. It is okay to use your EE as a part of the new way you see the world and the new environment in which you must live without your loved one. Consider for a moment the new beliefs your EE suggests. Only you can make that determination. The experience you have had is meant in part to help raise your conscious awareness of beliefs and your worldview. Review it as you ponder your thoughts about your present circumstances and whether some of your old beliefs are holding you back. For example, what are the implications of holding on to the worn beliefs that you can only be happy if you possess wealth or are married or that, "This should not be happening to me?"

Counter and utilize the wisdom of the ages: Attitudes and beliefs trigger *loneliness and a host of negative behaviors* .

Others who have experienced the extraordinary, whether when mourning or not, can be a special source of reinforcement for your beliefs. Many people have had contacts with deceased loved ones when they were not mourning and will be open to accepting you and your experience.

4. Beliefs are not beliefs unless you are living what you say you believe. Remind yourself that you will adapt to your new surroundings by drawing on your beliefs about yourself (I will prevail) and on the rich resources you possess (I have the courage and determination within). Remember what Rabbi Earl Grollman said about courage: "Courage is not the absence of fear or pain, but the affirmation of life despite fear and pain." Amelia Earhart, put it this way, "Courage is the price that life exacts for granting peace." Here is the acid test for your beliefs: if you don't live it, you don't believe it.

5. Go back to the section in this chapter entitled, *BELIEFS TO THINK ABOUT AND DISCUSS WHEN ONE HAS EXPERI-*

ENCED THE EXTRAORDINARY. Pick three beliefs that are most meaningful to you and print or type them on 3" by 5'" cards. Place them in your diary, prayer book, or use them as book marks in whatever you are currently reading. Review them each day and start living those beliefs.

6. Most fear is learned and directly associated with beliefs and perceptions. It paralyzes and limits the new beginnings that every mourner must initiate. If you will seek new information on how to deal with loss, be determined to uncover and change the beliefs causing fear, and trust the Unknown, you can control any fear. Honesty, openness, and the resolution to face fear will reduce its power over you. As Emerson said, "Do the thing you fear, and the death of fear is certain." Because you are the author of fear, use your EE as an initiator of the actions you must take to reduce fear of the future without your loved one. Fear carries with it deadly inner images that you have replayed thousands of times to build your fear base. With practice, you can replace those images with images based on your EE and in doing so create another reality to guide you through the pitfalls of change.

7. Einstein said: "Imagination is more important than knowledge." Employ the power of your imagination to decide how your extraordinary experience can be used to reawaken your interest in life and *why it was given to you* as a tool for altering beliefs and doing the undesirable in this time of adapting to change. Adopt Einstein's belief about imagination and it will change your life.

 Imagine where you want to be in your grief work four months from now.

 Lay it out clearly and decisively and each day do one thing that leads you in that direction. If you stick with it, you will be where you imagined you would be in the allotted time.

8. The only antidote for grief is to embrace the belief that you must go through it, not around it. Your mourning is a *natural* (though it

feels wholly unnatural) progressive process that leads ultimately to reconciliation and healing. Let it unfold; don't fight it. You don't get over it. You work, work, work, and get through it. Grief has a purpose: To remind us we have loved and that pain is part of loving.

9. Throughout life everyone undergoes belief changes based on new experiences. Its part of lifelong learning. When loss shatters tenuous beliefs and faith wavers, learning the lessons of suffering demands incorporating new understanding and beliefs about death, life, and accepting the oft forgotten fact that everyone suffers. Understanding that everyone suffers (the evidence is overwhelming) is the next step to a more realistic life perspective and a release from the hidden view that you have been singled out for sorrow. Persist in your need to develop new habits of thinking about yourself and your loss.

It is abundantly clear, what you choose to focus on grows and is what you control—or what controls you. Thus, if you only focus on what is painful you will draw more pain to yourself. Think of the amount of time you give to painful thoughts and how thinking about them seems to cause them to become more menacing. Conversely, if you focus on what is comforting and gives solace you will attract the same. Believe that you can manage your pain by what you decide to habitually dwell on.

10. Do not allow others' perceptions and beliefs about "proper mourning" to encroach upon what you know in your heart to be *your* path of mourning. In silence, listen to the wisdom of your inner voice. This is especially true in relation to your beliefs about your extraordinary experience. Hold fast to your beliefs about how you should mourn and embrace your gift from the Unknown.

11. Negative assumptions and beliefs have equal power to prolong unnecessary suffering. Persistent negative beliefs sever the flow of insights and creative ideas for going on with life and accepting death and loss as necessary conditions. Root them out by seeking

alternatives for them and take a lesson from your extraordinary experience, which is purely positive insight, if you will only receive it as such. That is the road to travel.

12. Are you aware of the messages you send yourself every day by the way you talk to yourself? Few are, especially when mourning. However, through self-talk (affirmations and other personal responses you repeatedly say silently or out loud to yourself), visualization (picturing yourself in your "mind's eye" doing the new task and coping well), and actually setting aside time to rehearse behavior associated with new beliefs, you can consciously and unconsciously strengthen those beliefs. For example, consider the belief that the relationship with your beloved is always only a thought away. He lives on within you and can be remembered in a joyous scene at any time of your choosing. Practice that reality. Or see yourself coping well with having to meet old friends for the first time after the death of your loved one. Say what you need to say to them as you picture the meeting. Practice. Practice. Practice. It simply takes persistent effort.

Change the nature of the pictures you create as time moves you to a different place in your journey of healing. You are in charge. Be motivated by the observation of William James: "The greatest revolution of our generation is the discovery that human beings, by changing the inner attitudes of their minds, can change the outer aspects of their lives."

As we close this chapter, let me emphasize the importance of the need for patience by the mourner *and* the helper. Grief is demanding and persistent patience is a hidden key for helper and mourner to practice. The goal is to outlast grief since it is so often discouraging, especially when progress is being made and a relapse is experienced. Look at relapse as a sign of progress, an expected part of the mourning process. You may think you are going backward when in fact you are simply following grief's way. To regress to an earlier stage of grief is not weakness. This is where you and your helping friend have to exercise patience, trust in the process, and be well aware that such a setback is a common occurrence. It has happened to millions of mourners, as it is part of a well-known pattern. And it can happen more than once during your grief work. Try focusing on this perspective: the power of patience is something to hold close and enjoy.

Grieve the best you can—with openness and the conviction that *you will be guided through*, albeit not around, the pain of your loss. As mentioned earlier, facing pain is an essential condition in coping with loss. It is one half of the twin belief underscoring one of the most important concepts in the literature on grief: the need to express emotions and feelings. This second "twin" is the challenge of the next chapter: learning to use the extraordinary experience as an outlet for pain and suffering.

4

Expressing Emotion: A Key To Healing

Tranquility of mind, so necessary for one's happiness and the accomplishment of good work, can be acquired.

William Lyon Phelps
Yale University

Anxiety Diminished

This experience greatly helped me in my grief. It served to comfort and console me. It reaffirmed my belief that my husband will continue to communicate on a spiritual level.

—Emma H.
On her EE after the death of her husband

∞   ∞   ∞   ∞   ∞   ∞

In *The Inner Voice of Love*, Henri Nouwen's "secret journal" written at a most trying time in his life, he poses a crucial question for anyone coping with difficult life-changes: "Do you own your pain?" If not, he suggests, you will expect others to take it away. In doing so you become a slave to their timetables and ineffective attempts, for no one except the bearer of pain can ultimately conquer torment and anguish. Owning your pain and not expecting others to relieve it is the prerequisite to eventual release. It follows that talking about what is happening inside becomes the leading *survival skill*, an ownership responsibility that casts a different light on the winter of grief.

At the same time, taking responsibility for facing pain and expressing it is a therapeutic force of inestimable value. In fact, the stress of grief is dealt a mighty blow when the mourner continually releases the turmoil within, because for every thought and emotion there is a corresponding physiological counterpart to that thought or emotion; every cell in the body heaves a mighty sigh of relief. As grief persists, most mourners realize that their naïve expectations of others for pain relief are at best unrealistic. In the final analysis, they alone must squarely face their suffering. Experiencing emotional (and sometimes physical) pain is inevitable, if healing is to occur. Expressing the feelings behind the pain, through the spoken word or any creative endeavor, is a little known but essential avenue for relief leading to reconstructing one's life.

In this chapter we will examine how extraordinary experiences can be easily used to provide a vehicle for ventilation of emotional pain and frustration as well as another resource to manage the stress of the grief process. But first, let me emphasize that it is difficult to be in the presence of those who are grieving the death of a loved one and need to express emotions. If you are helping someone who is bereaved your number one responsibility is to commit yourself to stay with the pain of the mourner when she expresses it. The temptation is to find an excuse to leave because of what you are witnessing or do something to stop a normal process. Her pain may include bursts of anger as well as incessant crying and real or imagined fears of the future. Be aware there is nothing you can say that will take away these feelings. However, being there to share them, without trying to impede the important process of release by saying "Don't cry" or "Don't feel that way" will be a great, though unsung service, which you can provide. Given the fact that early in life we are taught that emotional outbursts are not to be condoned, you may have to encourage the mourner to talk about those pent-up feelings and give her permission to allow them to surface in all their fury.

Begin the process of release by asking questions about life with the loved one, or whenever the mourner talks about the deceased, be willing to prolong the exchange and not end it prematurely. Those times are natural opportunities for intimate thoughts to become expressible liquid feelings in your presence. You will see that when an extraordinary experience is shared you will have much information from which to draw questions and a special point of departure for emotional release. The extraordinary can be used as passage into the past relationship the mourner had with the deceased. The more you gently assist the mourner to verbalize that relationship from beginning to end, as well as what it meant to her, the more you will be helping her confront and release feelings she can share and unashamedly cry about.

Let's take a closer look at the process by examining three experiences reported by Diane Zimmerman of Virginia Beach, Virginia. We will consider the types of questions to be asked which will create a helpful dialogue by pairing the EE with a review of past experiences with the deceased.

"THIS 'VISION' I SECRETLY HARBORED FOR MANY MONTHS"

*On October 15, 1998 my oldest brother Walt (our family affectionately referred to him as Buddy) succumbed to lymphoma cancer. Three weeks later, November 11, 1998, my father Walt senior, passed away, also from cancer. We were an **extremely** close* *family, always "together" by mail or phone no matter how many miles separated us. I was devastated upon hearing of my brother's death. Although we all knew how critical his condition was, nothing can really "prepare" a person fully. Being an ex-military man, Buddy was given a military funeral. As a hobby, Buddy spent many hours of enjoyment on his model railroad, hand-building trains and cars (that ran!) and an elaborate track plan so painstakingly done. Ours is a "Railroad" family being that my dad was an engineer for the Chicago Northwestern. Our lives centered on railroading.*

At Buddy's gravesite and after the 21-gun salute, the flag was folded and while it was being presented to Mary, his wife, the mournful wail of a train was heard in the distance. My brother's grave faces the railroad track that runs parallel to the cemetery. All of us heard the train approach—still the same sad, mournful wail of the whistle. As the freight train passed, what we witnessed is forever etched in our memories: a Chicago Northwestern engine was "hooked" on behind the lead engine—backwards. The analogy being somewhat like the boots on backward of the riderless horse at state funerals. Coincidence? I don't know? It's as if Buddy was bidding us all one final grand farewell.

Yes, we checked the timetables of the operation of the railroad. The train usually ran this particular course around noon-12: 30 each day. But on the day of Buddy's funeral the train had unexpected trouble, accounting for its lateness, thereby passing his grave and us at 3:00 p.m. The "backwards" Chicago Northwestern engine is certainly mind boggling as the CNW railroad changed over to the DMV line several years ago and all of the prior Chicago Northwestern engines were either repainted or retired. Remember, this occurred at the gravesite where 100 or more people had gathered. Was this Buddy's final farewell to let us all know that he was okay and in a better place? It's our belief that yes, this is exactly what it means.

*After returning home to Virginia Beach from Minnesota and my brother's funeral, I tried in vain to return to my regular routine. I returned home on Friday (he was buried the Tuesday before) and on Saturday morning I rose earlier than normal as I couldn't sleep. Soon, my cup of coffee finished, I was sitting by our kitchen table looking out at our pretty backyard. The tears came and memories came flooding back. It was 6: 00 a.m. In the quiet stillness of the morning I was alone with my thoughts and memories. After a few minutes of crying I was jolted by the sound of an ear deafening "Squawk Squawk Squawk." At first I ignored this sound, thinking to myself whatever it is I wish it would just go away and leave me alone!! The squawk was incessant to the point that I dried my tears and listened more intently. Now I'm beginning to think a little animal is hurt or in trouble—so out the back door I went in my pajamas, robe, and slippers. The squawking **did not let up!** I went around the perimeter of our yard looking for an animal either hurt or caught up in the fence. My search was futile. There wasn't anything there.*

*By this time this screeching is getting on my nerves. I came back in settling back down to my empty coffee cup and wondering, "What on earth could be making all this noise?" I went to the front room windows—but before doing so I cautiously opened our front door—nothing. This squawking has not let up for almost 10 minutes!! I was about to lose my mind! I opened one of the blinds to the front window—nothing. Upon opening the second window's blind's, I saw on the ledge outside **looking in,** the most beautiful Blue Jay ever! He was not startled at all by my opening the blinds, but instead squawked at me three very distinct times, and then flew away. This was before we started feeding the birds in the back!! Up to this point, no Blue Jay ever "came to visit." Remember, this was 6: 20 a.m. or so!! Although we now have Blue Jays in the back yard this "special" Blue Jay never returned at such an early hour.*

And why didn't it fly away when I opened the blind? Why did it **constantly** *squawk? To get my attention in order that I would find it perched on the ledge? Why three distinct squawks? Our family consisted of Mom and Dad, Buddy, myself, and my youngest brother Bob. Does this all somehow connect?*

A third experience involved my Mom, me, Mary (Buddy's wife), and one of Mary's friends. We all went to a college band concert, which took place in the lovely serene chapel at the college. Andy (Buddy's and Mary's son) had a major part playing a trumpet solo which was flawless. After the concert, I turned away from the friend sitting beside me to get my coat. Upon turning my eyes, I focused on the balcony and there I saw Buddy at the railing, standing like he always did. I was transfixed. He looked well, healthy, and smiling! Let me mention—the lights were all the way up— bright. No one was obscuring my sight. Sure, I wear glasses but who doesn't at 48? On the drive over we did not monopolize the conversation talking about Buddy. Anyway, this was something I needed Joanne (the friend) to see. I tore my sight away and turned to her saying, "Look!" immediately turning back and seeing…nothing where Buddy was. Joann kept saying, "What? What?" How could I possibly tell her? And no proof. So I brushed it off, "Oh nothing" as everyone was putting on coats and gloves and hats. It was 30 degrees outside.

I wasted time—taking my time while watching the people descend from the balcony. No one even remotely resembled my brother. I was heartbroken. If I could have seen **someone** *like Buddy—but no one. This "vision" I secretly harbored for many months before relating this to my husband. After reading your book, somehow it made it easier for me. So you see Professor, even skeptical people like me can have eye-opening experiences. I wouldn't call myself overly religious, but I do believe in a Supreme Being—God, Christ, Jesus—whichever you prefer to use. I find myself thinking of* *these several events and am hoping that someday my wonderful Dad will come to "visit" in a special way. Right now I'm content to believe Dad is much too busy in heaven—running the train!*

The unexpected—at the gravesite, at home, and on the balcony of the college chapel—were enough for Diane to have her natural skepticism challenged and set-aside for a new view of reality. She was propelled into a thought-life filled with hope and demanding openness to the Unknown. There *is* meaning in the unexpected; it teaches an alternative view about the borderland between physical reality and the invisible connections within and outside of the universe—connections that science has yet to explain, indeed may never be able to explain. Her spontaneous experiences brought meaning and expectations of good things to come, but most importantly they became a wonderful resource for talking about her brother and her love.

Diane's stress level also diminished, which is another common side effect of the EE that is frequently overlooked. Extraordinary experiences are literally immune system enhancers because they spark hope and eliminate the depression of endings without meaning. Persistent feelings that are buried within have a way of compromising the ability of the immune system to function often resulting in illness to the mourner. Persistent fear, in particular, is an exhausting emotion leading to impairment. Whether feelings are repressed (unconsciously held within) or suppressed (consciously held within), over time they take a damaging toll. The EE is a vehicle that begins the direct process of release, as it did for Diane.

QUESTIONS TO BE POSED TO DIANE

As you choose questions that will help a mourner express deep emotion, keep in mind that much will depend on appropriate follow-up questions after assessing her initial response. Here is where you can ask questions pertaining to when the deceased was alive. This is the central theme in helping anyone vent. For example, in talking about the vision on the balcony, if Diane said Buddy was smiling, you may want to inquire about the smile. "Do you remember when you last saw him smile that way?" or "In the past, what other ways did Buddy use to show how pleased he was with his son?" Take the cue from a response and build on it with questions that cause the mourner to recall other experiences involving the deceased. Tap into memories that elicit details and bring deep introspection. It is the recollection and discussion of past experiences with the deceased that allows venting of emotion, permission to mourn, and the normalizing of the entire process. The following questions can begin the process of examining the relationship between Diane and her brother.

1. What were your immediate thoughts when you spotted the "backward" Chicago Northwestern engine pass by the gravesite?
2. When you look back on that experience now, does it fill you with emotion?
   What does it bring to mind about Buddy and your relationship with him?
3. Who do you believe is behind the events that took place at Buddy's gravesite?
4. In what ways does Andy remind you of Buddy?
5. Can you remember the last time you saw Buddy well, healthy, and smiling like he was at the railing on the balcony?
6. What is the symbolic meaning of the Blue Jay squawking incessantly?
7. Why do you think it distinctly squawked three times before it flew away and has not returned at that early hour again?
8. Do you remember some of the conversations Buddy and your father had about railroading? Where did they take place?
9. What characteristics did Buddy and your father share?
10. What meaning do you draw from Buddy looking so well when you saw him in your vision at the concert?
11. How did the military funeral remind you of Buddy's service in the military?

12. What childhood memories of Buddy do you recall when you see his model railroad and the hand made railroad cars?
13. What memories came flooding back at 6:00 a.m. when you finished that cup of coffee?
14. What memories of Buddy have you shared with his wife and your husband? Have you recalled how you used to spend the holidays with him and his family? What comes to mind when you think of Buddy and the holidays?

Again, your goal in utilizing the EE is to initiate an exchange leading to a recall of events for discussing the life of the deceased, his values and goodness, and encouraging, primarily though your nonverbal behavior, the normal display of feelings. This is accomplished by helping the mourner bring out details of memories that plumb the depths of feelings. When the mourner opens to a particular emotion, recognize it ("You say that with deep love and respect.") so as to provide the atmosphere where the mourner senses the freedom to continue on, saying what she is feeling.

It has been said that perfect freedom is the freedom not to want. Your awareness of the mourner's need for freedom from her inner pain through sharing it can bring her search for that eventual freedom to fruition.

Is there a difference in approach when the mourner is unsure of the validity of his experiences? I will address that question through the series of experiences reported by a college professor who lives in the Midwest and has always been skeptical of unexplainable phenomena.

"I DO KNOW THAT THESE TYPES OF EXTRAORDINARY HAPPENINGS HAD NEVER OCCURRED BEFORE MY MOTHER'S DEATH"

On January 15, 1998, my mother was killed in a traffic accident. According to the coroner, she died instantly. She was the only person in the car. I would also like to tell you something about myself. I am an associate professor at a local community college. I have been trained in the scientific method and consider myself to be a very skeptical person.

Soon after my mother's death, several unexplainable incidences occurred. Some may have logical explanations; others do not seem to. The first three might be able to be explained.

1) *Around 2:00 p.m. on January 20 as I was leaving my house to attend the memorial service, I distinctly heard my name called out. I was locking my back door, and I was so startled that I jerked around quickly but did not see anyone. There were some children playing across the street, but they did not know me. The voice was not that of a child nor of my mother. It did not seem to be that of a man or a woman. It was very monotoned in sound.*

2) *On January 23 I was leaving for work. As I was going through my pockets, I found a roll of breathe mints which I had purchased for the memorial service. I think that I placed them on my wife's dresser. When I returned from work, they were on the bed next to the pillows. I re-enacted putting the mints on the bed over and over, and I just do not think I would have put them on the bed.*

3) *My mother's birthday is on February 25. In December my wife ordered several items from a mail order firm including a birthday present for my mother. The package did not arrive until after my mother's death. Everything that had been ordered was in the box except for the birthday present. My wife was charged for the present, but it was not included in the order. She has purchased products from this company on several occasions, but this has never happened previously. She did not contact the company about the missing item.*

The following three events have no explanation as far as I can see:

1) On January 19 at approximately 11:30 a.m., I noticed that our furnace thermostat was set at 72 degrees. For many years we have set the thermostat at 68 at the beginning of winter and have never changed it. On this day it had been changed. When we would go away, my mother would always take care of our cats. One of the things she would do is turn up our furnace because she thought that the house was too cold for the cats.

2) At about 4:45 p.m. on January 25, after my wife and I had returned from shopping, I noticed that the left door on my tape deck was open. Since we have a CD player with the tape deck, we don't use the tape deck. Also, it is the type of door that has to be pressed for it to be opened.

3) At 8:45 p.m. on the evening of February 2, I was setting my alarm clock for the next morning. The clock is a quartz clock. I noticed that the time was off by over 4 hours, and when I checked the alarm time setting, it was also off by over 4 hours. We have had this clock for over twelve years and it has never malfunctioned. I have watched it carefully since this episode and it has worked perfectly. It is a digital clock so it has to be manually set by pushing a series of buttons.

Nothing has happened since the evening of February 2. Later in February I purchased and read your book After Death Communication. *After reading it, I decided to write to you as you requested. You are the only person that I have discussed this with besides my wife who also witnessed most of this. I am going to send a copy of this letter to some of my relatives.*

I don't know the significance of these events. I do know that these types of extraordinary happenings had never occurred before my mother's death. I also know that my mother was a very strong-willed person, and if there was any way possible, she or her spirit would try to contact us to let us know that she is all right.

If, as William James suggested, "there is an unseen order of things," then perhaps it was at work here to initiate thoughts to help balance the healthy scientific skepticism that many people embrace. It is clear that this professor is torn between believing his experiences may be associated with his mother or not believing. However, these experiences were apparently real enough for him to search for information about them, particularly to take the time to contact me about their credibility. He would not have shared the experiences if he did not have some belief in their validity and the fact that "these types of extraordinary happenings never occurred before my mother's death." In any case, these events can be utilized to provide him with the opportunity to talk about feelings and emotions, and provide a platform for discussing the nature of the experiences and their authenticity. Obviously, a helper should first validate his EE's in order to initiate dialogue so he can begin to talk openly about his relationship with his mother.

QUESTIONS TO BE POSED TO THE PROFESSOR

Even though a mourner is unsure of the authenticity of his experiences, perhaps plagued by scientific conditioning, a helper should proceed in the same positive vein as if supporting a person who was convinced he had received an authentic contact.

1. At the memorial service what memories did the eulogy cause you to recall about your mother?
2. If you assumed these EE's were authentic, what do you think your mother is trying to get you to be aware of in your life or to say about her death?
3. Which of your EE's awakens feelings about your mother at her best?
4. Which EE is most meaningful and touches you emotionally? Why?
5. What feelings and emotions surfaced after the experience with the quartz clock?
6. Does the number of EE's that you have experienced suggest any insight regarding the consistency, determination or commitment

of your mother to your welfare? Is this reflective of your relationship with her as a child?

7. Have you or any members of your family ever had any similar
experiences prior to those occurring after the death of your
mother? Why do you think they have happened now?

8. Do you think your mother had something to do with the missing
present?

9. What do you talk to your wife about concerning your mother?

10. How have your experiences been a source of comfort? Do any of
your EE's bring back childhood memories of your relationship
with your mother and father?

11. Are any of the experiences characteristic of something your
mother would have done to get your attention?

12. Why didn't your wife contact the company about the missing present for your mother?

13. Would you be willing to talk with others who have had similar
experiences?

14. What would you need to learn in order to unquestionably believe
in the validity of your EE's and gain further insight into the origin
and meaning o your experiences?

15. When you think about your mother and your experiences what
emotions tend to surface?

16. Do you have anything that was left unsaid to your mother before
her unexpected death that you would like to say now?

17. Why do you believe these experiences have occurred to you and
not other relatives?

PRESSURE TO CONFORM

Let us recall a little known fact about mourning: Being around some
family members, co-workers, or friends breeds a certain conformity
that often inhibits the expression of feelings and emotions. There is a
clash of expectations about how to mourn that may include using or

not using the extraordinary experience in the mourning process. The person who has experienced the extraordinary—especially one who has been scientifically trained like the professor—needs opportunities to freely talk about it, unencumbered by fears of ridicule, just as he needs the freedom to mourn in a social environment in which trust and security are pervasive.

In providing support for someone who has an EE while describing himself as an intellectual, a rationalist, non-religious or highly skeptical it is especially important to emphasize two things: the vast historical record of the extraordinary in the lives of mourners and their acceptance of the phenomenon as a viable helpmate for dealing with loss. The historical record of EE's is virtually unknown to the general public although the literature in parapsychology clearly demonstrates its existence.

It is possible to help the mourner break the habit of conforming to being manipulated by the social community in which they belong. You can do this by first pointing out that only the mourner is in the best position to know what he has experienced. Furthermore, let him know that others will want him to talk about anything except the deceased because it makes them feel uncomfortable, and that friends and relatives are often afraid that by talking about the deceased they will cause him to cry or show emotion in their presence. This is way some friends often say how strong the mourner is ("You're doing so well.") and that he looks so good. This manipulation forces the mourner to keep his true feelings and his EE hidden. The latter becomes a closely guarded secret that cannot be fully utilized due to the social pressure to grieve according to the expectations of the social community.

In our next experience we find a young woman whose extraordinary experiences have been a major influence in how she mourned the death of her beloved grandmother. What was particularly helpful to Patti Carter of Alexandria, Virginia, is the openness with which she was able to talk to her husband about the events because he shared two of them with her. This sharing can be especially powerful for the primary mourner, for she now has validation from an important person in her life. This type of family confirmation—a critical response for all helpers to consider and emphasize—opens the way to further sharing and the building of trust so that deep feelings can flow freely. Furthermore, since some studies suggest that concealing emotion may well affect memory retention, finding that one person who "can hear anything and not be judgmental" may add significantly to healthy readjustment. Patti's experience is a good example of how a family member can positively influence grief work.

"WE HEARD MY GRANDMOTHER SAY MY NAME"

First I would like to give you some background information. I am a 22 year-old who less than three months ago lost my grandmother. My mother and I lived with my grandparents for over 10 years after my father left us. I became very close to my grandmother over the years. In 1995 my grandmother had a heart attack and over the next four years she had 15 different attacks. On May 17th we were told that she had less than a week to live. The next morning we signed the DNR and went in to say goodbye—but I couldn't say goodbye. At 8:20 a.m. we were told she was gone. I couldn't bring myself to go up to the casket at the viewing, so I waited until the funeral. I had my husband place a picture of my son and a copy of her favorite book in the casket because I couldn't.

Now about my contacts. The day she died I was feeling very guilty about not going in and saying goodbye. I was sitting on my living room couch just starring into space. All of a sudden my husband told me to look out the sliding glass window. There were 20-30 Monarch butterflies just flying around. What a wonderful sign.

A week later, I was having a problem dealing with not knowing what happened after we died. So I said out loud to my husband that, "I wish I could hear her say my name one last time." Three days later, my husband and I were getting ready for bed when we heard my grandmother say my name. That gave me so much comfort. Even now, three months later, I can still remember it so clearly.

One night, my husband woke up at 3:00 a.m. to see my grandmother standing at the window looking out. He said to her, "Grandmother, why don't you go and watch over Zachary (our 10 month old son)?" Well, as I heard him say this, I woke up to see my grandmother walk across our bedroom floor and through the door. I still see her to this day whenever I am feeling stressed, or I feel her give me one of her famous big hugs.

Patti's adventures after the death of her grandmother have caused her to think of the great questions that have always challenged humanity: Who am I? Why am I here? What happens when earthly life ends? Her view of life was profoundly altered and she wanted to share her experiences with others who believed in the possibility of her new found reality. As she indicated to me, "I have told my mom and aunt and they told me that they do believe me and they felt better knowing she has contacted someone...I felt I had the experiences because I was the only one in my family who has an open mind to ADC's and any other phenomena...I was having a fear that maybe after you die its like when you blow out a candle, nothing more. I had always wondered if there was life after death and now I know and I am not so afraid of dying when I am older."

QUESTIONS TO BE POSED TO PATTI
1. Were you encouraged to talk about feelings in your family when you were growing up? How has this influenced you with the loss of your grandmother?
2. What do you remember about your grandmother when you and your mother lived with her?
3. Where did your grandmother take you when she was taking care of you? Where did you like to go best of all? Why?

4. What did the monarch butterflies remind you of when your husband brought them to your attention?

5. How have your extraordinary experiences helped you in coping with the death of your grandmother?

6. Viewed as expressions of love, are your extraordinary experiences indicative of the way your grandmother loved you during the years you were close to her? How did she show her love?

7. In what ways has your behavior changed since the contacts from your grandmother?

8. What are some of the things your grandmother did in her life that you would like to incorporate into your lifestyle?

9. How did your husband respond after the apparition of your grandmother ended? What emotions were obvious? Were they similar to yours?

10. What have you and your husband discussed about your grandmother in the days after your experiences? What memories did those conversations bring back?

11. What will you tell your son about your grandmother as he gets older?

12. Tell me about the meaning and comfort you received when, after asking to hear your grandmother say your name, both you and your husband received the gift? What was the feeling?

13. Through the years, what is the most cherished experience you have had with your grandmother that you will never forget?

14. What do you feel is the main message of all of your extraordinary experiences involving your grandmother?

Focusing on the way that Patti and her grandmother interacted, especially when her grandmother took care of her and near the end of her grandmother's life, multiple opportunities for Patti to delve into her past and retrieve memories that stir emotion is provided. This method of life review allows the recall of many incidents that have long been forgotten but can now give rise to deep feelings, open the flow of emotions, and may even set the stage for introducing previous unresolved issues that need to be addressed. In using any EE for the purpose of emotional release, close attention has to be placed on the initial responses of the mourner so they can become the basis for deeper inquiry into the relationship.

In the final story of this section we examine the possibilities of building avenues for the expression of emotions through an auditory experience, and the resulting meditations by the mourner. The mourner, Cat Simril Ishikawa, a writer of radio plays, was moved to radically consider changing his belief about the existence of an afterlife. His daughter had died in an automobile accident at a very young age. His experiences after her death provide ample material to generate dialogue that could lead to uncovering deep feelings.

"NO COINCIDENCE EVER DID ME AS MUCH GOOD"

Our daughter, Monique Ishikawa, was born in Vancouver on October 25, 1978. We moved to Japan, to her mother Fumiyo's hometown near Tokyo, at the end of that year, and then returned to Vancouver in 1988. After graduating from high school here, she planned to return to Japan for a visit, the first time as an adult, in June, 1998. Monique and her friend Kim drove to Seattle in Kim's car in order for Monique to do some shopping for presents for her friends in Japan, on May 30, 1998. They finished shopping and were waiting at the border at 9:00 that evening. A woman from Seattle, hallucinating that a hockey player she was in love with was calling her on her car radio to fly to his arms in Vancouver, oblivious to the fact that she was at the border where everyone had to stop, ran her 1998 Grand Am into Kim's 1980 Honda at 100 mph. The Honda exploded. The woman from Seattle was not injured.

Sometime last fall, as I was driving in the afternoon, a time I would often pick Monique up from school or her friends' houses, I had the sensation of Monique being in the car with me and talking to me. I found this painful and depressing, but not particularly strange. I began to hear her voice more and more often. As I write radio plays (and featured Monique in one I wrote in 1997), this did not surprise me. I have spent most of my life talking into tape recorders and playing tapes, and I assumed I was just playing back memory tapes of almost 20 years of conversations I had with my daughter and imagining more. Oddly, Fumiyo and Monique's friends tell me they never hear her voice in their heads—but they don't write radio plays.

May 30th, 1999 was going to be a hard day. We were going to put flowers on Kim's grave in a distant suburb in the morning, then bury Monique's ashes in the afternoon at the local North Van cemetery, and do other related things. I awoke much earlier than usual. Monique and Kim's best friend Steph had given Fumiyo a birthday present in January, a book on extraordinary experiences. I had ignored the book, but that morning thought it might be interesting to read. I started it and finished it the following night. At the end of the book there are a series of meditations. As I read them, I heard Monique tell me to do them. I started doing them the next day, June 1st.

The conversations I began having with my daughter during meditation were of a different order than previous—almost always concrete advice. On one occasion, she told me to get some more books on meditation. I discovered through his web site that the author of the book I had read had another book out and I went and bought it. Its meditations were a little different. Before meditating that day, I had taken a sauna and the smell of cedar still permeated my skin as I meditated. Monique told me to use this smell as a meditation aid. My favorite thing about Japan, in the 17 years I lived there, was the smell of Sugi, a Japanese cedar, used for many things. Here in Vancouver, the Squamish people make boxes of cedar, and we have two small ones. I decided to use one for my next meditation.

This time during my meditation a smiling sun at the center of the earth met me. The sun was like you see in TV weather reports. This didn't surprise me, as the previous evening I had listened to an old favorite radio play, "Everything You Know is Wrong," by the Firesign Theater, which features a sun at the center of the earth. Back at the surface, I began reliving a train trip Monique and I had taken to Nagoya when she was 4. I remembered that somewhere I had some videotape of that trip that I hadn't seen in many years. After meditation, I began looking for it.

In a room we've used for storage for many years, I found 3 school notebooks that were put there when Monique was still alive, and which I had never opened. The top one was Earth Science 11. I opened the book—and discovered Monique's drawing of a smiling sun.

Up until that moment, I had never believed in life after death, and thought that Monique lived on only in memory. When her grandfather died in Japan in 1986, a large Buddhist ceremony welcomed him to the next world, but I told my 7 year-old daughter the only reincarnation was our atoms going to new life forms. Now I'm not so sure. She continues to pour good advice on me as I meditate. This is particularly helpful, as the trial of her killer comes up next month (Aug. 23). It seems the sort of thing that trickster Monique would do to convince me that she really was with me at this most trying time, that it wasn't just my memories of her but actually her. Everyone I told this to think I'm making too much out of what couldn't be more than coincidence—exactly what I would have told them before. Your chapter, Skeptics All, made me see how my previous skepticism was as least as suspect as my conversations with my daughter. The sun may well be a coincidence, but no coincidence ever did me as much good.

Thank you for your book. I may also write one about what I've learned from these meditations. When Monique was still alive, I began writing a play taking incidents from her life and putting them in the Mayan civilization a thousand years ago. This goes into production this fall. If you are interested in learning more about Monique's life, she has a web site at www.doctechnical.com/monique.

The jolt of coincidence is a frequent reflection of connectedness on an individual and collective level. No one has discovered the laws governing coincidence. Probability Theory (dealing with the laws of chance that a given event will occur) and the Clustering Effect (that certain events occur in clusters or bunches) do not explain the **origin** of coincidence. We have described and labeled some phenomena as "coincidence" but we have yet to fully explain it, especially the way it gives direction, guidance and timely inspiration. Could coincidence be a designed part of our connectedness to each other and to the world in which we live and die?

As with untold numbers of mourners before him, much in the grief work of this father hinges on that word coincidence. But all coincidences are not created equal. Was the smiling sun found in the Earth Science notebook Monique's (or the Universe's or Divine Providence's) way of helping her father on to a new path in his life? Was it a daughter's way of providing support at such a critical time? Was it a discovery he was supposed to make as a personal growth-producing measure? Or did the events arise capriciously out of a deep need to hold on to Monique? Who can definitively say? In any event, these constantly occurring experiences are the basis for special opportunities to talk about his daughter and provide him outlets for his deep sadness, and even to find meaning in a senseless tragedy. The drawing of the sun would be a wonderful way to create a healthy symbolic link to his daughter, allow him needed release, and promote solace in his relationship with her.

QUESTIONS TO BE POSED TO CAT

1. Have your extraordinary experiences been a source of comfort for both you and your wife? What emotions and thoughts of Monique do they evoke?

2. What have you discussed with your wife with regard to Monique and your extraordinary experiences?

3. As you think back of Monique as the trickster, what are some of the things she used to do when she was growing up that reflects this playfulness?

4. Have you been encouraged by others to talk about Monique and how her death has affected you? Who have you talked to? What have they said?

5. What have you done with Monique's smiling sun? Where can you place it to bring forth a beautiful memory and the feelings that accompany it? What action can it remind you to take when you are feeling low?

6. Would you say optimists or pessimists surround you as you deal with your loss each day? How does this affect your grief?

7. Do you encourage others in your family to talk about Monique?

8. When you meet Monique's Vancouver friends are you open to talking about her? What questions do they ask you?

9. How will you memorialize Monique on her special days?

10. Would you tell me about Monique's life in Japan? Her friends?

11. What is the most important piece of advice Monique has given you?

12. What memories of Monique most frequently come to mind when you are meditating?

13. What was your initial feeling and thoughts when you sensed Monique's presence in the car and heard her voice?

14. How has Monique's web site helped you deal with her loss?

15. What conversations have you had with Steph, Monique's best friend?

In posing the above questions it would be important to look for opportunities to link a particular response with further inquiries into Monique's childhood and her childhood friends. This would bring back sensitive childhood memories for Cat. For example, if Cat responded affirmatively to question 2, and said he discussed his EE extensively with his wife, then a good follow-up would be, "What serious discussions did you and your wife used to have with Monique about her friends when she was growing up?" Follow with, "Who was her best friend?" Another might be, "Did Monique ever have any dreams or experiences at school that she needed to share with you?" Cat's memories of Monique's childhood will likely open up deep feelings as he pictures his daughter in happier days.

CONCEPTS TO EXPLORE AND DEVELOP IN EXPRESSING EMOTIONS

Much more can be done to promote opportunities for the expression of emotions. In addition to the ideas, events, and past experiences to be discussed in conversations between the helper and the mourner, here are some concepts that are applicable to entertaining new approaches in dealing with emotions.

1. Decide who has been most open and accepting to your extraordinary experience, someone who as been comfortable in your presence. Consider that person as one to call on to listen in the months/years ahead when all others have decided that you "should be over it by now."

   Ask the person if it is okay for you to seek her advice and comfort when grief revisits. Make it clear that you are not in need of professional help but that you do need someone to listen as a normal part of the process of grief. Agree on a regular schedule where you and your helper meet and talk. Initially, it may be once or twice a week and at any mutually agreeable time. Later, the time between visits can lengthen as you get stronger. You may need that person to be there when grief resurfaces in the "year of the firsts" when you confront first-time circumstances without your loved one.

2. Use your extraordinary experience as a starting point to center your thoughts and express your feelings on an especially difficult

day that you are dreading (like going to the lawyer or returning to pick up his clothes at the hospital) or at the very beginning of any day before you get dressed. Meditate on the message and meaning of the EE. Open your heart and say what you are feeling at that time. As a support group participant once said, "Say it and let it bounce back off the walls at you."

3. Drop into your local church or synagogue and unburden yourself. Ask for help to understand "Why now?" Also consider, "Why not now?" Ask for the wisdom to make the right decisions and the strength to endure, and to look at the past as your teacher. Think about what you need to add to your life to conquer depression and to turn your focus away from yourself? If you believe in spirit guides or angels, ask them for the guidance to make the right choices in the days and weeks ahead as you adapt to your new "surroundings."

4. Write up the story of your extraordinary experience detailing the feelings and emotions that accompanied it. Try to recreate those positive feelings in your mind and body as you write about them. Describe them in as much detail as possible. Then add a note about one positive emotion or feeling that you wish to recall and cherish for the rest of your life. State how you will do this.

5. Go to a bereavement web site on the Internet (try www.griefnet.org). Ask for ideas on how to deal with a specific part of your grief that has been most troublesome. Take the ideas you receive and discuss them with a close friend.

6. Establish a mourning time each day where you focus on all your pain and what you have lost. Do not exceed one hour. Remember that grief is a friend, not the enemy; it is love's hidden companion. Bring a picture of your loved one to your mourning place. Lament about all aspects of your loss. Read something he has written or a poem that reminds you of him. Have something you plan to do at the end of the hour that will take you away from your mourning

place. As difficult as it will be, make every effort not to dwell on your loss for long periods of time for the remainder of the day. You will not be dishonoring your loved one; you will be applauding him or her and giving yourself time to regain strength. Do not be caught in the trap of thinking that by moving forward and not thinking of your loved one for a period of time you are forgetting him or banishing him to the past.

7. Keep a notebook on your nightstand. When you awake and can't get back to sleep, write what you are thinking and feeling at that time. Let it all come out. Call your notebook your "paper psychiatrist." When finished slowly read the story of your extraordinary experience that you have carefully written and placed in the back of the notebook. Concentrate on the descriptions of the feelings associated with the experience. Reread for the comfort and relaxation it brings. As you relax, try to get back to sleep by repeating a word or mantra associated with the EE that causes you to slowly let go of anxious thoughts.

8. Dedicate a particular domestic task that you have to do or an hour in your workday to the memory of your deceased loved one. Say in a soft voice that you are doing so, and then keep alive in your mind the purpose of your dedication. Let your thoughts or tears flow freely as you do the task.

9. Take some pictures, paintings, or drawings that remind you of your loved one and evoke strong feelings. Use them as visual signals for you to express feelings, especially when you want to show your emotions but have been unable to do so. Or make a piece of jewelry that will be your personal reminder of your EE. Permit yourself to openly express your feelings at the times you are drawn to reflecting on your memorial to your loved one.

10. Construct a collage of pictures or paint a collage in which you include a symbol of your extraordinary experience and other remembrances of your loved one's interests and values. Give it a

name and place it in your home or cottage in a location that will be helpful to you in maintaining the bond with your loved one and allowing your feelings to surface.

11. It is all right if you believe you have immediate duties or obligations that must come first (children, a new job, etc.) before you can deal fully with your emotions. Later, it is imperative to find the times and places necessary for you to openly grieve both alone and with others.

12. The best place to talk about your loss and be with others who are dealing with similar losses, if you have no one in your circle of friends who understands, is a bereavement support group. Seeking support is *not* a sign of weakness. Like going to a doctor, you may have to shop around until you find the right one.

    You will learn much from other participants who are at different places in their journey back to wholeness that will be useful. Ask about support groups at your local hospice, church, hospital, or mental health agency. The topic of extraordinary experiences will surface in one of the meetings. If you feel safe in the group, share your EE.

13. Do not hesitate to ask to be left alone to accommodate your need to express yourself out loud or silently without the intervention or presence of others. It is perfectly normal to talk to yourself by yourself. Do not compare your grief and the way you express it with the grief of others. Your way of mourning is unique to you. There is no right or wrong way to mourn; there is only your way.

14. Ask your best friend to attend a workshop or lecture with you on grief and/or extraordinary experiences. It will be a wonderful opportunity to talk about various issues and new information you will receive. Learning more about the normalcy of grief and extraordinary experiences is a significant part of grief work. It will counter the cultural misrepresentations that cause added pain.

ARE GENDER NEEDS REALLY DIFFERENT?

Over the years the literature on grief suggests that women often have better support networks and are more verbal and open to express emotions, giving them a therapeutic edge in coping with the death of a loved one. Men are said to be less willing to emote or be around when emotion is expressed and often need to work out or do other things to deal with their grief (work long hours, exercise, actively participate in funeral preparations). While all this may be true in a general way, let us remember that grief is still highly individual. Men as well as women often need opportunities to talk just as woman often need opportunities to get out and physically work out their grief. There are gender opposites when it comes to classifying characteristics of mourners but they do not hold up for all mourners.

Even though women generally outlive men and are most often the "survivors," letting out what builds within, finding someone who will listen to what it feels like inside, is a human need not a specifically male or female need. How and where the need is met, who or what will be the facilitator, can be surprising at times. As a helper, when the time comes, absorb the pain as though receiving a gift from a loved one. Gender is neutral in the throes of grief, especially when it comes to the repetition of feelings. Everyone likes to repeat certain events in expressing emotion and the need varies immensely. Much depends on who is trusted to be the listener. As you recall from Chapter 2, your willingness to listen repeatedly to the stories is important in lessening the deep emotional ties to the deceased and progressing to acceptance of the death. The repetition may come in the form of the story of the extraordinary or any other event between the mourner and the beloved. Allowing free flow of emotion is a health and healing initiative that you must embrace with all your heart. Although the methods of release of emotion will differ between the sexes, the basic need to say what is happening within is shared among all.

THE AMBIVALENT MOURNER

At times, most interpersonal relationships have some degree of ambivalence or opposite and conflicting feelings. The memories of such feelings almost always come back to haunt mourners after the death of a loved one inflicting unending guilt. If you are mourning, work toward bringing out your emotional secrets, submit and reconcile yourself to the faults as well as the disagreements you may have had with the deceased. Everyone has them. Proudly let your sadness at your great loss show without the added burden of false assumptions about yourself. By realizing ambivalent feelings are common and releasing them you will be letting your body and soul out of emotional solitary confinement and putting yourself on the road to peace. Let it become a habit, a lifesaving habit you can use for a lifetime. And there is a bonus: by practicing being consistently open and sharing feelings with the right person you will set the stage for your listener to share his inner Self with you. There will be a double victory, a strong mutually fulfilling relationship.

Until the repeated release of suppressed emotion is fulfilled, it will be most difficult to ever consider a major task of mourning: reinvesting in life. The pain will always be there, lying in wait, festering. Yet reinvesting emotional energy in life is the antidote for breaking the perception of isolation and fear that often pervades the journey through grief. Although many mourners express great emotion, sometimes they do little else to make sense of their loss and face life again. The essential task of reinvestment initially involves establishing a new relationship with the deceased loved one based on memory and living memorials, and then finding interpersonal relationships for sharing mutual interests and concerns. This is our next topic of discussion.

5

Establishing New Relationships: Breaking Through The Isolation Trap

Everything can be taken from a man but one thing: the last of human freedoms—to choose one's attitude in any given set of circumstances, to choose one's own way.

Viktor Frankl
Man's Search for Meaning

The Wisdom Within

Most of us go through life never really listening to or connecting with the little inner voice that is our soul. We are more inclined to deny the existence simply because of the strange looks and reactions that we receive when we mention such things. Our souls are ever connected to each other and those we come in contact with in our life times. That connection does not end when the vestiges of life leave our beings and the energy of our soul is liberated. When someone close to you dies, the subconscious mind is unlocked and these things open up....if you are open to it and allow it to happen. The departed one wishes to ease your pain, knowing full well that the loss is difficult, and to let you know that the relationship has not ended—that you are forever connected. We on this earth are all interconnected and we should embrace these connections and not deny their existence simply because we cannot prove it. The proof is in our subconscious and in our souls, the part of us that has been left behind in the modern world of science.

—Dianna K.
On her EE after the death of her sister.

∞　　∞　　∞　　∞　　∞

Grief will not go away if you simply wait for things to get better or if you try to medicate your way through it. I once heard a mother at a Compassionate Friends support group—whose 17 year-old son was killed in an automobile accident—put in perspective the work of grief when she said, "Time does not heal grief unless you work between the minutes." This chapter is about part of the work that needs to be accomplished between the minutes: building a new relationship with the deceased and with others who come into and out of our lives at this precarious time.

Any mourner's isolation from life and the world comes from three major sources: her emotions (as discussed in Chapter 3), friends of the mourner who are dealing with their own fears and do everything to avoid her, and from poor choices based on questionable assumptions. The perception of isolation from friends and loved ones is commonly a major source of stress for most people because each of us needs our own particular type of intimacy and community—and from the "right" person or persons. This is especially true of those who are mourning. If one is convinced that she is all alone, perceives that she has been avoided or abandoned by those she thought were friends, is convinced that no one understands or is there to reach out and help in time of need, then the sense of isolation becomes almost unbearable. It is further heightened when others encourage her to let go and forget the past, including the deceased loved one.

A sense of deep isolation can also occur with the mourner whose loved one committed suicide. The stigma of suicide often causes the mourner to withdraw from others out of shame or self-blame. Some survivors say they sense the awkwardness of friends who try to avoid them because they don't know what to say.

The state of isolation is a constant threat if the mourner has been conditioned to believe that living alone or being alone is in itself equated with not being loved and persistent never-ending loneliness. Unfortunately, such a negative belief has been fostered by our highly affluent and technologically oriented culture. This conditioning prevails because society minimizes the importance of silence and solitude and maximizes the need to depend on and be around others for entertainment and happiness.

SHYNESS AND COPING WITH THE DEATH OF A LOVED ONE

Whenever a mourner isolates himself he automatically gives his fears, feelings, and doubts freedom to reign, grow, and complicate the reconstruction of confidence in social interaction. This ultimately leads to unnecessary suffering instead of gradual acceptance of change. Yet it is common for mourners to have people around them for a week or ten days after the death and then suddenly feel alone as people gradually drift away. At this time, mourners feel no one really understands their pain, or that those who should still be giving a helping hand are growing weary of their commitment. Such thoughts are major barriers to the social connections desperately needed when mourning.

Shyness also exacerbates feelings of loneliness and isolation, not to mention the anxiety of self-doubt that is created. And since it is estimated that millions of people are shy—by some estimates nearly half of the population—those providing support need to be especially cognizant of the mourner's personality before the death occurred. Support persons will need to be especially proactive, maybe even a little aggressive, in their efforts to give assistance.

If you the reader are a shy person mourning the death of a loved one, now more than ever you need to reach out for help, find someone to trust, and share your extraordinary experience (or at least your deep feelings of sadness). This is easier said than done when your history has been one of withdrawal and distancing. However, your choice to trust and share your gift with the right person can be the single most important factor in reconciling your loss.

It may help to know that many others need the opportunity to provide support for you as much as you need to receive their attempts to understand your plight. There will be people around you who will welcome your call for assistance because they don't know what to do. This is one time when you need to reach out instead of in. So whether your shyness is due to overprotective parents, distorted self-perceptions, physical appearance, or a long series of putdowns by others in your life, make every effort to look for someone—clergy, counselor, parent, relative, friend—to be the sounding board you need in your sorrow. Take the risk of possible rejection that has long been your scourge; we all must take risks in order to grow and adapt to massive change. Life is all about taking risks or simply continuing to live deep within self-imposed limitations. I know all too well of what I speak for I am one who has known shyness.

REMEMBER QUESTIONABLE CULTURAL CONDITIONING

As suggested earlier, a patently false view of grieving advances the belief that the grief process is relatively short and one should soon be "over it" and be "like his old Self again." A companion myth further suggests that the mourner should let go of the deceased and try not to think about him. "Put the past behind you," they say. In short, what well-meaning friends are saying is that the relationship has ended, and you should not try to keep it alive. This is unrealistic at best. Furthermore, friends and relatives learn early on not to mention the deceased in the presence of the mourner because "it will only cause more pain." The truth is, by not mentioning the deceased the mourner has to keep her pain within where it causes great turmoil both physically and mentally. She will always have thoughts about the deceased. Other mourners fear that not talking about the deceased means he or she will be forgotten. Relationships thrive on attention and communication—both verbal and nonverbal.

In reality, it is essential for the mourner to develop a new relationship with the deceased, one in which the death is accepted and memories of their lives together can be looked upon in a healthy way. This transformative process occurs more easily once helpers become aware of the importance of their support in the construction of the new bond. The relationship with the deceased proceeds unconsciously and consciously in the work of grief. Establishing a new relationship with the deceased is essentially establishing a new inner image, a bridge between the living and the dead. The EE is part of the superstructure of that bridge.

Even if the mourner tries to suppress the relationship because of the pressure from her immediate social group, or because of her choice to persist out of a misguided need to conquer grief, the relationship will persist. However, the type of relationship developed, one in which the survivor recognizes and accepts the death yet cherishes the memories and associations with the deceased, depends on honestly mourning all of the implications of the loss. That can only be accomplished by coming face to face with change and new responsibilities, not sidestepping them. Specifically, it means recognizing all the secondary losses as suggested in Chapter 1 (things like financial , social, sexual, and geographical changes imposed by the death as well as unspoken shattered dreams) and mourning them. This is always a long-term process and needs good listeners

Although death does end the visible interaction between two people it never ends the inner relationship. It is the internal relationship that has to be built and nourished. There are clearly many healthy ways in which a new relationship can be initiated and maintained that do not impede the growth and adaptation of the survivor. In this regard, it is healthy to consider the values and rich experiences in life that the survivor received from association with the loved one. For example, the mourner can write a history of the spousal relationship and what she was grateful for. She could dedicate a fund or scholarship to honor the deceased or celebrate a special holiday by recognizing a wonderful blessing received. All of this nourishes the inner relationship. These are not only important considerations when grieving, but also years later when reminiscing with family and friends they help nourish the continuous bond. Sometimes friends provide rich observations for the new relationship as illustrated in the sentiments of a note received by a woman who came to me for counseling after the death of her husband. Her friends had written:

> *And while nothing can make this time any easier for you*
> *maybe it will touch your heart to know that while we mourn*
> *the loss, we also celebrate the gifts we never would have*
> *known if we hadn't known such a wonderful person.*

On the other side of the card was a single sentence of inestimable value: *"Your loved one made such a difference in so many lives."* Needless to say, this thoughtful note did touch her heart deeply, provided much comfort to a grieving widow, and became part of the new inner image of her husband.

The topic of lessons learned and gifts received from the deceased may become a meaningful source for establishing new memory relationships, especially when a mourner experiences the extraordinary. Mourners often perceive the extraordinary experience as a carryover of the love and concern the deceased still shows for those left behind. If that is not openly expressed, you may want to bring it to the attention of the mourner when appropriate. It is a sound basis for establishing the new relationship and also giving the mourner permission to begin her new life as a different person.

TYPES OF RELATIONSHIPS

New relationships can be established on three levels. First, the mourner can initiate healthy memory relationships with the past ("We had a good life together.") This can be accomplished in writing the history of her relationship with the deceased loved one. Promoting healthy memories is the foundation for a strong inner relationship. Sometimes the relationship with the deceased after death is stronger than when the person was alive. Secondly, she can establish a new relationship with the deceased in the present ("I will always love him, although he is gone and in a better place now.") Also in the present, she can establish interpersonal relationships as a result of meeting others who have had similar experiences.

Thirdly, a mourner can relate to others in her world with a whole new perspective as a result of an EE. As one woman said, "I am closer to others. I am making my beliefs more known. I am less introverted." Some EE's, coupled with the experience of mourning a major loss, can be the basis for strengthening relationships within the family, cultivating a new social circle, or rejoining an old one. The experience may easily change the way the mourner views her world.

Let's examine three accounts of spontaneous experiences that illustrate how each type of relationship can be developed to assist one's grief work in the establishment of new relationships and possibilities.

This first brush with the extraordinary occurred to Kern Loughran, the mother of Meredith, whose twenty-six year old aviator daughter was killed when the jet she was in crashed on the deck of the USS Enterprise on November 8, 1998. Meredith's cats gave her mother much comfort in the days following the accident that also claimed the lives of three other naval aviators. One of those cats was of special significance in her experience.

"THIS EMPTY TO FULL BOTTLE TRANSFORMED ME FROM A DOUBTING THOMAS"

On November 16, 1998 I was in the hallway crying and talking to Meredith and I said, "Meredith, I know that you're okay but I'm not. I need some comfort." I went down the hall and went into the bathroom and sat down. Pumpkin jumped in my lap and kissed and kissed my hands and rolled around and gave me the biggest love-in and I said out loud, "Oh, isn't this nice." Then I realized that it was Meredith sending me comfort through her beloved cat and I said, "Oh Meredith, it's you. How nice." I enjoyed it so much and all of a sudden Pumpkin stopped and jumped out of my lap.

I had a terrible week of sorrow and on December 9th I was so distraught that I essentially cried all day long and wailed and prayed to God for comfort. My daughter Katherine called me seven times that day to check on me. The first thing on the morning of the 10th she called again to see if I was better and as I was talking on the phone I picked up the medicine bottle. It had been brought back from the vet for Dusty by our Goddaughter, Amy, the month before during the week of Meredith's accident. Dusty had developed a cancer on her lip in September. Meredith and I had e-mailed each other trying to decide what to do for the fourteen year old cat and we finally had her operated on, the stitches removed, and the medicine obtained by Amy. The medicine was only to last for a month, which it did.

As I was talking with Katherine, Meredith's sister, I picked up the bottle to get the name of the medication so I could call the vet to make sure they had some, in order to give me a refill. It had been totally empty on Tuesday and I'd been in too much grief to get it refilled. I couldn't believe it—the bottle was full! Right away I knew it was a sign of comfort from Meredith and once again it involved one of her cats. It was appropriate that Katherine was on the phone with me to share this miraculous sign of comfort.

That day I was able to get to the vet to have the contents first checked by the assistant and then verified by the vet. She tasted and smelled the contents herself and said it was exactly what was supposed to be in the bottle. This empty to full bottle transformed me from a doubting Thomas to a believer in every aspect of my Christian education. This caused me to believe in the transubstantiation during Catholic communion and as a result of this I now take communion with John in the Catholic Church with our priest's blessing. This event also opened my eyes to the Christmas celebration, like it was my first Christmas.

Kern's experiences have led her to a new relationship with her daughter as she believes that Meredith lives on "but merely in a different realm." She made it clear to me that she is working on integrating the spiritual and earthly worlds in her goal "to make the necessary adjustments in life to go on and live a full life." This is a very important statement and goal that needs to be discussed in terms of specific actions she is taking and will continue to take in the future. It is also a part of the third level of relationships, strengthening friendships with others, which can be developed as a result of her EE. As a result of her experience, I have learned that others have shared their EE's with Kern and they have reinforced the validity of her own experience and changed the quality of her social interactions.

QUESTIONS TO BE POSED TO KERN
1. What do you believe are the attributes and limitations of the realm in which Meredith resides?
2. What caused you to think that Meredith was behind the cat jumping up into your lap and kissing your hands?

3. What is different about the relationship you now have with Meredith?

4. What differences do you see in the way you think of and relate to those in your social circle? How has your relationship with yourself changed?

5. How has your experience affected the way you interact with other family members?

6. How did the veterinarian and his assistant respond when you explained to them the purpose of your visit?

7. What specific things are you doing that illustrate your change from a doubting Thomas to a believer?

8. How has your experience motivated you to reach out to others in need? Has it rescued you from your turmoil and returned a sense of control?

9. Has your experience brought your family closer together? If so, in what ways?

10. How has the bond between you and your daughter Katherine changed?

11. Have you met others who have experienced the extraordinary? How has learning of their experiences helped you?

12. Who has provided the most helpful support through these difficult days?

13. Have you drawn especially close to anyone since Meredith's death? In what ways?

14. What part of your relationship with Meredith and Katherine will you forever cherish ?

15. With whom do you spend most of your time as you continue to cope with Meredith's death? Have these relationships become stronger?

16. Have you met anyone in your support group that you have spoken with outside of the group setting? Had lunch with?

Encouraging Kern to develop her relationships with others in the family and outside of it, as well as with Meredith as a loving daughter, can flow naturally from the answers to the above questions. In this regard, a helper could ask Kern if she has a scrapbook of Meredith's life and how she could go about rearranging it and bringing it up to date. At the same time, she should also be aware of Katherine's need for nurturance and not to idealize Meredith to such a degree that Katherine feels her mother is not giving her enough attention at this critical time. It is not unusual for a sibling to feel she is being overlooked during the mourning process. Though decidedly different, the relationship with both daughters can be maintained and made stronger.

In the following EE Nancy Allen has been able to use several dream experiences to strengthen her beliefs in an afterlife and in the freedom that death brings to the soul. She also discovered that the relationship with her deceased loved ones never dies but requires new modes of interaction. Furthermore, her mother and great-grandmother's dream visitations have brought much change in Nancy's image of death and are considered to be great treasures in her life. Her relationships with her deceased loved ones have taken on new meaning.

"LEARNING TO RELATE TO A LOVED ONE IN A DIFFERENT WAY WAS A PROFOUND THOUGHT FOR ME"

My mother moved on to her new life in April of this year. Through my Christian grounding, my readings on the spirit world, and my personal experiences I very much believe in life after life. But your thoughts about the grieving process being one of learning to relate to a loved one in a different way was a profound thought for me. Even though I believe I can communicate with my mother and she with me, I'd never thought about the fact that those of us left behind have to learn a new way to communicate, and to receive communication. Thank you for opening that door of thought, among others, for me.

Until "Mom" Hayes' death in August of 1980, I had not given much thought to signs or communication. "Mom" Hayes was my great grandmother and was close to my family. She spent many hours with us. Her most regular visits were on Sundays when she would come home with us after church to have lunch and to spend the afternoon. The day she died was a Sunday. We had taken her to her home to change into more comfortable clothes with the understanding that we would leave her and come back later to pick her up for lunch. I was the designated "picker upper." When I arrived at her house I noticed that her door was open and not on the chain lock, which was unusual. After knocking and calling for her and getting no response, I walked into her house. What I found was her in the middle of having a stroke. Our last earthly nonverbal communication was me looking at her, and her looking back with the understanding in her eyes of what was taking place and the fact that I was there. She then lost consciousness. Later that evening she passed on to the next life surrounded by the love of her family.

During this time, "Mom" Hayes' daughter, my Grandma Mae, was dying a slow bed-ridden death. She would die in December of 1980. So it was hard losing "Mom" but even harder for me to see Grandma Mae die a suffering death.

About two weeks after "Mom" moved on I had a dream. I was outside of "Mom's" house looking at a beautiful yellow rose. Suddenly that rose "died" into a beautiful golden color. Dead, but still as awesome in color as ever. Out of that rose then rose up a butterfly that flew off into the heavens. Then I walked into "Mom's" house. Standing in the front foyer of her house I could see into her bedroom. My Grandma Mae was lying on "Mom's" bed. She was dressed in a white wedding-like gown and seemed to shimmer with light. She floated off the bed, into the room where I was standing, came and still floating, rested on my shoulders. I could feel no weight. I heard the words from "Mom," "She's dying, but that's okay." I awoke to the knowledge that I'd had no ordinary dream, that "Mom" had paid me a special visit to let me know that death is a beautiful, freeing thing, and that Grandma Mae was headed for the same wonderful journey. My image of death will always be of that of yellow roses and butterflies flying free.

After my mother died, on the plane ride back after her funeral, I had a dream of her coming up and hugging me. I woke to the special feeling that she had been right there. I could feel her warmth and love. That was a special hug. Then on July 3rd I had another dream (this is the one that caused me to buy your book). Mother and I were in a camp cabin, talking about everyday things. She then said, "I'm okay you know. God kept my body going for so long." Off to her left was her Dad. Her comment about him was, "He was sure glad to get out of that old body." Off to his left was another figure. It was a human shape but with no features. It was dirty yellow in color—like a form ready to be filled in. I looked at it and Mom said, "He committed suicide, you know." Initially I thought she made that comment about her Dad, because the suicide statement came right on the heels of her comment about her Dad being glad to get out of his body. But given the fact that her dad did not commit suicide, and given the fact that I was looking at the yellow form when she made the comment, I think now that she was referring to whoever will fill up that form. I've asked for clarification, especially if I am supposed to do something about whoever this is committing suicide. Mom's been no help in clearing up this matter yet. I'm still waiting! Now the part that made me cry and laugh at the same time was that Mom was wearing her red, white, and blue top. Given that it was July 3rd she was right on target with holiday wear. Typical Mom!

Obviously I've held on to this dream as something very special. Like "Mom" Hayes' dream to me, Mother's coming to me has helped me know that she's okay, earthly death is okay, and that the release of the soul from the body is a wonderful freeing thing. They are experiences that I will treasure all my life.

The extraordinary most often brings connection, affiliation, cohesion, a sense of belonging—needs which are imbedded deep in the psyche and long for continuous fulfillment throughout life. As we have seen, these needs can be met in a dream, then validated through discussion with a support person, and treasured as inspirational resources to build new relationships.

QUESTIONS TO BE POSED TO NANCY

1. How often did you visit with "Mom" Hayes before she died? What did you used to talk about?
2. How would you describe the new relationship that you have with your grandmother?
3. How has the experience of finding "Mom" Hayes at her home affected you and your view of life?
4. How were you able to assist your Grandma Mae during the time of her lingering illness?
5. How did the words of "Mom" Hayes in your dream help you in the way you related to Grandma Mae during her illness?
6. In what ways have your experiences helped you in the way you relate to other family members?
7. How have you filled the void in your life due to the deaths of your loved ones?
8. Do you think "Mom" Hayes would be the first to say, "Reach out to others and enjoy their company?" Why would she feel this is so important?
9. How will you reach out to others and the future?
10. Have you joined any clubs or initiated any new hobbies to find others who have mutual interests? How do you think this could be helpful to your well-being? What would it do with some of your emotional energy?
11. What is the message(s) you have received about living life from the dreams you were fortunate to have?

12. If "Mom's" purpose for visiting you in your dream was to tell you she is okay, what would you think she would like to see you doing so that you will be happy again?

13. What choices have you made about life and the people in your life that are different as a result of your dreams?

14. How will you promote new relationships in your life given what you have learned?

15. As you look back on your experiences what are you most grateful for? How do "Mom" and Grandma Mae live within you now?

Nancy's awareness of the importance of "learning to relate to a loved one in a different way" presents a significant introduction to the discussion of relationships, what they entail and demand. The discussion can center on the quality and meaning of her relationships with those who are deceased and, of equal importance, the quality of relationships with those in her circle of friends. Particular attention should be focused on the health implications of interpersonal relationships and the need to cultivate and work on maintaining them. The nature of interpersonal relationships—particularly the specifics of trust, openness, caring, and commitment—provides a review of factors that brings awareness of mutual assistance and need satisfaction. Reminders about what makes for solid interpersonal relationships, especially the major role of social skills, are something all of us can benefit from given the mental and physical health implications.

When the extraordinary experience involves the deceased voicing words of love, it becomes a special vehicle for transformation and building the new relationship while accepting the death of the loved one. Here is an example of a message of love raising self-esteem, so essential in regaining a sense of control and in relating to the deceased. This is exemplified in the life of twenty year-old Angela Greer, who at a relatively young age, was given an experience that she said she used to widen her horizon.

"I COULD FINALLY UNDERSTAND WHY SHE CAME TO ME"

This experience happened about one year ago, actually one year and four months.

It was October 4, 1997 and I was up early on a Saturday morning, which was quite unusual for a 20 year-old, especially after a Friday night. I was having a hard time sleeping so I laid in bed and watched television. Then I received a telephone call from my father at 7:30 a.m. informing me that my grandmother had had a massive heart attack. So I went to the hospital. When I arrived there, she was already gone.

This was a shock to everyone in my family since my grandmother (Nancy Walde) was only fifty-eight years old. She had a successful health examination one-week prior to her death. Words cannot define the feeling of sadness I felt. My grandmother was a wonderful person. She was like a mother and a best friend to me. My parents were very young when I was born (seventeen & eighteen years old) so my grandmother became my sense of security and stability. I was her only granddaughter and we bonded from the beginning of my life and on into her afterlife.

The funeral was horrible as expected. I dropped out of college because it was too hard to study full-time through all this. I continued modeling and I was taking medication for depression. A few months later, I was informed that my grandfather became ill and that his days were limited. Grandpa (Larry Greer) was also only fifty-eight years old. I went to see him at my father's house and he looked horrible. It was very difficult to see him because he had lost over seventy pounds and had a yellow coloration to his skin due to liver failure. I couldn't visit very long because I couldn't fight my tears. I knew it would upset him to see me crying.

I went home and continued on with daily duties. It was a few days later that I woke up in a crying frenzy. I had a dream of my grandmother and it seemed so real. What I mean is that I was con-

scious, and I seemed to be aware of reality. Usually in dreams I don't have a sense of reality, nor do the dreams make sense. I believe this was not a dream, rather some form of communication with the deceased.

It began with my grandmother sitting on the side of my bed and I sat up to see if it were really she. She was wearing a regular shorts outfit but there was a light surrounding her. I looked at her and said, "Oh my God, what are you doing here? Are you okay?" She said, "Yes, I am fine. I know you are not doing so well. I am so sorry for leaving you." I said, "Grandma I understand, it's not your fault. I am sorry that you are gone. Why are you worrying about me?" She said, "Angie, I love you very much" as a steady stream of tears were rolling down her face. I asked her, "Did it hurt when you had the heart attack?" She replied, "No, I was not in any pain. There are a few things I want you to do." "Okay, grandma." "Well first of all, you have to realize that just because I am not here with you physically, it doesn't mean that I am gone forever. You have to be strong and move on with your life and think of your future. I want you to remain close to your dad and let go of your anger toward him (dad and I had normal relationship problems). And I would like you to finish your college. I know you can do it. Make me proud of you. It is very important to me. I have to go now, but I love you and I will always be watching over you." I said, "Bye grandma, I love you too." Then I woke up.

Even though I was crying, I also felt a sense of relief and peace. It was February 12, 1998, and I telephoned my dad to inform him of my encounter. I was crying. Dad then informed me that my grandfather had passed away. It was all making sense to me now. I could finally understand why she came to me. Grandma's intentions were to relieve me from the sadness and grief that I felt after her death so that I would be able to cope with my grandfather's passing.

It is really odd, because I was raised as a Roman Catholic and I attended a Catholic school for about nine years. I never really *believed in ghosts or any afterlife stuff. So this was very hard for me to understand. I haven't had any other encounters, but I would love to see my grandma again.*

The importance of Angie's feelings when she awoke from her visit with her grandmother should be emphasized in discussing her experience. The sense of relief and peace that were part of the event are significant factors in her awareness of her grandmother's ongoing love, the relationship they share, and her growth and maturity in facing the continuing losses in life. It would also be appropriate to explore her views on the meaning of life now that she has had an EE, the example that her grandmother has set for her, and how love has proved to be a major factor in dealing with the sadness that occurs in life. Of course, the advice Angie received should be given particular attention for its usefulness in the months ahead.

QUESTIONS TO BE POSED TO ANGIE
1. What was the feeling when your grandma said, "Angie, I love you very much."
2. Knowing that your grandma is loving you from the other world, how can you use that knowledge in reconstructing your life?
3. What is different in the way you are dealing with your grandfather's death since the visit from your grandma?
4. How do you interpret your grandma's meaning in the phrase, "it doesn't mean that I am gone forever."
5. How did your grandma continually show her love for you in the years prior to her death?
6. Who would you turn to now for emotional and attitudinal information?
7. What has been most helpful in dealing with your depression?
8. Who do you think about when it comes to making choices and decisions about future plans?
9. How will you go about modeling your grandmother's love?

10. What action will you take with regard to the requests your grand-mother made about finishing college and letting go of the anger toward your dad?

11. Why were you able to better cope with your grandfather's death as a result of the visit from your grandma?

12. Are you familiar with the doctrine of the Communion of Saints in your church and that you can pray to your grandma and she can intercede and pray for you? (In the broadest sense, the Communion of Saints includes all who die in the friendship of God, irrespective of religious persuasion, and not just the holy or Christians. There can be communication between the living and those in spirit.)

13. Have you asked for another visitation dream?

14. Do you have a spiritual practice that helps you connect with the wisdom that lies within? Would you like to explore how others have made this connection?

15. What parts of your relationship with your grandma do you want to develop in building other relationships in your life?

The special need for maintaining an intimate connection, a sense of belonging and being understood is no greater than at times of loss. As we see in the relationship of Angie with her grandmother, a departed loved one as well as the conventional support system of family or friends, all can fulfill the intimacy need. Angie wielded considerable strength and determination in making efforts to fulfill her grand-mother's wishes, as she told me later. She has gone back to school and plans on making her grandmother and family proud of her "because that is the last gift I can give."

Can a new relationship with the deceased be fashioned if there is an unresolved issue? Can others be enlisted in forming a new bond with the deceased? Could a deceased friend play a part in preparing for the death of a loved one and the acceptance of that death? In considering these questions witness the experience of Virginia Povraznik, a Health Consultant from Van Nuys, California.

"EVEN THOUGH I KNEW HE WAS GONE AND I WAS CRYING, I WAS NOT SAD"

Background

My after death communication experiences involve both my best friend Kathy, who committed suicide in April 1996, and my husband, John, who died on July

17, 1999. This was a second marriage for both of us and it had its problems, primarily two episodes of infidelity on the part of my husband. My best friend had helped me through both of these, including a particularly bad time between November 1995 and March 1996.

That November, my husband was diagnosed with colon cancer. He announced to me that he was leaving me and moving in with a woman he had known before we married. Both he and this woman had strong beliefs in the power of spiritual healing. It was my husband's feeling that, because of my occupation in the health care field, I was preventing perfect health from being expressed in him. This resulted in his cancer. He was gone for three months.

During this time, my best friend was there for me. She was a physician and helped me both with the normal trauma of being left for another woman and with the fear I had because my husband was not seeking any medical treatment for his cancer. After three months my husband returned. I was able to reconcile with him since I believe he had simply gone a little "crazy" with fear when he heard the diagnosis with cancer and this had made him behave as he did. In my career, I have often seen people who do some pretty drastic things when given this diagnosis. His behavior was not the worst I'd seen. He had been home one month when my best friend killed herself. I suffered greatly at that time going into true clinical depression. My husband helped me through this, which strengthened our relationship significantly.

When my husband returned, he chose to be treated with chemotherapy and radiation and not surgery, which was the treatment recommended. With the treatment he chose, and the power of his belief system, all traces of the cancer disappeared. He remained in remission for over a year. In November of 1998, however, he was diagnosed with metastatic disease to the liver. The surgeons felt that this could be completely removed, and his liver would regenerate. This surgery was done in April 1999.

His post-operative progress was amazing, even by the standards of his physicians. By June 1, 1999, his liver had regenerated. All tests showed no signs of any residual cancer. The medical oncologist, who pre-operatively had recommended a course of systemic chemotherapy to begin four weeks after surgery, said that was no longer necessary. A four-week course on an oral agent was all that would be needed. In short, he was a "poster boy" patient.

There was only one problem. After the liver surgery, one of the temporary drains they had left in place broke when they tried to remove it and retracted back into the abdomen. Several attempts were made to remove it. On July 2, 1999, it was removed through an upper GI endoscopy procedure called an ERCP. One of the risks associated with that procedure is pancreatitis. This is often fatal and was so in the case of my husband.

After death Communication – My Best Friend Kathy

My husband had the retracted drain removed by ERCP on July 2, 1999. This was an outpatient procedure and he came home that afternoon. He had considerable pain during the night and the next morning I took him back to the hospital to be admitted for what everyone thought was some intravenous pain control. He was expected to be in the hospital for twenty-four hours. I did not go back to see him since I knew he needed his rest and the situation did not appear serious. The next morning, July 4th, I received a call that he had been transferred to the ICU on a ventilator and was in critical condition. He never recovered enough to talk with me or to give me any visible sign that he knew I was there.

From the time of his admission to the ICU, the physicians gave him only a 5% chance of recovering. However, they did stress that he was fighting and was certainly responding like the 5% that do recover. He was treated aggressively both with medication and mechanical assistance including dialysis. For the first week I had no strong inner feeling as to whether he would recover or not. Sometimes I thought he would, other times I felt the opposite.

On the morning of August 11, 1999, before I went to see him, I went to church. I am Russian Orthodox by faith. My best friend who had committed suicide in 1996 was Jewish. In my church, parishioners tend to sit in the same pews every week. While I was praying, something made me turn around and look over my shoulder. I saw a woman walk in who looked just like my best friend. She was even dressed like her—impeccably, very European, linen dress, low heeled dress pumps, right down to the scarf around her neck. The only thing slightly out of place was that she was carrying a backpack, not the tiny purse she usually carried. She sat in a pew about 5 rows behind me, on the opposite side of the church and on the aisle. A couple with 2 high school age girls usually sit there. My first thought was, "God, that looks like Kathy. What is she doing in a Christian church?" Right on top of that thought, I felt something that was more than a thought but it said, "It is Kathy. She's come for John." Then I thought, "You're crazy."

I finished my prayer (about 1-2 minutes). Before I stood up, I played a mind game with myself where I said, "When I turn around, if she is gone it was Kathy and she did come for John." I did this because I was a little scared and I firmly believed that I would see this woman when I turned around and this would prove that I was just having a bout of over imagination. When I did turn around, however, the woman was gone and sitting where she had been was the couple with the 2 high school girls. I have to say that I do not know if these people had been sitting in that pew before I saw my friend or not, because the first time I looked back was when I saw her.

At that moment I knew my husband was going to die no matter what the doctors said. I knew it so strongly that I arranged for his cremation, for a private autopsy, and for a legal firm to start on malpractice litigation during the six days he remained alive, even though the doctors kept saying he still had a chance. I must stress here that I had never had any prior communication with my friend after she killed herself although I had wished for it, had prayed for it. I wanted to know what had made her take her own life, but she never communicated with me in any way. Another thing that should be noted is that she and my husband were alike in many ways. She and her "significant other" and my husband and I used to do a lot of things together and the 4 of us had often joked about how much those two were alike. I believe that she showed herself to me in church because she knew I had a strong faith and would not be afraid if it was in church that I saw her. But what she came to tell me, by her presence, was that John would not be alone and that she was OK. The things I had heard about sui-cides being "punished" were not true and I could be at ease that she was not suffering and my husband would be taken care of. She had been his physician when she was alive so her "taking care" of him was almost a normal condition. I have never seen her again since, nor have I had any other type of communication from her.

After Death Communication – My husband John

Some of the most significant communication I had with my husband occurred at the moment of his death. When it became apparent to his physicians that he was not going to recover, we talked about how we would remove life support and still keep him comfortable. It was decided to leave the ventilator on as removing it would cause a very uncomfortable death. What we would do is stop the dialysis and antibiotics and give him morphine for pain. This would take longer (about 2 days I was told) but would be easier.

When they told me this, I knew it wouldn't be 2 days. I knew he was ready and someone was there to go with him. He only needed to be released by me to move on and would not go until I did this. I went home to tend to some necessary chores secure in the knowledge that he would not die while I was not there. I don't know how I knew these things. I just know that I did, and with great certainty. During our marriage, my husband had traveled extensively all over the world, and I had always felt very "in touch" with him no matter where he was. Even he thought it was strange how I "read his thoughts" so perhaps he was communicating with me by spirit in those hours before death.

When I returned to the hospital, I sat with John and talked. The nurse had turned off all the alarms on the monitors since there was no need for them any more. The only machine you could hear operating was the ventilator that was breathing for him. I told him we had no unfinished business, that I knew he was sorry if he had ever hurt me and I had forgiven him for anything he had ever done. I asked him, if he could, to send a butterfly (his personal symbol) to me after he was gone to let me know he was all right. I read him some prayers that had meaning for him, and then I told him to take his beloved dog (who had died some 8 years before) and go for a walk out over the mountains he loved so much. I was holding his hand the second time I said this and I felt him slip out of this world by passing right through me. I knew he was gone even though, because the ventilator kept him "breathing," it still looked like he was alive.

I know this sounds impossible, but that is what I felt. For a second I was lifted to this state that was almost like rapture. I can't describe the sensation exactly. It was something like a hug, but I think it must be more of what a baby feels when it is held and enveloped in comforting arms. Even though I knew he was gone and I was crying, I was not sad. I know I was smiling when I turned to look at the monitor to confirm that his heart had stopped. The nurse had looked up at the same time and she looked at me, she was crying and smiling too, and said, "He heard you." The one thing I had been praying for through all this was that he would give me some sign that he knew I was there and that everything was all right between us. In that moment he gave me that sign. It was only about an hour after I sat with him that he died, not 2 days.

My communication with John did not stop at the moment of his death. The next day when I went outside, there was a small white butterfly in my shade garden. Butterflies don't usually come to that part of the yard. It was there all day for 3 days. I talked to it and it never seemed afraid of me. On the fourth day I didn't see it and I was really sad. The next day, I saw what I thought was it and went outside. I felt this happy feeling again but this time the butterfly flew away. Then I saw one just like it sitting on a leaf. It was not afraid of me and I knew this was the one I had been seeing for the past 3 days. It looked like it had gotten wet in the sprinklers and was drying its wings. I picked it up and it sat on my finger for quite a while. Then I put it on a leaf and went inside.

The next day I went out and there was a white butterfly in the garden. It was quite friendly so I thought it was "my" butterfly. Then, I noticed that there was a dead butterfly on the ground under the leaf where I had placed "mine" the day before. At the exact same instant that I noticed this, I felt a voice say to me, "I will always see that there is a comforter here for you. If it is not one butterfly, it will be another, or it will be something else, but whatever it is, even if it is God or Christ, or a sunset, it will comfort you." Later that day when I was cleaning out his organizer case I found a very old "refrigerator" magnet in the shape of a butterfly. It had a Bible verse from Matthew on it: "I will be with you always."

There hasn't been a butterfly in my shade garden since but I haven't felt the sadness I felt the first day there was no butterfly. Each time that I have become sad when thinking about my husband being gone, after a short time I get a feeling that comforts me. Sometimes it is something I see that reminds me of him, or of the beauty still in this world, but sometimes it is just a feeling. But, it is very real.

I have had 2 more instances of what I believe is after death communication from my husband during the first month following his death. The first was on my birthday which was one week after he died. During the almost 25 years John and I had known each other, he had always given me a very unusual kind of rose for my birthday—it's white with a dark pink rim on the petals. I don't recall ever seeing it in our local stores. He used to order it from the florist I think. On my birthday a friend stopped by with her 2 girls who are 5 and 3 years old. She said the girls had made her stop so they could pick out flowers for me for my birthday. The flowers they brought were the same roses John had always given me. My friend commented how unusual they were and said she had never seen them before but her girls were insistent that these were the ones I should have. I have been back to that store several times since and have never yet seen that particular rose.

The second instance was one evening when I was sitting on the couch writing thank you notes for cards and memorial gifts made for John. I keep a bowl of scented flower petals on the coffee table and this is all you can smell in that room. All of a sudden I got a very strong scent of pine. I need to tell you that John had a very special love for Lake Tahoe. He had lived there for a year and always said that he would return. He had scattered the ashes of his dog up there and had asked that we do the same with his ashes should he die. I believe he was letting me know that his spirit was there already even though I have not yet been able to make the trip with his ashes.

Consider the parts that others played in the new relationship that Virginia began to establish with her husband at the moment of death. A very sensitive nurse validated her experience at his bedside. Her experience in church involved her best friend Kathy, her husband's former physician. The gift of unusual roses on her birthday after his death came from another friend and her two little girls. All were part of a mosaic that helped her cope with her husband's death and realize he was in good hands. The security of his journey, as with many mourners, is often another significant factor in the nature of the new bond being established.

QUESTIONS TO BE POSED TO VIRGINIA
1. Do you have a picture or a gift John gave you that most exemplifies the relationship you and he shared?
2. Having wished for and prayed for a sign from Kathy, do you feel your prayers were answered with your experience in church? How has this affected your beliefs about an afterlife and your relationship with her?

3. How has the scent of pine indicating your husband's presence served as a symbol of your ongoing relationship with him?

4. How do you explain your ability to be "in touch" with your husband no matter where he was? What does this suggest about your relationship then and now?

5. Does the church have any special meaning in regard to the relationship you now have with John? Have you returned to that same church pew you were in when you received the message from Kathy?

6. What other conversations about death did you have with John other than the one when he talked about the disposal of his ashes?

7. When the doctors told you John would die in about two days, how did you know that his death would come sooner? Where do you think this insight came from?

8. What does the symbolic meaning of the butterfly suggest about the relationship you have with John and Kathy?

9. Have the experiences you have had with John and Kathy influenced the way you relate to relatives or friends?

10. Whose voice do you feel you heard speak to you in the shade garden? A divine figure? John? Kathy? Your unconscious?

11. How do you account for not feeling the sadness you felt the first day there was no butterfly in your garden? What has caused this change?

12 How did John most frequently show his love for you during your years of marriage? Is that same love showing in the EE's you have experienced?

13. What are some of the alternative messages that could be deduced from your extraordinary experiences?

14. What is an example of "the beauty still in this world" that helps you overcome the sadness?

15. Did you ever talk to your friend who brought the roses on your birthday about how important they were to you as a sign from John? How did she respond?

16. After the experience with the strong scent of pine, did you ever look back at the pattern of experiences you have had and consider that perhaps there is an overall message? What are all of these experiences suggesting?

Every strong relationship between people, whether living or deceased, is built on the 4 A's—a foundation of appreciation, acceptance, affection, and attention. There is no place for relationships of dominance, where one is related to in a dependent way. Everyone likes and needs attention, regardless of age, as long as it comes from the right person, in the right way, and at the right time. Likewise, everyone wants to know that a friend or loved one accepts them as they are and appreciates them for what they do. In times of anguish and disorganization, affection is an effective antidote for reactive depression. Building a personal repertoire of behaviors to meet the 4A's in the lives of those we touch is an ongoing task for helpers and mourners. The more adept we become in matching these needs with practical behaviors the more solid and lasting will our relationships become.

Various forms of appreciation, acceptance, affection, and attention say, "I care," in no uncertain terms. In various ways, most extraordinary experiences fulfill these four relationship needs as they did for Virginia in forming her new relationship with John. *The EE makes clear for all survivors that the loved one has died while giving attention to the deceased and the survivor. This is the crucial framework for the establishment of the new relationship with the deceased loved one.* The deceased accepts and is reciprocating the love of the survivor. He appreciates and understands the struggle being endured by the survivor, wishes to assist in the transition, and is maintaining the relationship.

FIND A VISIBLE CONNECTION

A fruitful approach to establishing a new relationship with the deceased is to find physically tangible connections to the loved one. Begin with considering "his favorites." This could be from favorite meals, colors, and clothes to shows, tools, paintings, or other personal objects. For example, I once had a woman in a support group who showed all of us the wallet of her beloved sister that she carried in her purse and which brought her great comfort and pleasant memories. It was part of her sister bringing comfort and a sense of closeness to her. The object could even be something connected with the death or a gift that had been previously received.

To assist the mourner in this regard, listen carefully to what she says about the deceased's favorites and the emotion she invests in the description of them. Determine which ones have special meaning and bring comfort and joy when she talks about them. If there was an object or piece of clothing or jewelry worn by the deceased in the mourner's extraordinary experience, consider how that can be used as a connection to the deceased, a way to express love or find solace. In the three accounts presented in this chapter a grief facilitator might explore the meaning and use of pine scent, the yellow rose and the butterflies, the cat and the medicine bottle, the refrigerator magnet, and something from the home of "Mom" Hayes. Validate the normalcy of connection to the object, its significance, and the legitimate comfort the object provides.

If there are no objects immediately identifiable from the extraordinary experience, you may want to discuss whether or not the experience suggests anything else the deceased loved one was especially attached to that the mourner would cherish. If an item does have meaning and cannot be located, for whatever reason, consider a substitute or a symbolic duplicate of the object.

RELATIONSHIPS WITH THE LIVING

The extraordinary or scientifically unexplainable event can also be the springboard for establishing new relationships with the living or strengthening existing ones. All too frequently, other relatives and friends have had, or know others who have had, similar experiences.

Even when they have not had an experience themselves, if they believe in the phenomena, they are eager and willing to be good listeners and encouraging resources, if not companions, for the mourner. These discussions can lead to enhanced feelings of security for the mourner and a reduction in fear and anxiety, as she believes she is understood.

Therefore, the extraordinary experience, like any other subject of deep mutual interest, can become a strong bonding source for people. I have experienced this myself in my associations with mourners and colleagues who have shared their experiences with me. ("I'm glad I can talk to you and not feel you think I'm crazy.") The general public would be surprised at the large number of people in the country who have come together solely because of the EE.

Another source for new relationships comes through meeting others in support groups who have had an EE. The many possibilities for meeting others with similar interests through web sites and conferences are there and need to be explored and facilitated with discretion by both mourners and helpers. New meaning and insights often develop when the bereaved discuss their experiences with each other. A sense of community settles in when one believes she is in the company of others with like beliefs.

CONCEPTS TO EXPLORE AND DEVELOP IN ESTABLISHING NEW RELATIONSHIPS

The research shows quite clearly that strong interpersonal relationships offer significant protection from illness, are an adjunct to stress management, and as Leon Eisenberg, M.D. puts it, "Good friends are an essential ingredient for good health." I would also add that a healthy relationship with a deceased loved one will further add to the mourner's well-being. With that in mind, here are some concepts to consider in building connections to a changing world.

1. Write a personal letter to your deceased loved one sharing all your feelings. It will help clarify your thoughts, allow you to be totally

honest with her, and give you insight on where you are in your grief work. It will keep your loved one close to you in spirit and allow you to share your deepest feelings. Write when you feel it is needed. You need not share the letters with anyone.

2. Work between the minutes. On rising (or if you prefer, the night before) take pencil and paper and plan your entire day. Make to-do lists. Each hour indicate what you will be doing or where you will be. Be sure to schedule something active to do like cleaning, going shopping, exercising or gardening. Also include times when you will talk to at least two other people during the day, weather you feel like it or not. Schedule some form of self-care where you give yourself a treat. Self-care is extremely important to your grief work because the one who gave so much care is gone. Your care has been diminished. Your daily planning will help you to stay in charge of your grief, bring balance into your life, and help establish patterns of interaction with others. *If you make a plan that takes you outside of yourself, you will always survive and prosper.* Here is an additional monthly treat. Most florists have a monthly plan where you can stop by and pick up flowers for your home. The fee for a year is quite reasonable ($20-$25) for twelve bouquets of flowers. It is also a great gift to give someone you care about.

3. As difficult as it may be, let others know you are approachable during your mourning by saying things like, "Thank you for coming to help, please stop by again" or "I appreciate all that you are doing," or "You have been a great listener." There is a tendency for mourners to cut themselves off from those trying to help by inadvertently failing to fully acknowledge them. It is understandable but detrimental to an ongoing relationship.

We all tend to forget that the need to feel appreciated tops all emotional needs. Remember Mark Twain's sage remark: "I can live for two months on a good compliment." It will work wonders in establishing and strengthening all of your relationships if you put compliments high on your list of social skills to develop. Why? Because to feel appreciated is to feel loved.

4. Know that your deceased loved one is aware of your sorrow over her death and through the sign or contact you have experienced she wants you to be happy again, to interact with others, to initiate new pursuits. She wants you to celebrate her life and the gift of the extraordinary she was allowed to give you. What forms will your celebration take and who will you celebrate with?

5. Establishing new relationships—whether with the deceased or with the living—takes time. Although we live in a culture that promotes time saving procedures in every facet of life, a sort of instant everything expectation, lasting relationships take commitment and practice. And practice means repetition. Decide what you want to keep alive from your life together as a lasting bond with the deceased and what you know you must let go of and not bring into your new life. Take the repetitive steps to do two things: Cement the lasting bond that will make the relationship with your loved one visibly permanent and reach out to make the casual relationships of the past stronger.

6. Consider what the deceased was wearing when you had your EE. If you had a visitation dream, vision or apparition and he was wearing familiar clothes, think of a creative way you might use some of his clothing that you have not given away. For example, some people make quilted pillows out of shirts that can be placed on sofas or a bed. Or you may take some of his socks to make holiday stockings at Christmas time. You may wish to save a particular piece of clothing as a reminder of a happy event. This too will be part of the new relationship you are establishing with your loved one.

7. Educate your support system. Tell those who are helping you what you need, whether it be a hug, to be alone for a while, to be able to call them when feeling low, or to pick up something at the grocery

store. One of your needs might even be to have them call you on the telephone at a specific hour or do laundry.

Tell them not to get upset at your crying and think it is a sign of weakness. Tears are a sign of love, sadness, and progress in dealing with your deep loss. Crying is coping. Let them know they can help you in these or other ways. Take special effort to be humble, sincere, and open when telling people how they can best assist. Be prepared to seek out others who are willing and able to fill your needs if someone you ask is unable to accept your request.

It seems unfair that you have to tell people what your needs are when you really feel they should know. And it takes a lot of strength on your part to tell them at a time when strength is very limited. But remember, friends and family can't read your mind, they won't know what you need unless you tell them. And sometimes you may not even be sure what you need. So do what you have to do.

8. *There are no perfect relationships.* Good relationships are a product of connecting on any one of several levels: intellectual, spiritual, emotional, behavioral, mental or common interest. Beware of looking for the so-called perfect friendship with the living or with your deceased loved one. The perfect friendship myth is common; however, the perfect friendship doesn't exist. We all have to accept some personal idiosyncrasies we may not like in the people we interact with and love. Beware of idealizing your deceased loved one.

Also, are there any people in your life you have prematurely stopped being friendly with because you both did not agree on everything? Reach out and right the wrong. When we change relationships change.

To strengthen your relationship with a good friend, try the following. Make a list of the things you appreciate about her. Then on two separate occasions tell her one thing you appreciate about her.

9. Alcoholics Anonymous, the largest and arguably the most successful self-help group in the world, has among its slogans the following: "Fake it, till you make it." In other words, act as you wish to feel. Acting as you wish to feel is a mood-changing process that has been used by millions. Your emotions and feelings will eventually change for the better and so will your relationships. Simple deliberate actions will influence how you see and feel about a particular problem or a relationship. But it takes persistent effort. It begins by a commitment to do what you dislike doing. No one likes to start something when feeling blue. Getting started is the hard part, but it will pay off in enlarging your circle of friends. How will you reach out? How will you change self-pity? Feel joy? Nurture old friendships? Act with a purpose.

There are no rewards for simply possessing the right beliefs, determination or intentions about what has to be accomplished; the only payoff comes through faking it until you make it. The ability to pretend is an incalculably important attitude for dealing with grief, stress, and a new environment.

10. Search for a loving supportive community (I don't necessarily mean a bereavement support group, although that too may be necessary, especially in the second year of grief). It could be a small group of friends who have mutual interests. It could be a group who has experienced the extraordinary. It could be a church or community center group. Like anything else, you will have to pick and choose. Do not get discouraged if one group does not meet your expectations. Try another, or start your own group built around mutual interests (like the dining-at-a-new-restaurant group each week). After her EE Kern Loughran started a reading group called "The Beyonds." The purpose of the group is to "read all about death, to learn as much as we can to erase the fear factor."

An outstanding hospice nurse, after the death of her husband, wrote the following: "Some good advice given to me was—try every group at least three times. The first time you won't really be comfortable. The second, you'll recognize some more faces and be more sure of yourself. The third time you'll start to feel 'at home,' if it's the right group for you."

11. The holidays are special relationship days with family, friends, and your deceased loved one. They are also high stress days because family togetherness is not the same without your loved one. Here are five guides used by many over the years in making it through holiday stress. (a) **Reduce time spent in situations that maximize your stress.** You don't have to spend the same amount of time with others as in the past. You don't have to bake, send cards, cook a turkey or follow family traditions. Cut down on stress exposure by changing or eliminating some family traditions. Simplify. (b) **Conserve energy.** Holiday celebrations, especially anticipating what it will be like without the loved one, are heavy energy drains. Talk about the pain of anticipation with someone you trust. Take care of your body by doing some light exercise, eating wisely, avoiding too much caffeine or alcohol, and sticking to a reasonable schedule for sleep. (c) **Celebrate the memory of your loved one.** This means adding something new to your celebration. Decide on how you would like to remember or honor him/her on this special day. Some bring out a favorite picture, make his favorite dessert, or honor him with a place setting at the table. Others remember through telling favorite stories about the holiday and the loved one. Some widows buy a gift for themselves from their deceased loved one. (d) **Recognize that there is no magical way to take away the pain of not having your loved one with you at holiday time.** Everyone is not happy over holidays. But you can decide what to do to manage the inevitable. And it is okay to cry. Circumstances can easily reduce us to tears. Talk openly about the normalcy of that

possibility. (e) **Tell your family all of the above well before the holiday begins.** Let them know what you want to do and what you will not do and how they can help. They must know your special holiday needs in advance and only you can tell them.

12. Regardless of your age, be open to listening to the advice of those around you. This does not mean you have to follow their advice. However, there is wisdom out there, solutions to every problem in life. Start with the belief that those who come into and out of your life have something to teach you. Study the lessons others teach by focusing on what they are doing and saying. You will learn who and what to stay away from and what to pursue, if you will think in terms of what you can learn from those you interact with. Ask yourself from time to time, "What is this person teaching by word and action and can I use it or should I discard it?"

The construction of a new life and the development of the needed skills of change is a long-term part of adapting to major loss, a part of grief that often goes unrecognized. Few like to admit that they must start a new life, different from the one so familiar, that they have to do things they have never done before. The reconstruction process may begin by putting into place rituals specific to the needs of the mourner. The extraordinary experience often provides rich insights and memories to become fertile soil for the creation of rituals and traditions that can be comforting and sustaining for years to come. We turn now to examine the power of rituals and traditions and how to create them from the extraordinary events in life.

6

Creating Rituals And Traditions: Structure For Adapting To Change

Ritual provides the bridge between inner and outer worlds, and creates a context of connecting to our souls. The result of all ritual is increased balance, strength, energy, and comfort.

-Angeles Arrien-

Conviction

I know without question that after we leave this earth, we continue to live in a different form. This belief is so long instilled in me, that I can't even imagine a person going through life questioning whether there is life after death.

—Patricia D., age forty
On her EE at age nine, after the death of her father

∞   ∞   ∞   ∞   ∞   ∞

We have seen in earlier chapters that lasting connections are an integral part of feeling whole and nurturing self-esteem throughout life. This observation is graphically illustrated in the temporary—and sometimes not so temporary—loss of self-esteem that occurs when a marriage ends in divorce or death takes a marriage partner. When connections are broken reconnecting to life and people comes from new habits and traditions as well as initiating new rituals or celebrating old ones. Reconnection is the centerpiece for adapting to change imposed by separation and loss. Indeed it is crucial to the adaptation process. Regrettably, the processes involved in the creation and maintenance of routines, traditions, and rituals are commonly resisted, even though they bring comfort while giving structure to seemingly chaotic circumstances. Traditional formal rituals after the death of a loved one also provide a public forum for grief, making grief and the strong emotions associated with it much more socially acceptable.

Rituals and new traditions evolving from extraordinary experiences not only help create acceptance of the death but help reduce frequency of thoughts like, "I keep expecting him to walk through the door at 5 o'clock." Such thinking, part of entrenched old habits involving denial and expectations of the deceased, has to be confronted by most mourners.

Traditions establish points of recognition and honor, boosting morale and instilling pride. But rituals and traditions are much more than mere sources for gaining strength to deal with the pain of life without loved ones who gave the living so much. They are major guides in the transition from one phase of life to another as they assist in forming a new identity, acting as tools of transition. Ultimately, rituals and traditions free the mourner to think about life and the practical matters of living again. New traditions, in particular, can be started and become part of family life, marking a turning point in family history, and giving inner direction to all members. They also become a resource for recalling how the past is part of the present and how they help create the future. Family traditions may even be passed on from generation to generation when applicable.

Informal rituals engaged in on a daily or weekly basis (perhaps writing a note or letter or pausing to remember at a specific time) with the deceased in mind can be especially potent factors in fashioning a new life. These same informal rituals allow a mourner to say things he may not be ready to say out loud to others. One may also prefer to express an informal ritual in the beauty of silence in order to give example and teach children a way to honor the deceased.

Rituals and traditions are as old as humanity, highlighting purpose, honor, and often transition between life and death. They may be symbolic and sacred or practical and transforming. Most important of all, rituals and traditions provide a road to healing and a means of coping with adversity while generating new and lasting relationships.

In addition to being important resources for gaining strength to deal with the pain of life without loved ones, ritual provides a way to either maintain a strong living connection to the deceased or a means to let go and say a temporary goodbye. Thus rituals may be one-time services (to say goodbye), less frequent yet regular celebrations of life such as on anniversaries, or daily routines like sitting in a particular place at home, remembering the deceased at bedtime prayers, when meditating, or when giving thanks before meals. A mourner may also fashion a ritual to let go of anger or guilt. As we shall see, there are many rituals and traditions that can be initiated through extraordinary experiences that have deep personal meaning for the mourner and commemorate the life of the beloved.

In particular, rituals involving extraordinary experiences are a personal way each mourner relates to the deceased loved one. Expressing beliefs and facilitating emotional transactions are commonly fashioned in these rituals and ceremonies. Thus symbolic remembrance through an extraordinary experience has positive psychological and spiritual effects. In particular, spiritual growth and renewed spiritual strength is not an uncommon result of using the extraordinary in ritual formation. Carl Jung said that a key question we all need to address is: "Are we related to something infinite or not?" For most who experience the extraordinary the question is easily answered; they have connected with something greater than the Self and can express it through ritual.

Let us flip our mental calendars back to 1979 and examine the experience of Gloria Thornton of Auburn, CA to explore how an EE could be incorporated into a particular ritual or initiate a tradition to be carried on for years to come. Gloria's son died unexpectedly but she received indication of the death before she was officially notified.

"THAT WAS THE SIGN I HAD WAITED FOR!"

In July of 1979 my son Donn died alone in his apartment from a convulsion. He was dead a few days before they found him. Before I found out about his death, I was walking down the hall of my house and a voice said to me, "One of your children is dead." This was a voice in my mind; it wasn't a loud voice. I said to myself, "That is not true. I am going to die before any of my six children." A few days later the police came and said they found him dead in his apartment. The time of death would have been about the same time I heard the voice.

His 33rd birthday was on August 27, 1979, a few weeks after his death. Although I do not go to church, I asked God to give me a sign on that day that he was all right. I waited all day for the sign. About 10:00 PM I received a call from a woman I had met at a retreat I had attended after my son's death. She was an alcoholic who needed help and after talking to her for a while I told her I would send her some books that might help her. As I was trying to put the books in a manila envelope the edge of the envelope caught one of the books and flipped it open to a page with my son's handwriting on it. This is what he wrote on one of the pages from a quote he had found. "When I was born I cried while all around me smiled. When I die I will smile while all around me cry." That was the sign I had waited for! I kept the book and treasure it. The name of the book is AS A MAN THINKETH. I had loaned it to him. I had no idea he had written anything in it.

For others, a fairly trivial incident, but not for Gloria. She knew, without a doubt, it was the guidance she had sought. When speaking with Gloria she told me she had had a second unusual experience involving her son and a picture of him that was hanging in the back room of her home. As a result of these and other life-affirming experiences she was convinced that life goes on in another existence, that there is communication from that existence, and that her experience with the book was "God's way of saying Donn was okay. It was also Donn's way of saying he was okay." A double confirmation.

How then could her experience be used in creating a ritual that could mold a new bond in the relationship with her son or, if desired, used to say farewell and we will meet again? Since Gloria has already begun to create the ritual of maintaining the relationship by treasuring the book in which she found her son's handwriting, she could be encouraged to open the book and read the message as well as other segments of the book on key anniversary dates. The readings would be rituals of *continuity*, expressing the continuing bond with her son. (*As A Man Thinketh* is a book is filled with great wisdom about the power of thought and could easily become a source for inspiration and motivation for years to come.) Or the book could be placed on her nightstand or an end table as a ritualistic reminder of the answer to her prayer. On the other hand, if she chose to use her experience as a ritual for saying good bye, she might wish to go to the cemetery, a park or other significant place frequented by her son and read the piece out loud as part of her goodbye session. Then in a symbolic gesture of goodbye she could tie a copy of the written verse to a balloon and let it go in the wind or leave it at the gravesite. The tradition of reading from the book at the gravesite on the anniversary of his death could also be started.

Another approach could be suggested along the lines of spreading the knowledge in the book to others and in so doing commemorating her son by placing his name on the inside cover with an "In memory of" inscription. Choosing to buy copies of the book to give to libraries in her area could be broadened to include high schools and colleges as well. On certain occasions, because of the nature of the book, it could be given to a friend or relative as a gift. Each time the bond with her son is recognized and revitalized.

Gloria might also decide to do any or all of the above depending on specific needs at a given time at intervals throughout the year. It doesn't have to be done all at once. The most important consideration in planning her ritual is to help Gloria search for how she would like to honor her son, make a statement about salient characteristics of his life and what he means to her. What she chooses will become indelibly imprinted in her memories through ritualization. Because symbols are an inherent part of ritual and hold deep meaning for the individual, search for and discuss with the mourner the significant symbols that express the messages and meanings she cherishes and wishes to convey. In this instance, where an educational tool is involved in an extraordinary experience, the motivation to enhance the education of others as a way of honoring the deceased should be discussed. Many mourners can find a very special satisfaction when others are served and the deceased honored at the same time.

QUESTIONS TO BE POSED TO GLORIA
1. What would you like to always remember about your son?
2. How would you like to include the extraordinary experience as part of a memorialization?
3. Where would you like to have the ritual? What time of day? Alone or with others?
4. Would you like to include a passage or passages from the book in a reading?

5. Where have you kept the book? Can you use it as an inspiration by putting it in a particular place where you will see it?

6. Can the book be used as part of a daily ritual in conjunction with other readings that you do, say with the Bible or other inspirational reading?

7. Do you prefer to use your choice of ritual only on certain anniversaries?

8. Would you like to include any family or friends? Have you asked them for input on creating new traditions or rituals?

9. What do you want the ritual to accomplish? Saying a final good-bye? Ongoing remembrance?

10. Is there a tradition or a legacy that you think Donn would like you to begin in his honor?

11. What is your interpretation of the quote Donn wrote on one of the pages of the book? Is there a special message that you draw from it?

12. Would you like to use the quote Donn wrote as part of a ritual?

13. Have you considered giving a copy of the book as a gift to a library or other agency?

14. Has your family had other rituals or ongoing traditions that are associated with other deceased family members? Would you like this ritual to be similar to or different from those you have mentioned?

As time goes on, Gloria may choose to change any of the rituals or traditions she has created in order to meet other needs as the years go by. For example, she may move away or at some point no longer be able to go the cemetery. On an anniversary, she may then substitute going to a new location other than the cemetery that reminds her of her son. She may also decide to discontinue or limit a ritual or tradition. Flexibility is always an option.

Let's consider several experiences as reported by attorney Louisa N., who lives in the northeast, which resulted in an increase in spirituality, the elimination of her fear of death, and acceptance in coping with her loss. Her ritual of remembrance and honor is typical in coping with major loss.

"I HAVE FOUND THAT HE HAS BEEN AS LOYAL A FRIEND AND AS MUCH A MENTOR IN DEATH AS DURING HIS LIFE"

I was fortunate to be the primary caregiver and support system to my best friend and mentor Jerry. He died August 5, 1995. My communications began the day after his funeral. We had always laughed and joked about his dislike of red carnations. As luck would have it, a large bouquet was delivered to the funeral home. After the services, his son, some friends, and I decided to toss the red carnations off a local bridge in a sort of tribute to him. This went well. The next morning, I discovered two red carnations **underneath** *the floor mat in the back seat of my car. I wrote it off to coincidence but kept them in a bag.*

The next instance of coincidence occurred on my birthday, November 13, 1995. His birthday had been November 11, and he always made me cheese cakes to celebrate our birthdays. I woke up feeling that I would not be surprised to find one on my desk when I arrived at work. Instead, when I stopped for gasoline, as I was paying, a woman I had never seen before accosted me, calling me "Gigi." The only Gigi I had ever met, or even heard of, was Jerry's ex-wife. I laughed and started thinking these events were more than coincidences.

In the months that followed I had three "big dreams." While reading **After Death Communication: Final Farewells**, *I could completely relate to descriptions of dreams unlike any others. In the first dream, I was sitting on my front porch drinking coffee on a beautiful sunny morning with my mother. Jerry appeared in the middle of my driveway, walked on to my porch, held out his hands and said, "My hands aren't cold anymore." He then vanished. In* *the dream, I knew that he was dead but I was not scared or shocked to see him appear and disappear.*

*In the second dream, he sat on the edge of my bed. He was talking to me. I was not paying attention, but being rather nonchalant. He was chastising me, and I asked him to reveal all of life's secrets. He responded, "Come on, you know I can't do that." The final dream occurred at a particularly stressful period at work. In the dream, he appeared in the middle of the hallway, put his hands on my shoulders and told me everything would be all right. I have had other normal dreams involving him, but in those, he was always alive. In these three I knew he was dead, and he always just appeared. In **Final Farewells**, I liked the explanation that the dreams, unlike awake contacts, eliminate fear and shock to the recipient.*

Because of my experiences, I have become more spiritual, no longer fear death, and have conquered my grief over his death. I have found that he has been as loyal a friend and as much a mentor in death as during his life. I hope that my experiences can be beneficial to others suffering the great loss of a loved one and who are feeling the "am-I-crazy-or-over-reacting" syndrome following an after death communication.

Spirituality remade. The fear of death disarmed. Loyalty reaffirmed. Although meaningful synchronous events are still considered relics of superstition or wishful thinking by many, for this attorney deep inner meaning was gleaned from the unexpected. She was inspired to continue to explore her spiritual quest, to fill an empty void. How might we help her usher in and further strengthen these deep inner changes and develop ritual to facilitate the transition she is confronting? Consider the questions to follow and the potential dialogue that could flow from them.

QUESTIONS TO BE POSED TO LOUISA

It is interesting to note that Louisa and her friends had already used the red carnations as a ritual of remembrance of Jerry by throwing them off a local bridge. One could easily suggest the use of the two carnations found under the floor mat in additional rituals of goodbye, remembrance, or reconciliation. They could be wonderful reminders of any number of times (or ideas) when Jerry had been there to provide Louisa support or direction in taking action. More about this later. Let's look at some questions for Louisa to open up some of the possible uses of her extraordinary experiences as one time, daily, or periodic rituals.

1. Do you recall the time and the conversation you had with Jerry when he first told you about his dislike for red carnations? What did he say?
2. Did the topic of red carnations come up again? What was said?
3. What did all of you talk about when you had the tribute to Jerry of throwing the flowers off the bridge? What were your thoughts at that time?
4. What was the personal meaning for you of the woman calling you Gigi on your birthday?
5. Are there any traditions you would like to start to honor your friendship with Jerry and his role of mentor in your life? Are there times you know he would have been celebrating and so you can celebrate him and his life?
6. What was the significance of his comment that "My hands aren't cold anymore?"
7. What will you do to keep Jerry's memory alive? To show you have learned from him?
8. Why was Jerry chastising you in the second dream?
9. What did you mean when you asked him to reveal all of life's secrets? What were you hoping to hear him say?

10. How did your final big dream affect you when you went into work the next day? What were your feelings?
11. Was it meaningful to you that he put his hands on your shoulders? In what way?
12. Would you comment on why you feel more spiritual? Could you give an example?
13. Why is it that since you have had these experiences you no longer fear death?
14. How have you used your experiences in dealing with Jerry's death? Is there a daily ritual at the office that gives a happy thought of your mentor?
15. What legacy of Jerry's would you like to recognize, perpetuate, and carry on?

Depending on Louisa's responses it might be appropriate to inquire if she has given any thought to how she might use the two red carnations in remembering her friend. If interest is shown, then some of the following suggestions could be made:

Have one of the carnations encased in lucite to place in a special place at home or at the office as a loving reminder of his counsel and example. Such a ritual of *affirmation* could become one way of dealing with work problems by way of thinking of the inspiration Jerry might give.

Use a carnation in a special private service or visit to the cemetery at a later date as a ritual of *transition* recognizing Jerry's death and giving thanks for the relationship.

Plan an anniversary or holiday remembrance celebration in which the story of the carnations is told and other memories of Jerry are talked about.

Have color pictures of the carnations taken or a painting commissioned to display in an appropriate setting.

Audrey Port is a professional broadcast journalist in Spokane, Washington whose experiences after the death of her father have been a resource for coping with her loss, and if she chooses, a way to create rituals and traditions for lifetime use. First, here is her story.

"IMAGINE DREAMING YOU'RE EATING A BOX OF CHOCOLATES, THEN WAKING UP AND ACTUALLY TASTING THE CHOCOLATE IN YOUR MOUTH"

Since my father's collapse on St Patrick's Day 1998 and subsequent death a week or so later, I've had some extraordinary, unexplainable experiences. They are like nothing I'd ever experienced before. I'm a television reporter/anchor and my father was a prominent veterinarian pathologist (a D.V.M. Ph.D.) known nationwide for his research. We were extremely close my entire 32 years of life. Our bond was unbreakable.

My final farewells started while my father was still alive—but after his collapse from a brain hemorrhage. My brother (a physician) and mother and I decided within days to let him go—it was really the only logical choice since he would never have any quality of life. The night of the day we made the decision to let him go, my experiences began. He came to me in a dream, still in his hospital bed, but awake from his coma (brain surgery dressing still on his head) and turned and looked at me. He smiled a huge, bright, vibrant smile. He said nothing. I was shocked and startled within the dream, because he scared me when he woke up! It was only days later I recognized this signal and accepted it as his endorsement of our decision.

Surprisingly, when he died March 23, 1998, I did not feel any traumatic sensation or breaking of our bond at the moment he died. Although that disturbed me (I always thought I'd know the exact moment) what has come after has been interesting.

When I flew back from Florida to my Spokane, Washington

home—I was absolutely at the lowest point of my life. I was a broken woman by his death. He must have known. I had a dream that I documented and here is the description: Dad was in the dream. He didn't speak, but I was startled to see him. I was in a hallway with two other people and there he was, leaning against a doorjamb. He had on blue jeans and a plaid shirt. Later, I was sitting on the edge of my bed, grieving him. I felt awake within my dream—very aware. His spirit floated down to me, slowly reaching over, and he touched my hand. He was light, floating, and it didn't look like him, yet I knew it was him. His hand was transparent, but it became one with mine. Even more incredible, when I awakened hours later, I KNEW someone had physically touched and held my hand the entire evening. The sensation was unique—His hand came over the top of my hand and I could feel pressure as his fingers entwined with mine. I remember thinking, "Wow! I can actually feel this. And wow, I didn't think a transparent hand would be able to actually touch me!" When I actually woke up, I remember lifting up my left hand from under the covers and rubbing my fingers together—knowing I'd been touched. Even more incredible, later on, my mother told me the way he held my hand (not palm to palm), but putting his hand over the top of the back of mine, is always the way he held hands with her. His preferred fashion. I'd liken this experience to the following: Imagine dreaming you're eat colate in your mouth.

Shortly after that, I had a dream we were in church and there was a man several pews in front of me—It was my father, a younger version of him. People were singing hymns, etc...and then I got his attention. He turned around and I said,

"Do you like it"? He said, "Yes!!" smiled, and turned around facing forward. I've also had dreams where I visited his house, wherever he's living now. He said nothing, but led me through the rooms. A fireplace and a balcony with a view from above the

clouds, looking down at the sparkling skyline of whatever city he chooses. Upstairs, a bedroom with a window view of clouds below and a sheer drop off a mountainside into nothingness.

Last summer, I asked him for a sign. I asked him, because he's energy, to tamper with energy here on earth. Screw up a television, turn off a light, flicker a lamp, screw up my phone. Whatever you can do. Of course, on demand, nothing happened. Twenty minutes later, a friend of mine from Portland, Oregon called to talk. I told her I'd made this request of him. She asked a little more about what he was like and I launched into a great, funny story about him. We kidded and gave each other a lot of shit for fun all the time. Just at the part of the story where I was really ragging on him in good fun—the phone line went deader than a doornail, the phone clicked twice, then a dial tone came up. Amazing!!!! My girlfriend and I hooked up again and she said, "My God! That was him! He couldn't let you get away with teasing him like that! Just at the part of the story where he was taking it on the chin—he cut you off!!!"

Additionally, as a Swedish family, making Christmas Gloog was a tradition he carried on every year. It's a hot, alcoholic beverage that's delightful. You make up the pot of this wine drink, then light it on fire as a festive celebration of Christmas. My heart was heavy Christmas 1998. I knew someone in our family had to take up the mantle and make the gloog. Being so close to him, I decided I would. Just after I lit the pot on fire, then put out the flames, I picked up a mug to dip it into the beverage to take a taste. This was the time when we all gathered around the stove to hug, kiss, and celebrate the holidays. I touched my mug to the wine—the phone rang, startling me. I said, "If that's my mother, I know he's here right now in this kitchen." My husband picked up the phone and tears came to his eyes. It was my mother and upon learning I was at the point of tasting our special tradition, she also believed he had brought us together at that moment.

There's more, which falls under your unusual animal behavior category. After my father was cremated, we decided to donate to hospice and put his name on a plaque in a butterfly garden/habitat being constructed at the hospice where he passed. The day the garden was dedicated, my mother attended. Each person attending was given a refrigerated butterfly in an envelope. Celebrants opened the envelope, exposed the butterfly to the Florida sunshine, and the butterfly awakened and slowly fluttered out of the paper and into the garden. Such a lovely way to do a dedication. My mother opened her envelope, the butterfly came to and flew out slowly—then landed on her skirt. She shooed it away and it flew back, landing on her shoulder. People started to notice what was happening. Everyone else's butterfly left them immediately for the garden. She shooed the butterfly away again, only to have it come back to her again. Tears filled her eyes. She told me, "It was him...it was a sign. It's as if he didn't want to leave me." She said she'd been waiting for a sign from him and felt this was it. He was clinging to her, in the garden of the hospice where he died. Finally, the butterfly flew away. She called my brother and me and told us what had happened to her—her special moment. I'm still speechless.

The butterfly experience could be a strong continuing bond between Audrey and her mother as well as the source of a ritual for the family. For many, butterflies may symbolize change, rebirth, transition from one life to another, new life or ongoing life. The butterfly imagery of hope—rising triumphantly from the chrysalis—could be used as a demonstration of passage to a new and better life, as a belief in reunion, as a reminder of something from the life of the deceased, or as a symbol of farewell. Some people have obtained larvae and raised butterflies each year as a joyous reminder of the deceased. Still others view the butterfly as a symbol of starting life anew each day. They rise, come out of their cocoon, and greet the day with new resolve and commitment. Purchasing a butterfly pin could be the beginning of a ritual of remembrance for mother and daughter.

Because of their close bond, Audrey should have many golden memories of her father that she may want to use in conjunction with establishing new traditions and rituals of hope to keep her father alive in her heart. In using her experiences for this purpose, the support person should present questions to review her relationship with her father, to discover both the insights she has gained in her years with him and the rituals she would like to focus on that represent his unique characteristics. She may also wish to add to the family traditions something that will include open acknowledgement of her father. For example, when making Christmas Gloog in the Swedish tradition, she might create a toast to her dad (a ritual of *continuity*). A family tradition could include the retelling of the story of her asking for a sign and her ensuing telephone conversation.

QUESTIONS TO BE POSED TO AUDREY
1. What is your father saying to you and your mother through the EE's that you would like to remember by way of a new tradition you can start in your family?
2. What memorials have you established for your father?
3. What personal messages have you received from the extraordinary experiences you had?
4. Have you thought about the possibility of drawing or painting a scene from one your dreams about your father?
5. Will there be an annual formal remembrance on the anniversary of his death? If so, what form might that take?
6. In what ways has your behavior changed since experiencing the extraordinary?
   Can this be put into a ritual or become part of a new tradition?

7. How will you honor your father through living the lessons he taught?

8. Has your mother considered having someone draw or paint a butterfly for display, similar to the one that came to her, as a positive way of remembering your father?

9. Have you and your family openly discussed the highlights of your father's life? How would you like to add to some of his accomplishments?

10. Is it possible that one of the messages your father is conveying through the EE's is "continue to take care of each other through the years?"

11. At some time during the year, would you like to have a ritual of remembrance of your father with just your mother and you participating?

12. Is there a symbol you could create based on your extraordinary experiences that would be indicative of your father's love or the way he cared for his family?

13. Did you do anything different when making the Christmas gloog that will be your new tradition and a remembrance to continue next year?

14. Is there something your family (including your mother and brother) might want to initiate, based in part on the extraordinary experiences, as an annual ritual to celebrate your father's life?

I asked Audrey if her extraordinary experiences had influenced her beliefs. She replied: "My father's death and subsequent ADC's with him have really solidified my belief that our energy lives on and the veil between this life and eternity is quite thin. These experiences were unique and unexplainable, and I'm probably the most grounded, rational, reality-based person you'll meet!!!—and I believe in them fully with all my body and soul. My ADC's have beefed up my reading and interest on the subject. One other important note—the ADC's have vastly increased my sensitivity to energy, sensations, and events related to him. I really felt he was near the first six to eight months after he died, but truly don't feel he's around anymore. It's just a feeling I can't articulate. It will be interesting to see if I feel him near again at some point and can differentiate the feeling of his presence or energy."

New insights and comfort are results of these unexpected gifts. If, as Einstein said, "The only source of knowledge is experience," then Audrey and her mother have indeed been fortunate.

STARTING FAMILY TRADITIONS

Losses always bring new beginnings; endings and beginnings go hand in hand (a good point to make to family members). It can also be helpful to all family members to consider starting new traditions for two essential reasons: *to strengthen family ties and to keep the memory of the loved one alive.* In most instances, new traditions can be initiated by involving all family members in providing input on what to do and how to do it. Even families with young children can be given a voice in where they would like to go or what they would like to do to honor the deceased. On certain dates or during particular seasons of the year, the family can decide on beginning a new tradition or slightly changing an old one while honoring the deceased as Audrey did. Here are some examples:

1. Meet at a place the deceased especially liked or where his ashes were scattered if appropriate. Bring a picnic lunch, celebrate the day, and talk about the loved one as part of the festivities.

2. Plan a get together involving activities like hiking, fishing, swimming, clamming, roller blading, or any other activity that the deceased engaged in with the family. Do it for a Sunday afternoon once a month.

3. On the deceased's birthday, meet for breakfast at a local restaurant to be followed by a drive to a scenic view. Another option would be to start the tradition of making homemade pizza on a special day that honors the deceased for an achievement or on a national holiday.

4. Start a tradition honoring the loved one on the date of his death by
   attending a show, professional athletic event, or other social event.
   (On the anniversary of the death of my father-in-law, my mother-
   in-law takes my wife and I out to dinner in his honor.)

These and other new traditions, depending on their nature, can be
weekly, monthly or yearly events or planned around holidays and
anniversaries.

Can one look back and come to realize that perhaps experiences previously disregarded were connected to the deceased and should be
taken advantage of in planning new traditions and rituals? Can someone receive a final farewell or reassurance and not be aware of it? Listen
to Catherine Hayes.

"I COULD HEAR HIM, FEEL HIM, AND EVEN SMELL HIM"

*Your book made me realize that what I experienced when my
father died was not just coincidence or my imagination. It gave
me peace of mind. Three separate incidents occurred in the first
four months after my father's death that have stuck out in my
mind as rather peculiar. Nothing else out of the ordinary has
ever happened again.*

*To give you background; My father was 47 years old when he
had a series of heart attacks. He had experienced a major heart
attack earlier in the week while he was at home alone. When he
survived it, he assumed he would be all right. (We now know that
immediate hospitalization can make the difference.) Later in the
week, he experienced another and was admitted to the hospital.
The third and final attack came the second day of hospitalization.
His mother and I were at his bedside when he said, "I'm getting
dizzy." The monitors went off, and a barrage of doctors and equipment were rushed into the room. We were ushered out of the room
to anxiously wait in the corridor.*

Death did not cross my mind. After all, he was in the hospital, and they would fix him. When the doctor finally came out and told us he had died, I collapsed. I wailed. My heart broke. He had no spouse, so I being the oldest child, assumed the responsibility of organ donation, arranging funeral home transport, etc. After a couple of hours, all the other family and friends had left the hospital, I had signed all the necessary papers, and gathered myself together enough to walk out to my mini-van. It seemed like a dream leaving the hospital with my father's lifeless body still inside. It was only three hours ago that I had spoken with him. It didn't seem real.

#1 From the hospital steps, I could easily see my red Chevy Astro van in the parking lot surrounded by hundreds of cars. What was unusual about it was this large black bird sitting on top of my van. I remember how odd that seemed; that out of all the cars on the lot, this lone bird had perched on top of mine. He was huge. And black. I watched him the whole time I approached my car. He watched me, too. I got right up to the back bumper of my car and was looking up at this bird, who was looking down at me. I remember how strange it was that the bird did not seem afraid of me. At this time, I did not make the connection that this might be a sign. I finally said, "Shoo!" and the bird flew away. That was the first incident.

#2 I went against family wishes and buried my father in the National Cemetery as he had told me he wanted. Instead of having cousins be pallbearers, I requested a full military funeral. It was a stressful time. At night, I had many dreams, or nightmares, about my father. Things like the rain washing out of the ground, etc. However, there was one dream that was different. It was in color, for one thing. I remember telling my husband the next morning that I could actually hear my dad's voice and feel his arm around me; that it felt like I had actually visited with dad. In the dream, we were walking through a field of yellow flowers, and he had his arm around me. I was telling him about the funeral and explaining why

I made the decisions I did. He assured me that I had handled everything just fine. I could hear him, feel him, and even smell him. I hated to wake up. Of course, I just chalked it up to my psychological need to know that I had made the right decisions. Still, the dream is very real to me even today, nine years later.

#3 The third and final event happened on my 30th birthday. Dad had only been gone three and a half months. I woke up that morning sad because my dad didn't live to see me turn 30 years old. I remember speaking out loud to him, saying, "Well, dad, your little girl is 30 now. Wish you were here to help me celebrate." I finally quit moping about it and went out to check the mail. Our mailbox was free-standing, and on the ground by the post was a little spiral memo notebook. All the pages were blank, but the cover was imprinted with a finger with string around it and the words, "Never forget."

My first thought was it was odd that this little book had no writing in it and how did it get at the base of my mailbox? A kid threw it there, perhaps? But here is the catch: My dad ALWAYS carried a little spiral memo book in his pocket with family addresses and birthdays, important numbers, etc. in it. In fact, when the hospital gave me his personal belongings, his little spiral memo book was among the items. So here it was, my 30th birthday, I was missing my father, and this memo book appears at MY mailbox. Out of all the mailboxes in the neighborhood.

After reading all the similar stories in your book, I am convinced that these three incidents were not just coincidences. I am convinced that my father was communicating with me. Sadly, that memo book was the last peculiar occurrence related to my father. I guess it was his final farewell.

Timing, need, direction, unity, and connection—all come together to facilitate change in one person's life. Catherine's story is most interesting because it highlights two dynamics: she learned that others have had similar experiences that run counter to conventional interpretation and she learned that others have used unconventional experiences to deal with their losses. The result introduced a whole new set of possibilities for coping with her loss. Specifically, it helped her remove the stigma of using hard-to-explain experiences as a source of comfort. In discussing her EE's with her as a helper it would be appropriate to begin with her final observation that the memo book experience was her Dad's final farewell. Would she like to use that event in creating a ritual of goodbye? Or, would she like to use her dream experience in a ritual of thanks for her father's love and caring? Guidance from deceased loved ones sometimes comes in redirection, consolation, and encouragement. Catherine received all three.

QUESTIONS TO BE POSED TO CATHERINE

1. What is the meaning you have found in the words on the spiral memo book found at the mailbox on your birthday? How will you make the most of the insight gained?
2. What new tradition or ritual can you start on *your* birthday that will keep alive the memory of the memo book?
3. How would you like to take the words on the memo book and use them in a ritual of farewell or remembrance or to start a tradition in your family?
4. How do the words illuminate characteristics of your father you would like to point out to young and old alike?
5. What rituals are presently parts of your family history? Are they open to change?
6. How did your dream, in which your Dad reassured you, motivate you to follow your beliefs about his wishes?
7. Is there any part of the dream that is most precious to you? How would you like to use it in a ritual to honor him and signal a new start in life?

8. Do you usually dream in color? What is the significance of this for you?

9. What were your thoughts and feelings when you woke up from your dream?

10. Are there any lessons to be learned from the demeanor, appearance, or actions of your father in the dream that you can use in the future?

11. Now that you know others have had similar experiences, what does the bird on your van mean to you now? Is it symbolic of anything associated with your father?

12. How would you like to show that your father will always be an important part of your life?

13. Do you know if others in your family had any extraordinary experiences that could be used as part of family ritual?

14. What have you learned from your father and your relationship with him that you should never forget? How would you like to express those things in an informal or formal ritual?

Catherine found new nourishment for coping with her loss as she recalled her three experiences and the messages she gleaned from them. She can use her previously disregarded experiences to bridge the divide between her father and herself. Any rituals that she plans and carries out will, as with most rituals, provide a tangible way, some evidence, that the death is real, did in fact occur, and she is visibly dealing with it. At the same time, her rituals and traditions will honor her father as they provide an avenue for sharing emotions with friends, relatives, or neighbors.

CONCEPTS TO EXPLORE AND DEVELOP FOR CREATING RITUALS AND TRADITIONS

Because rituals have a strong influence on memories, mourner and helpers can collaborate to build ritual or tradition as part of the resolution of grief, to create a form of communication with the deceased, and to provide an avenue of action or doing something that counters feelings of powerlessness. Below are some additional concepts to include in the review of the choices available to meet these needs.

1. Consider what rituals or traditions can be developed so that you can *symbolize the presence of your deceased loved* one at specific family celebrations, anniversaries, or in circumstances when you are alone. For example, it could be the lighting of a candle, the display and acknowledgement of a special picture or an object that was made by the deceased, playing a recording of his favorite song, or something associated with the extraordinary experience.

2. Is there a ritual of expression you wish to initiate based on the extraordinary experience? For example, do you need to say good-bye, let go of anger or guilt, use the EE as a memory trigger for a specific event in his life, say something you didn't get a chance to say, or use it to affirm the death and your belief that death brings a new beginning? (One woman who had an EE involving pennies uses it in the following way: Any time she finds a penny she uses it to trigger recognition of her deceased husband and greets him with a "Hi Harold.") How will you remind yourself to use your EE ritual of behavior?

3. Try this anniversary ritual. Spend a quiet time of your day alone and look over photographs of the life of your loved one. Dig out all your old photo albums that go back to the first pictures you have of the deceased. Review her life and your relationship with her through pictures. Then spend time with other members of the family, share a meal, and discuss the past.

4. Tape-record a description of your EE, memories of your early life, and the memories of your relationship with your loved one to preserve as part of family history. Play it back in whole or in part on appropriate days. Tell your children where the tape is located.

5. Build a daily informal ritual or start a tradition that expresses one of the four beliefs associated with successful coping found in Chapter 3.

6. Create a ritual in which you use your extraordinary experience to tell your loved one that you need to rein in your grief and find some control, but that it does not mean you love him or miss him any less. Use the ritual at least once a day at a convenient time. Begin by reviewing the EE, then make your statement for changing the course of your grief work. You know he would want you to be happy again and not prolong your suffering.

7. Plan to use your EE to include others in your family as part of a ritual of *remembrance* and to strengthen family ties. Use the telling of the experience to invite others in the group to exchange their memories of the deceased.

8. Create a ritual in which you seek forgiveness or say to the deceased that you extend forgiveness. A forgiveness ritual can be utilized in a church, home, or out-of-doors setting. This ritual of *reconciliation* will be a gift to yourself as well as your loved one.

9. Begin the ritual of keeping a "coincidence" diary that includes not only the extraordinary experiences you have had, but especially all the little things that occur at the right time that help you move along in your grief work. A phone call when you are feeling down, a thought that suddenly buoys your hopes, an invitation to dinner, a visit from an old friend who offers to fix a plumbing problem on the spot—and the list will go on. Over time look at the numerous occasions when the ritual of recording coincidences and the unexpected have played an important role in your growth through grief. Use the results to build trust in mystery and the unseen to enhance your life in the years ahead.

Perhaps you may want to keep in mind this quote from Michael Shallis in *On Time:* "As there are as least as many unconnected or acausal events as there are causal ones, a coincidence can be seen as pointing to this missing half of reality."

10. Use your extraordinary experience as entry into a daily listening ritual. Take yourself away from the daily bombardment of the

physical world with a time of nurturance that features listening. Call it "sacred time" where you first relax and think about your EE. Then ask a question on a topic of concern and listen for what answers come into your mind. Listening becomes a ritualistic discipline. Your "sacred time" will bring new ideas and insights to help bring passion back into your life. With passion you will achieve many goals.

11. Make plans to use your extraordinary experience as part of a yearly anniversary remembrance of the death, or on Memorial Day, or on the day the EE occurred. Decide what messages you wish to convey in the formal or informal ritual you create? Some examples of messages are as follows: my love for you will grow; I will never forget you; thank you for everything; we will meet again; you have taught me so much; you are in my prayers; thank you for your continuing help.

RITUAL NEED NOT BE ELABORATE

When thinking of rituals or traditions to pass down from generation to generation, there is a tendency to think big, that bigger is better. Not so! A ritual or tradition can be as simple as regularly using an object belonging to or crafted by the deceased or wearing a particular piece of jewelry or clothing that he used to wear. Or it can be as simple as a nightly prayer of petition or thanks, a calming daily recollection of memorable words from a dream, or a weekly visit to a contemplative, peaceful place that reminds one of the deceased. These and many other overt signs involving the extraordinary experience can be used in bringing structure and direction in the process of adjusting to the death of the beloved while reinforcing an important belief—that the loved one is gone but never forgotten.

Another basic approach is to create ritual that enacts the message of the extraordinary experience. If the basic message is interpreted as the deceased saying, "I'm okay," then think about a celebratory ritual such as a toast, a short trip, a daily walk to the park, playing a favorite song, or reciting a poem created by the mourner thus joyfully acknowledging he is okay. Or suggest keeping that message on the bulletin board in her kitchen.

One can also create a ritual in which the mourner responds to the message in the experience. If the message is interpreted as, "I love you," and the mourner wants to say the same in return, then find a way to put it into ritual. For example, she can purchase a coffee cup with "I love you" printed on it. It can be used daily or only on special occasions in honor of the deceased. Using her "I love you cup" can have enormous conscious and unconscious implications for expressing emotions. Or help the mourner create a ritual to use for coming-home-after-work or when coming back from a visit or long journey. At these times a simple ritual can help in coping with the absence of the loved one, ease the anxiety of coming back to an empty house, and by doing so give a feeling of control. Emphasize that the mourner can make a plan to deal with any of the troubling parts of her grief work through a ritual of *continuity* that recognizes the absence of the deceased but says, "I can continue on and always remember you."

Whether formally planned or instinctively adapted a ritual can bring a welcome sense of achievement, a channeling of one's grief into more acceptable proportions. Any ritual can be a participatory event that permits release of inner tensions through physical expression. Equally important is the role that simple ongoing rituals play in reuniting families and giving them a sense of identity and belonging by reaffirming one's beliefs and memories concerning the loved one.

Rituals and new traditions lay the groundwork for beginning the task of recognizing one has been changed by the death of a loved one. They also begin the needed formation of the old Self and the new Self into an identity previously unknown to the mourner. Next we explore using the extraordinary to help the mourner form the new identity needed to face the future.

Hold that thought.

7

Forming A New Identity: Combining The Old And The New

The irrational fullness of life taught me never to discard anything, even when it goes against all our theories...security, certitude, and peace do not lead to discoveries.

C.G. Jung

A New Identity

I believe I had these experiences to help me heal myself through this very rough time in my life. I know in my heart that my parents are always with me, watching over me, guiding me, helping me in my life. I feel a calming come over me and I know what I have to do. But these experiences (my EE's) are their way of letting me know that they are okay where they are. I am not to worry about them because they are together and happy. I feel I am a stronger person for going through what I did. I believe I was somehow chosen to deliver a message (and

I do) about what I have experienced, so that people will not be afraid of what they do not understand.

—RoseAnn M.
On her EE's after the deaths of her parents

∞   ∞   ∞   ∞   ∞   ∞

When death takes a loved one we were particularly close to it also takes a part of the Self. We lose that core of the Self that related so intimately to the deceased. That part of us that interacted with the loved one dies, and it is mourned just as we mourn our loved one. All at once we begin to recognize that we are suddenly less than whole. We feel different. We act different. We are especially related to differently by some friends and acquaintences. In fact, we sometimes feel as if there was big gaping hole right in the middle of our heart. We suffer a loss of identity. If widowed, one is no longer invited to couples social events; if you are a parent who lost a child, you no longer get together with other parents at the park or at school. If your loved one was primarily the only source of meaningful social interaction you feel all alone. Life and identity is not the same as it used to be.

Identity is essentially the product of what one thinks about the Self in the deeper recesses of the mind. It's who we think we are, our roles, our essence, our mystery. Often when we are mourning we are confronted with a key question: Who am I now that my loved one has died? Those who are absent from our lives will continue to be a part of our identity, but not in the same way; we are changed by death. In addition, if a mourner's identity is tied solely to many shifting or variable factors affected by loss (appearance, skills, house, car, collections, the loved one, etc.), one's identity can be severely threatened. Regrettably, social and physical changes are often highlighted and reinforced by the way others unwittingly tend to isolate the bereaved. These omissions seem to be the most painful for any mourner.

Sometimes bereaved people are avoided out of a false fear that simple conversation might lead to talking about the deceased and precipitate emotional upheaval. At other times, the bereaved person is excluded from social gatherings for reasons ranging from awkwardness to forget-fulness, sometimes out of fear that a widow or widower might be a threat to one's marriage. All of this affects the way a mourner thinks about herself. Her identity is assaulted because she believes she is now of less importance to those she thought were friends. She wonders what she could have done to deserve such treatment and sometimes tries to act solely to please others. This complicity in acting as others would want her to must be challenged in order for the grief process to natu-rally unfold and be expressed.

In instances where the bereaved had substantially given up his or her identity by relying too heavily on the deceased loved one—not an uncommon happening—the mourner must establish a whole new identity. This new identity will be a mix of the old and the new, in most instances, as one must decide what to leave behind and what to take with her into her new life. He or she has to assume new roles and responsibilities, and develop skills and behaviors necessitated by a range of needs formerly filled by the deceased loved one. Previous ways of being have to be abandoned, unless one chooses to live in the past, insu-lated from responsibility, and resist necessary social interaction. Directing the time, energy, and interaction originally given to the deceased, into other rewarding pursuits, will result in further recon-struction of identity.

Let me emphasize the bold fact that *friends, family or other helpers do not change a mourner's identity.* The mourner is the only change agent; others may facilitate, but the mourner orchestrates all. But what you do as a helper can have a major impact on the mourner's choices, how she perceives her social support, and how she reconstructs her identity. Still, there is no guarantee your efforts will be totally successful simply because there are too many variables over which there is no control.

TASKS OF HELPERS IN IDENTITY FORMATION

Friends or family members do not have to be therapists—only concerned caregivers—to accomplish four tasks in assisting identity formation after major loss.

1. *Always show deep respect.* As a helper, you are a powerful stabilizing force in the life of the mourner. You may be her primary lifeline during this turbulent time. What you say and how you say it will affect the way she perceives herself and the supportive relationship. You are communicating that the mourner is valuable and you will be supportive of her changing identity. Be careful about how you suggest alternatives and *never* talk down or act authoritarian. Being consistently respectful, as though you were helping the most important person you had ever met, will generate mutual respect and freedom of open exchange. The latter is of critical importance. Your respect must not diminish if the mourner fails to respond as you would like.

   Deep respect is especially significant in the discussion of the extraordinary experience. That respect will be a strong motivator for the long road full of changes the mourner will have to make. The mourner's goodness, her value (her intimate identity) will be reflected in your eyes. That is why the mourner/helper relationship is a special factor in reshaping identity—because it tells the mourner that under the worst of circumstances she is forever a person who is highly valued.

2. *Identify and strengthen existing skills and positive beliefs.* What we do well and what optimistic beliefs we hold play crucial roles in how we see the world and ourselves; in a big way they shape our identity. Skills and beliefs that are to be retained from the old identity (organizational, work, and recreational skills; positive attitudes and beliefs about life, the deceased, and his contributions) should be talked about at length and highlighted as being important parts of the mourner's life that can never be taken away. The extraordinary

experience will be part of that belief system with its implications for positive action and reconstruction of life. Part of the action and reconstruction will revolve around how those existing strengths and skills, buttressed by the incorporation of new skills, can fit into new roles the mourner must assume.

This is a time where the EE can be used as a resource to encourage the formation of new skills and hone others that have gone unused for long periods of time. It can also suggest the release of self-defeating attitudes through awareness of the positive response expected from the gift of the EE.

("You have been given a gift to assist you. What does it say about the need for hope-filled action on your part?")

3. *Create opportunities to establish a diverse social network.* A major factor in the establishment of a new identity is the mourner's perception of existing relationships. Strong social relationships are to identity as blood is to life.

People need people. Assessing the needs for interaction with others at the appropriate time and creating situations where the mourner is comfortable in mixing with new and old friends will be an integral factor in her identity formation. This is an ongoing practice in which you and the mourner will have much trial and error learning. Persist. Use the EE as a reminder that the deceased loved one wants the mourner to find fulfillment in the satisfaction that comes from rewarding participation in social communities and organizations.

4. *Talk about the deceased as one who has lived and died.* An integral part of establishing a new identity is the realization that the loved one has lived *and* died. Therefore, your willingness to openly talk about the deceased in the past tense (He *liked* this or that. He *was* happy about that.), pointing out attributes and contributions, will become a part of the memory life that is ingrained in the new identity. This carefully reinforces again and again that life has

changed and the mourner must respond accordingly. As simple as this may sound, in reality, the full meaning of the death may not be fully realized for months, and in some instances, for years. Although discussion often centers on the past or one's old life, the major thrust is progressively on what is to come. Chapter 10 addresses the way one can use the extraordinary to maintain positive memories to help bridge the old life and the new one with all of the changes involved.

The awareness and acceptance of the role of identity-changes, through the demands of adaptation, can be a major step forward in reconciling oneself to major loss. ("I am a different person now than before the death of Matt.") Helpers can facilitate this awareness through an extraordinary experience. Let's examine how by way of the following pattern of EE's that occurred to Martha after the death of her husband.

"I HAVE ALWAYS BEEN A SKEPTIC UNTIL NOW"

(1) The first thing I noticed when my husband became gravely ill during the last few days of his life was this band of small white butterflies; they hovered outside of the Florida room window where he lay dying of lung cancer. I have never seen these butterflies here before and we've lived in this house since 1980. They were there, like I said, a few days, and then when he died they were gone.

(2) A month or so after my husband died a bush sprung up out of the ground near where the white butterflies had been. The white flowers on it are the same size as the white butterflies. I did not cultivate it. It grows without any help and it looks as though it came from a nursery.

(3) It rained "cats and dogs" all night long the night he died (2:30 a.m.) as well as thundered and stormed. But when they opened the door to take his body to the funeral home, the rain turned off as if it had been a faucet with a turn-off valve.

(4) *As you can tell by the letter, I'm in Florida, which is where he died. We have no oak trees here in Florida like we have up north; however, when I returned from burying my husband in Ohio, on my top doorstep, right where I have to step to get into the house, there was this huge oak leaf. It was about 8-9 inches long and was old, brown, and weatherworn. This was a tremendous jolt to me. My father had built our home in Kentucky under all the big oak trees and this immediately told me he was near. He died in 1964.*

(5) *Then there was the Sunday in church when I had gotten altar flowers in memory of my husband. As I was sitting there I felt a "presence" or breathing on my skin that made me shiver two or three times. When I acknowledged what it was—a connection with my husband—I stopped shivering and was not scared.*

(6) *And so I told you my husband died on April 12, 1997. Our wedding anniversary is October 1ˢᵗ. On October 1ˢᵗ at 6:30 a.m. I was in bed, the shades were down, and it was dark. Soft voices and a light coming through the doorway awakened me. I thought it might be the neighbors next door talking and their porch light was on. I was getting a little upset with them so I got out of bed, marched out toward the light and voices, only to find that my TV had come on all by itself. And the really odd thing is when I saw it was the TV—I merely said, "Happy anniversary Kent," turned the TV off, and went back to bed. My daughter asked if I checked to see if anyone else was in the house or if the door was still locked. I live alone and the door was locked. But I knew somehow I did not need to check the door. My TV continues to come on by itself. It came on four times in November and once each in December, January, and February. I have called the Cable Company about my TV; they are unable to explain it. My son works on*

TV's and electronics and he said he never ran across a TV that comes on by itself.

I have always been a skeptic until now—and I will always believe from this day forward that there are "spirits" or "forces" that are around us. And they are lovely to behold. I have no fear of death and I know my husband is in a beautiful place. I often ask myself why I have been so specially blessed—I am not worthy to have seen these things take place.

From skeptic to believer, from egotism to other centeredness is not an uncommon shift in these situations. The pattern of symbols in Martha's experiences have been the basis for drawing strength and finding new meaning that leads her to conclude her husband is happy and whole again and she is a different person. There are no substitutes for these patterns of experience and they come together in a one-of-a kind way. The personal meaning to the mourner is both a complex and highly significant factor to assess as an outside observer. One thing is certain: her beliefs about her EE's are an extremely powerful motivator in the process of adapting to change. Therefore, her convictions are a potent coping tool to be explored and used. In this instance, a helper might begin to inquire about Martha's statement that she no longer fears death (she has changed) and believes the spirits of her loved ones are with her. What will be the implications of those beliefs in the formation of her new identity?

QUESTIONS TO BE POSED TO MARTHA

How will Martha choose to live her life if she has no fear of death and knows her loved ones are near? With this question as a focus in the process of identity formation and recognizing accompanying changes in the way she sees herself, here are some questions that should be explored and expanded upon.

1. What do you believe that your husband is saying about you as a person and your capabilities in dealing with his death?
2. How do you feel about yourself now that you have experienced these gifts?
3. In what way have your experiences affected your views on life and death?
4. In what ways do you think you are stronger and better prepared to deal with your new life? Are you more aware of and sensitive to signs and symbols that are part of your life, like the butterflies that appeared outside of your Florida room when your husband was dying?
5. How do you feel you might be able to help others who are in need of support now that you have come this far?
6. Was there one particular experience that has been most meaningful to you or is it the fact that you have had several experiences which are associated with your husband that has given you a new direction?
7. What was the special significance for you in having the sense of presence experience that occurred in the church?
8. What is the symbolic significance of butterflies for you?
9. What does the appearance and growth of the bush with the white flowers indicate?
10. What role, if any, do you believe that love plays in what you have experienced? Where do you think love originates?
11. Do you see yourself as a different person now than before your husband died? If so, how are you different and what have you learned that you can take with you into your new life? More capable? Less fearful?
12. What meaning have you deduced from the signs received from the TV coming on by itself on your anniversary and then in succeeding months? How has it influenced your life?
13. How can you use these experiences to discover your gift to the world?

14. How will your experiences cause you to initiate new traditions of remembrance, new routines at home, or observance of special anniversaries?

15. How have these experiences changed the way you think about yourself and what you expect from yourself. Have they made you aware of what will never change about you?

Helping Martha become more aware of establishing her new identity means helping her clarify her new roles and responsibilities now that she is widowed. How she can adapt to these new demands and find comfort and satisfaction are topics that will need to be continually addressed. A significant part of providing support in this regard is to think about and present to her the choices she has in her confrontation with change.

STRENGTHENING SELF-IMAGE

In whole or in part, redefining oneself is a necessary part of grief work and coping with massive change. Rebuilding identity necessarily includes strengthening self-confidence and self-esteem. Therefore, a key question for both the mourner and those providing support is "How can self-confidence and self-esteem be restored or at least revitalized?" Put another way, "How can you help the mourner experience success in *any* endeavor to strengthen a sagging self-image?" Patterns of poor coping behavior are often rooted in a poor self-image. Recognizing that reestablishing identity is a long-term project, here are several ways to begin the journey of strengthening self-image.

1. *Help the mourner experience success.* Because powerlessness has the characteristic of making the mourner feel insignificant and believe the world is an unjust place, finding success is pivotal. Her success may begin by finding a way to get through the next hour or the day. It may mean finding a new way to do an old chore or going to a social event for the first time without the beloved. The extraordinary experience often suggests a new sense of purpose, a

deeper understanding of the meaning of life that far surpasses anything previously imagined. Consider it carefully for the wisdom it holds that points to the development of a higher consciousness through study and practice. The event itself is a success experience (the mourner has been honored) leading to successful transition. Bring this fact to the mourner's attention.

Success may also mean sharpening work, communication or social skills by taking a class in a specific area of interest. It could mean teaching a particular skill to children or adults. Whatever it is, recognition and reassurance by a trusted helper will be instrumental in forming the new identity as self-image is restored. The mourner's self-image plays a major role in the determination to deal with her loss.

Reassurance can also be drawn from the extraordinary experience by exploring it in terms of what it is saying about the mourner's ability to deal with the loss. Whether spoken or unspoken, most extraordinary experiences *imply* support and reassurance for going on. Examine parts of the experience that are applicable and point out that the loved one "knows you are capable and wants you to reach out and experience life (and success) again."

2. *Help the mourner achieve recognition of progress in her grief work.* Reaching out and taking risks to make changes is a courageous act by the bereaved and needs the reassurance of key friends and family members. Your sincere willingness to help by recognizing the effort will go a long way toward bolstering self-esteem and continual commitment. Nothing can be more helpful at this time than allowing the person to talk through his thoughts and feelings about progress or a lack of it. But be prepared to show how he has been moving forward.

Recognize progress but do not overstate or imply an unrealistic picture. ("You made it through this first week back at work by your courage.") Emphasize a slow one-day-at-a-time approach and remind the mourner it is normal to desire a quick adjustment and relief from pain. Regrettably, emotional pain visits and revisits before it eventually fades in its persistence. But she should know that, "The day will come when you can recall your loved one, smile, and be happy about the time you had together."

3. *Help the mourner develop ways to deal with being devalued.* Loss itself is often humbling as well as imposing a sense of lowered respect. It is in being devalued that we need to be reminded that the death of a loved one is a universal human experience, not a punishment. No one escapes that experience although most of us refuse to recognize this universal truth and live as though death never comes.

The first step in handling devaluation is to recognize its normalcy given the circumstances; it is to be expected when someone so loved and valued is taken from us. We feel crushed, insignificant. So, too, is the experience of being labeled a widow or widower demeaning to many who are mourning. Talk about it. Expect it as a common though seldom talked about reality of grief. Some losses make us feel betrayed by those we expected would help.

Many who are not mourning have little insight into what the mourner is dealing with in her transition. When helping a mourner who is isolated by others, I try to explain the role that fear of death and ignorance plays in the hurtful behavior shown by friends and neighbors. Sometimes fear of death causes friends to limit or end their relationships with the mourner.

The second step is to encourage talking out any anger that exists toward those who have said or done something devaluing in the eyes of the mourner. Help her normalize, consider the source, express, and leave anger in the past. Then comes the task of recognizing and replacing the negative self-talk and self-pity with reassurances that one will prevail, endure, and find meaning in life, that there are people out there who will "walk the talk" with them. Be sure to talk about the "surprise people" who unexpectedly stepped forward to help—and those who where expected to help but did not. The mourner must not forever write off those who are now abandoning her. Some of those people change; they learn and grow and see their mistakes. We all have to be willing to readmit them into our lives and not forever carry a grudge.

4. *Help the mourner reestablish confidence in her decision-making and problem-solving.* Making decisions and solving problems is the lot of every mourner at a most devastating time in life. And it is not unusual to be hesitant and unsure when decisions have to be made. Therefore, recommend the importance of seeking input on problems from experts when feasible. It is sound thinking, as well as a critical problem-solving strategy, to seek out a mentor, a coach, or a respected friend and consider her input—then make a decision. Millions do so every day. You, as a helper, as well as the mourner, may have to tread the same path at some point. Helpers and mourners may have to speak to a grief counselor or a bereavement coordinator at a hospice for ideas and direction if they are at a loss for what to do in a specific situation. In either case, there is nothing wrong with having a lifetime mentor, confidant, or coach. In fact, they are highly recommended for all. No one can be expected to have all the answers.

Seeking alternative ways of dealing with a problem, obtaining the best information available, often gives insights and new opportunities to consider before deciding on a course of action. All helpers can certainly give their opinions to mourners when asked. However, they provide invaluable assistance by learning who to consult in the community, given a particular problem a mourner is confronting. Financial analysts, RN's, social service workers, occupational therapists, legal experts, academic counselors, to name a few, may have to be consulted before a decision is made.

And don't forget to ask for the counsel of those who have preceded the mourner in a major loss and have had an extraordinary experience. They often have much wisdom and reassurance to offer. In the end, the mourner always chooses what to use and what to discard; it is her grief, her loss, her responsibility to cope.

A mourner can also review (with the help of a trusted friend) her strengths at work, with hobbies, athletics, or any area of endeavor where she feels confident or skillful and assess what it is that provides the level of success enjoyed. Write down the thought processes and skills involved that led to the present level of expertise and begin to consider how these same thoughts and skills could be used in planning to cope with the many changes imposed by the death of the loved one.

Suggest reviewing her loss history; everyone has one. How did she cope with previous losses in her life? What did she do then that helped her, and can she employ similar thoughts and behaviors in dealing with her current loss? The support person can remind the mourner that she already has assets that have brought her growth and ability to deal with other problems. Bring them out into the open, see how they can be applied to the present obstacles.

Ask her what she thinks her EE *implies that she should be able to do* under the circumstances.

5. *Help the mourner live by her values and beliefs.* Major loss commonly calls for self-examination and clarification of one's values and beliefs because they have been challenged and often changed by death. In order to regain a sense of control of her life much thought, prayer or meditation, and sharing is needed, especially when the mourner feels that her perception of the world and her belief system lack meaning. As new beliefs about her identity and her place in the world are formed they will affect how she views her remaining grief work. The extraordinary experience will play a

major role in her value system and reevaluating what is truly important in life.

Here is where helpers can support the bereaved by creating an atmosphere where her deepest thoughts and beliefs, including thoughts about extraordinary experiences, can be sorted out and worked through. Suggesting alternatives and options will mean bringing to the helping relationship the fruits of your labor in searching for useful information. You will be challenged to become aware of the great opportunity for rapt attention and care. By being a good listener (this is not as simple as it sounds) you are allowing the bereaved person to prepare to make her choices and to reorder and live by what she values.

Again, the unfolding of all of the above processes is gradual and ongoing and immediate results cannot be expected. There will be advances and declines as well as lack of movement. Be there when needed and you assist the mourner in believing in herself and her ability to adapt.

ESTABLISHING IDENTITY WITH NEW ROUTINES

One of the salient approaches to coping with the death of a loved one or a divorce is the importance of giving up the *anticipation of old routines* involving the deceased (or the ex) and beginning the essential task of establishing new routines. This means attempting to intervene in anticipating his or her arrival home from work, the Sunday drive to the beach or the park, the 5 o'clock glass of wine, perhaps the dinner out on Friday evenings. Whatever the cherished rituals of the past involving the person who is gone, to continue their anticipation, is to court unnecessary pain.

Planning and initiating new routines as simple as having breakfast in a different room, deciding to try a new restaurant, or choosing a recreational facility not previously frequented is part of adjusting to life without the person. Making deliberate changes in routines is fundamental to coping well. It is also an integral part of identity formation—and it takes strong commitment to turn new routines into old ones. Once more, recognizing and grieving the loss of old routines involving the deceased (talking and crying about them as necessary) are key factors in replacing them with the new. Everything the mourner does as a new routine or ritual becomes a part of her new life and who she is becoming in her adaptation to change. She is molding an identity that necessarily demands advancement toward greater independence as she takes over added responsibilities for herself and those in her care.

In the following visual experience that occurred to Nedra Hendrickson of Wichita, KS, she reports how in a great time of emotional upheaval, she received a visit from her father that strengthened her resolve to deal with her dilemma. The EE also reinforced her identity with the reassurance that her father was still looking out for her and that she was capable of managing her stress-filled life. This is a particularly extraordinary experience given the fact that her father had died twelve years previously. She believed she had completed her grief work and had not been thinking of her father at the time of his appearance. Her great anxiety, due to the hoped for heart transplant for her husband, was the precipitating factor in this EE.

"I THINK MY DAD KNEW HOW STRESSED I WAS"

In October of 1991 my husband Harold had a massive heart attack which led to a 30-day hospitalization. His stay ended with him being placed on the waiting list for a heart transplant. In March of 1992 we received the call that a heart had become available, but we needed to be at the hospital within 30 minutes. I was working across town which meant speeding home to pick up Harold, then to the hospital. After we arrived at St. Francis we were rushed up stairs to cardiac ICU where he was immediately prepped for surgery. At this point we began to wait. All of our family arrived to wait with us. We took turns going into ICU to wait, which meant fully gowning up, complete with facemask. After approximately 4 hours we were told that the donor heart was not acceptable for transplant and everything was stopped. No surgery. IV's removed, etc. Since he was admitted to the hospital, Harold was held overnight so that his heart function could be tested.

After arriving back home that evening our sons and I took our baths and proceeded to get ready for bed. It was approximately 10:30 when I finally retired for the night turning out all the lights. I rolled over facing my husband's side of the bed when I sensed someone was in the room. Thinking it was our 12 year-old son, I turned back over to see what he needed. The day had been an extremely stressful one for all of us. But instead of my son, my father was sitting in a chair beside the bed. I spontaneously spoke to him asking, "Daddy, did you know they thought they had a heart for Harold?" He responded, "No, no they didn't." He then asked me, "Girl, are you all right?" I responded that "Yes, I was okay." At this point I started to get up out of bed when suddenly he was gone. He did not fade out, but was just not there anymore.

I know I did not dream this event as I had just turned out the lights and lay down.

My father passed away January 2, 1984, so he had been gone for 12 years. Having gotten past the grief of his death many years ago, I hadn't consciously thought about him in a long time. I felt no fear at his presence and spoke to him automatically. The only odd thing about his presence was his sitting in a chair, for there are no chairs in our bedroom.

When I realized he was gone I didn't feel let down or disappointed, but had a calm feeling and a certainty that Daddy had been here but was now gone.

I didn't tell anyone about this experience for a long time because I thought they would think I was either crazy or had *dreamed the entire event. At the time of his presence he was in as solid a form as you or I.*

We went through 2 more false alarms before receiving our transplant, but I never experienced any more visits from my father. It only happened the one time. I feel that the stress level was so high during the first "dry run" that my Dad's appearance was to reassure himself of my well-being as well as being a comfort to me.

It is interesting to note Nedra's observation that her father came because he needed reassurance as much as she did. Some researchers and parapsychologists speculate that among the reasons for the return of the deceased is self-need. Some have returned asking for prayers from the living.

QUESTIONS TO BE POSED TO NEDRA

Keeping in mind that identity is made up of all of our interactions with those in the present as well as those in the past (our perceptions of the old life), let us consider the questions we might ask in order to reinforce a positive identity for coping with the stress experienced by Nedra. In answering some of the following questions that include people in her life, and beliefs that support her observations, friends and family would do well to validate her remarks both verbally and nonverbally.

1. How do you see yourself now that you have experienced an entirely different dimension of life?
2. How does knowing that your father is still concerned about your well-being influence the way you feel about life and the way you deal with it?
3. Would you describe how waiting for a donor heart is a pressure-filled experience? What did you need at the time?
4. How were you able to deal with the stress of waiting at the hospital?
5. Do you find comfort in sharing your hopes and fears with family members?

What has been most comforting through these difficult days?

6. How do your children influence the way you deal with your husband's heart trouble?

7. How do you feel you have set an example for your children?

8. Why do you think the appearance of your father did not frighten you at all?

9. In what way did the appearance of your father reduce your stress?

10. What has been the most transformative part of your EE that has made you who you are right now?

11. In what way does your EE fit in with the personal experiences you had in relating to your father when he was alive?

12. As a result of your dad's visit, how will you try to find peaceful, restorative time each day to deal with the stress in your life?

13. Have you wrestled with the question of why you were given the extraordinary experience?

14. What do you want to change about the way you deal with adversity as a result of your experience? What will be the first step you will take to incorporate this change into your life?

IDENTITY AND INTERPERSONAL RELATIONSHIPS

Popular workshop leader and psychologist John Bradshaw, in *Bradshaw On The Family*, says, "We cannot have an identity all alone. Our reality is shaped from the beginning by a relationship." A single relationship can be an integral part of one's identity. As suggested in Chapter 5, the relationship between the mourner and the deceased must change from one of physical presence to one based on past experiences and symbols in the present that speak to the importance of the deceased in the life of the mourner. The recollection of past experiences combined with the EE will be of special importance in the building of useful symbols. The mourner needs to be willing to talk about and expand on the meaning of his lifelong relationship with the deceased as he goes through the process of reforming the way he looks at himself and building his symbolic relationship. This will set the stage for the development of an unseen but very real inner relationship between the mourner and the deceased loved one. This invisible relationship is an integral part of the way the person views himself and his world.

The renewal of Nedra's relationship with her father is an important source of strength and revitalization. It is symbol building at its best. Recognizing her powerful bond has not been broken, and highlighting her importance through her father's visit, will be most rewarding and will enhance her feelings about herself. She knows her family and her father will always care about her.

THE USE OF OBJECTS AS PART OF A NEW IDENTITY

There are many symbols that can be factors in forming a new identity by confirming that loving relationships with the deceased are ongoing and purposeful. They can be symbolic memories or tangible objects. Symbols have often helped the bereaved deal with the loss of a loved one by acting as reminders that the deceased always is near and his love continues. Sometimes the symbolic sign can involve natural phenomena or an animal. Many extraordinary experiences involve objects that become treasured for their symbolic meaning. Flowers, stones, personal items belonging to the deceased, a Christmas tree ornament, any object involved in the EE may be used by a mourner as a reminder that love is eternal and forever strong. For the mourner, a physical object involves tangible evidence of the reality of the EE, a lasting bond to the loved one, and recognition that she has changed. Here is an example from Janet Haines of Jaffrey, NH.

"THE RELIEF I FELT WAS IMMEDIATE"

My experience of after death communication has been inside of me for five years waiting for the right person to tell. In the summer of 1993 my father suffered a heart attack. While he was hospitalized, my Mom suffered an asthma attack and she was also hospitalized. Rather nerve wracking having both parents ill and hospitalized at the same time! It was discovered that during the asthma attack my mother had torn a hole in her heart, which put both parents in cardiac intensive care. My mother had open heart surgery to repair the hole in her heart and my father had quadruple by-pass surgery a week later. Because of my Mom's many years of asthma, she was never able to be taken off the respirator. The day after my Dad was released from the hospital, my Mom passed away. I lost not only my Mom, but my dear friend.

Because we are not from NH originally, but from Long Island, the funeral was to take place there. This meant getting my Mom's body to NY and getting my Dad, who at this time was only five days out of surgery, on a plane to NY for the funeral services. Once this was over and we were back in NH, my Dad stayed with us while he recuperated from surgery. We tried to help him deal with that plus the loss of his partner of 47 years. Needless to say, my own grieving had to be put on hold so that I could be strong for my Dad.

Once my dad returned to his own home, my husband and I headed for the coast of Maine. I guess it's my LI upbringing, but every time I have a really big problem to work out I head for the ocean. When we arrived I put on my running shoes and took off down the beach by myself. While running, I just let go and tried to get everything out. I cried, screamed, did whatever to try and get some relief. One thing I was saying, and I guess in a way I was talking to my Mom, was that the last thing she had said to me was that I would always be in her heart. I was asking her if I was still in her heart and telling her how much I missed her.

After running for about two miles I turned around and started walking back. As I walked, I looked down, and there on the sand was a smooth stone in the exact shape of a heart! Some might say this was just a coincidence, but I believe it was a sign from either God or my Mom, or maybe even my guardian angel. I do know the relief I felt was immediate. It seemed to me I was being told my

Mom was okay and that she knew how much I loved her and missed her, and that she loved me too and knew what I was going through. I, of course, still miss her and have sad times, but I kept that stone and it is a comfort. The experience also left me with a great love for angels, which I collect in many different forms, and a desire to read and learn all I can about what happens after death.

LOVE AS AN IDENTITY BUILDER

Love, particularly the belief that one is not loved, is at the core of most abandonment issues and life's problems. In mourning the death of a friend, relative or family member, love is a pivotal force in picking oneself up again and again and going forward to integrate loss into life. We can survive anything if we feel loved. With the death of the loved one, the perceived absence of love by the mourner adds immeasurably to the pain of loss. However, restoring love is found through the consistent actions of those in one's support network *and* in the EE. In the case where the mourner has had an extraordinary experience, the deceased is one of the main love providers.

In terms of identity, let us remember that love says the mourner is important, a somebody. It confers a critical sense of value identity at a time when the questions "Who am I now?" and "Where am I going?" loom as challenges. Who we are and what we are worth are often called into question in the course of grief work. A true friend or helper confers a quality of love and value that helps meet the challenges and answers the questions. It is easy to overlook that *how others see us* is an integral part of *how we see ourselves.* The mourner who believes that her helper and/or the departed see her as someone who will prevail, with a little help, who believes she is loving and loveable, and who is convinced she is perceived as normal in her reactions, will have made a positive beginning in the construction of her new life.

No one can fully understand or appreciate the meaning for Janet of finding the heart-shaped stone. This is simply because no one can fully understand this mother and daughter's love for each other, the death bed conversation regarding always being in her mother's heart, and the deep symbolic significance of the heart-shaped stone. Only the person who has such an experience is privy to the profound implications of the event and its authenticity. We can speculate that the stone is an obvious symbol of eternal love and a meaningful message of reciprocal love that will be integral parts of her new identity. This linking object is a tangible way to perpetuate a healthy relationship with her mother and help shape her new identity.

Your task as a helper would be to validate the meaning and connection to the object as a legitimate means of relating to her mother. It is okay to cherish the stone. It's a reminder that her mother has died, lives on in her heart and soul, and is part of her being. They will always be mother and daughter. Also, pursuing her interest in angels and learning more about what happens after death, by being prepared to suggest readings and other resources, is necessary.

I asked Janet what she had done with the heart-shaped stone. "I have placed it in a special place," she said "and I have an angel from my collection watching over it. It makes me feel peaceful to look at it and think of my Mom." This behavior is highly significant for a helper to consider. Depending on the object involved in the experience and the personal and symbolic meaning to the mourner, exploring how to use it as a way to inspire, to accept, to modify emotion, to recall loving moments, and to reinforce beliefs is significant to your role.

Another effective way to help fill love and worth needs is to emphasize the mourner's ability to create. I cannot emphasize enough that with a little help everyone can create, can make something new—everyone. Creating is life giving and identity forming. The mourner who has an extraordinary experience can be encouraged to use it to make something new. Adding one's creative touch (as Janet did) can be extremely useful in the process of coping, in adding to or strengthening one's philosophy of life, and in seeing death as a door and not a wall. All of the above can augur well for the positive identity of the mourner.

QUESTIONS TO BE POSED TO JANET

1. Do you remember what started the conversation with your mother in the hospital when she told you that you would always be in her heart?

2. After your experience of finding the stone, what was the first indication that you were coping better with your mother's death?

3. What changes in your behavior did your husband notice after you found the stone? Has it affected the way you relate to your children?

4. What will you do to demonstrate your belief that your mother lives on?

5. It took you five years to openly share your experience. What is different about how you think of the death of your mother now than when she first died?

6. How has your self-talk (how you talk to yourself about your mother) changed since you had your extraordinary experience?

7. How did you come to decide how you would use the stone as a reminder of your mother's love?

8. Have you considered using the stone as part of celebrating your mother's life and love on special anniversaries or holidays?

9. What has your experience motivated you to do differently in your work or relationships?

10. What is different in the way you think about life and death since you had the experience on the beach?

11. What gifts of wisdom and understanding have you received from your mother that you will be passing on to your children? Education with stories is a universal practice.

12. Has your experience influenced the expression of love to your husband or other family members?

Although part of our identity is bound up in who we identify with early in life, it is also influenced by those with whom we choose to interact with when we grieve, and the new relationships we form in the course of accepting loss. We will identify with our support group, others who have experienced the gift of the extraordinary, or any other group we join where we find compatibility. The interpersonal exchanges through the sharing of experiences seeps into the Self and becomes part of the "new me."

By necessity the mourner interacts with a variety of people during the grief process. As suggested, they include specific family members who can be highly influential in identity formation. This is especially so if another family member also has an extraordinary experience which corroborates the beliefs of the mourner. Doris Stowell of Hammond, NY had two extraordinary experiences. In addition, her son's dream visitation from his father further reinforced her beliefs about herself, her experiences, and eventual reunion with her husband.

"I UNDERSTAND NOW THAT DEATH IS NOT AN END, BUT A BEGINNING"

My husband of 26 years died suddenly a little over a year ago. Two weeks after he died, I had a vivid "dream" about him. I was walking through the living room late that night and passed his chair on my way to my room. The night-light was on and I heard him before I saw him. He was getting up from his chair and acted weak, sort of uncoordinated. I knew he was dead and wondered if things were so terrible where he was that he decided to come home, so I said to him, "Oh,—what is it?" He reached for me and I nearly lost my balance when he leaned into me. My left hand reached out for support and landed in a funeral arrangement on the TV. He stood upright and held me in his arms and looked deeply into my eyes. He bent and kissed me—a long lingering kiss. All during this embrace I am so amazed to feel his arms around me, holding me tight. I could feel his body—his broad shoulders under my hands. I hugged him tighter and put my face against his as I've done so many times. I could feel his cheek against mine. I had my lips close to his ear and I sobbed as I whispered, "Oh, I love you so, I will always love you." He just faded away and I woke up crying.

Now I never believed this was just a dream and I'll tell you why I know it was real. After the funeral, I was so devastated that I never had the chance to say goodbye. He died while I was at work, on the road, out of reach (social worker). He died at 2:05 p.m. I didn't arrive home till 5:30 and our son was waiting on the lawn to break the news. I had no way to handle the sorrow other than starting what I called a journal that was actually letters to my husband. I poured out all my pain and heartache in those letters at not having the chance to hold him one last time to say goodbye. You see, he had three other heart attacks and I was always there for him, to get him to the hospital and to stay by his side all night, till he was out of danger. He knew I needed to say goodbye and I felt he needed to hear me say, "I love you" once more.

This is not the only contact I have had. Six months after he died, I was alone in the house cleaning, when the song "The Dance" by Garth Brooks came on the radio and I totally lost it. I was in the kitchen cleaning out my junk drawer and I just screamed his name and told him I didn't think I could handle this pain of missing him. After awhile I resumed cleaning and at the very bottom of the drawer were two small pink slips of paper. One said, "Hi, I love you—Clark." The other said, "I love you and miss you." Both are in his writing, signed by him.

These two contacts with Clark have helped me to understand that although the bonds of marriage are broken by death—love goes on and I will one day be with my soul mate again. I understand now that death is not the end, but a beginning.

I have had other contacts, but these two are etched in my mind *for life. I'm an open-minded, 53 year-old woman, with a Master's Degree in counseling. I know reality when confronted—this was real and thus began my healing. It has also helped me to help a friend who lost her husband on Memorial Day.*

I know science can pick my gift apart; they are welcome to their narrow perceptions. Our son saw his dad shortly after the funeral in a "dream." He says his dad is okay, but he misses us. I don't look a gift horse in the mouth. I feel blessed to have ADC. I'm happy that I have not lost my beloved completely.

An important asset to be discussed with Doris would be the way she will be counseling others based on her experiences. Having already helped a friend, a support person might explore how she went about giving help, how she felt about the results, and how she will implement the approach in her formal or informal counseling when the opportunity arises. The skill base developed, based on Doris' experiences and resulting beliefs, could become a significant part of her counseling expertise and her new identity. Other counselors who have experienced the extraordinary when mourning have also developed and implemented the insights gained into their counseling practices. These insights have led to strong identity beliefs assisting them in the process of adapting to their losses.

Identity beliefs are at the core of who we think we are. An example would be Doris' conviction that "having been blessed with an ADC I have an obligation to use this knowledge in my interaction with other bereaved people." Part of her identity beliefs is to spread the word about EE's and what they can do. Determining and reinforcing positive identity beliefs will be a major coping force for anyone who is confronting a major life-change.

QUESTIONS TO BE POSED TO DORIS

1. What is different about the way you are coping with the death of your husband since finding the two slips of paper?
2. How have the extraordinary experiences altered the way you think about life and death?
3. How have your experiences helped you in placing great value on the work you do in counseling others?
4. What new routines have you begun since your husband died that you are trying to firmly establish?
5. What has changed in the perception and meaning of love in your life?
6. What is the most important message you have received from your extraordinary experiences that you have incorporated into your life?
7. In what ways has it been helpful for you and your son to discuss your ADC experiences? Has it strengthened your relationship?
8. What have you done with the pink slips of paper from Clark?
9. Is there a way you would like to use them as a reminder of your goals and mission in life?
10. How has it helped you to help your son cope with the loss of his father?
11. How were you able to help your friend who recently lost her husband? What did you say and do?
12. Knowing your husband is in good hands, how will you go about finding ways to reinvest your energy and time in new interests?
13. In what ways have your worries about the future changed since you believe "I have not lost my beloved completely?"
14. How have you and your son's interlocking experiences affected your spiritual life? How has it affected the way your son views nonphysical reality?
15. How have your experiences deepened your sensitivities to the mysteries of life and the world? How has your husband's death and your EE changed you as a person?

A major part of Doris' identity is in her work as a counselor and mother. Building on these two factors, and her knowledge gained from her EE's, will be a significant step in the establishment of her new identity. A support person could aid in the process by reminding Doris of the skills she possesses, her past commitment in assisting those in need, the impact of her interaction with others, and the relationship with her son that can be nurtured through their extraordinary experiences. Showing admiration for specific characteristics she possesses can also be utilized.

It may be necessary to help Doris forgive herself for not being with her husband before his death. At least giving her an opportunity to express guilt could be useful and set the stage for later discussion at an opportune time. Not having been with a loved one at the time of death is a common dilemma when mourning. It is not considered true cause and effect guilt, or what some counselors call real or healthy guilt, which prods one to seek wholeness and healing. For Doris, one might address her neurotic guilt feelings with a question like "Based on your EE's don't you feel your husband has forgiven you and perhaps you should consider forgiving yourself?"

Finally, since Doris can affect the lives of others with her skills, enlarging her professional contacts within the county in which she works could be an additional approach in identity formation for the new relationships it will offer.

CONCEPTS TO EXPLORE AND DEVELOP IN ESTABLISHING A NEW IDENTITY

Doing something you value and doing it well reinforces a positive identity. One approach to molding a positive identity is to choose little goals, meet them, and then become more ambitious in the goals you set for yourself. Here are some ideas to contemplate in building a success base leading to things you value and/or wish to pursue.

1. Grief is not just about loss; it is also about gain. Specifically, it is a journey of discovery. What have you discovered about yourself, your extraordinary experience, and your pain and suffering that will be a meaningful part of your new identity? Consider the following very carefully: Ask yourself what makes you feel most loved. Is it when someone does something for you, or when you are hugged? Is it when you receive compliments, gifts, or are simply in the presence of someone who cares (so-called quality time) when you are sad? Is it a specific combination of the above? Make every effort to give this much thought in seeking to strengthen your relationships with others by understanding your needs and who meets them *and* in understanding what others in your life need from you. There is really not much difference between your basic needs and their needs. Make an assessment and in both instances you will be on your way to filling love needs—yours and theirs.

2. Life will never be the same again. This is a hard cold fact to face. Yet life has to be different if a special person in your life is not there. It is okay to accept that reality as part of your new identity. But remember that through trial and error learning you will find joy and goodness reentering your life. The day will dawn when you feel better about life again; that is the history of grief and the experience of millions who have gone before you. Keep reminding yourself of this fact (say it to yourself again and again). And, as occurs in most major transitions, mistakes are bound to be made. Be willing to talk about them with your helper or confidant. Learn what you can from them, refuse to let them dominate your thoughts, and continue on with the reestablishment of your life.

3. Macramé or crochet a response to the message you have received from your EE (or find someone at your local craft shop that does macramé). For example, if you interpret the message you received from you EE as saying, "You can do it, you are capable" then you

might respond with three messages to build into your macramé: "I can, I will, I did it." Put one response on each side of an 8" by 2" long triangle and place it on your desk or table. Each time you initiate a course of action and/or progress in dealing with a problem associated with your grief work display the appropriate sign from your response macramé.

4. Perhaps your loved one, by his life and example, has made it clear that the greatest among all of us is whoever serves. Look at the ways you might serve. This can have a powerful effect on your identity. Albert Schweitzer, medical doctor and missionary, put it this way, "I do not know what your destiny will be, but one thing I do know: the only ones among you who will be really happy are those who have sought and found how to serve." It takes time to get to the point where you are ready to serve when your grief is still fresh. But look for the opportunities, for you will also be helping yourself in a most effective way—and developing new roles, habits, and needed relationships.

5. Coping with the death of a loved one is not about what others say or think about you. It is about the thoughts you entertain, the choices you make, and most important of all, the commitment you make. How will you deal with well-meaning friends who applaud you for "doing so well" so you will not grieve in their presence? You can only rise from your great loss by *first lifting your thoughts to a higher level,* then following your inner wisdom. Listen to the suggestions that spontaneously come from within at various times. Discuss them with the person you most trust, then assert yourself and proceed to do the difficult.

6. How you decide to memorialize and celebrate the life of the loved one who died will be part of the memory base that becomes enmeshed in your new identity. Decide on a special memorial that is most meaningful to you, that you are proud of, that depicts your loved one's life, personality and symbol of the EE, and that brings

satisfaction and comfort when you think about it. It can range from having her name engraved with an inscription in a sacred place to starting a charity in her name, dedicating a book or project, or beginning a scholarship.

7. Think about this ancient wisdom: We don't feel things in a vacuum; we feel things in relation to a thought. Ask yourself what painful thoughts you are keeping alive and giving power to impede your progress to grow and change through your loss. What thoughts will you work on to replace in order to change feelings?

8. Visit places that reinforce the sense of belonging. One's old homestead, high school, college, or favorite nature scene can stir inner feelings of attachment and community. Nature has long been considered a landscape for the soul allowing us to think of the place we all have in the mysterious stream of life. Visit the place where the extraordinary experience occurred if it was outside.

9. Alone time is critical because we easily forget how much energy it takes to socialize. It is also essential for thinking through social, philosophical, and emotional dilemmas that are part of grief work. For example, how will you deal with the emptiness you feel due to the death of your loved one? Will you tell someone about this feeling, or will you keep it hidden? Alone time is a lifelong need in the process of living life to the fullest and sorting out the many ways of dealing with loss and change. Learning to be comfortable with alone time, especially if you have been raised to always be around others or counseled to constantly keep busy, is an integral part of the process of doing grief work. Look at it as a needed coping skill for the rest of your life. Because alone time is consistently devalued in our culture, search diligently to find new ways to entertain yourself, find life-affirming activities, and add to your personal growth. Everyone experiences times when they feel all alone and yet it is healthy to learn to be with and entertain yourself at these times. Learning to deal with being alone *begins* with the recognition and

acceptance that being alone is not abnormal. Then start learning about how to develop creative solitude. There is much information out there that will challenge you and reflect your ability to deal with aloneness and use alone time wisely. Start by reading *The Call of Solitude* by Esther Schaler Bucholz.

10. Give something away every day. There are a host of things you can give away that will not cost you a dime. Give away thanks, your time, your smile, a friendly wave, your laughter, a hand shake, or something you no longer need. The point is: decide that you are going to give on a daily basis. Make a list of what you can give. Each gift is a gift of encouragement. The returns will flow in beyond your wildest expectations and your identity will grow. You may want to consider giving your helper a gift to show your appreciation. It does not have to be an expensive gift, just something that makes the statement that you are thankful for all of the time and energy she has devoted to you over the weeks and months.

11. Like the EE, grief in all of its manifestations is a profound messenger. Some evening, which is classically the most difficult time of the day for most mourners, sit quietly with paper and pencil and ask yourself this question: "What is my grief telling me at this moment about my loved one, myself, and my life?" Take notes on the answers that pop into your thoughts. The next day discuss with your best friend what you came up with and the implications of your insights for your grief work.

12. Think back to your childhood and those you looked up to as heroes. Now add those in the present you think are heroic. Review the characteristics of your heroes and the losses and changes they had to deal with. (For example, Abraham Lincoln had three children, ages 18, 11, and 4 who predeceased him. How did he and his wife cope with those deaths?) What can you learn from your heroes to apply to your circumstances? Perhaps you will need to pull out some old books, a family album, or go to the library to

refresh your memory about your heroes. It will be well worth the effort to seek their wisdom because they will supply useful ideas for coping with your loss.

13. Change your physical surroundings. Add a new piece of furniture, paint a room, hang new pictures, get another potted plant or an artificial one, burn scented candles or put up an inspiring poster. Use these changes as part of your declaration of beginning your new life.

Does identity have an impact on hope for the present and the future? Is hope—that nebulous will-of-the-wisp—so often turned to when circumstances seem at their worst, a factor in the work of mourning? How can friends and family members be images of hope for mourners? How does the unexpected facilitate the reestablishment of hope? Let's explore some answers to these questions as we turn to the subject of reestablishing hope through the extraordinary.

8

Reestablishing Hope:
Renewing The Future

What the caterpillar calls the end of the world the rest of the world calls butterfly.

Richard Bach

Hope Reinstated

This communication has made all the difference in my outlook on life. I no longer need to grieve for her because I know that she is still able to feel and convey love. If this is still possible after life, the world is worth preserving and there is meaning for my life. I hope I can take some of this feeling of meaning and returned joy and pass it on to others.

—Karen—

On her EE after the death of her adult daughter

∞   ∞   ∞   ∞   ∞

Hope comes with the package. That is, it is an integral part of what we all start out with on our individual paths, although it is given scant attention, especially early in life. But hope is the hidden sustaining force in adapting to any loss or change. It silently emerges in an expansive variety of forms. From the struggle to get though the next minute or hour and the determination that one will go back to work and fulfill responsibilities, to the confidence that a friend will stand by and assist in finding a solution to a problem, hope invisibly permeates every forward-looking effort. There are probably as many forms of hope as there are people and tasks to complete.

THE EXTRAORDINARY EXPERIENCE: SYMBOL OF HOPE

Clearly, hope is often the last thing that people openly turn to when faced with a crisis. However, hope generated by the EE is actually a hidden foundation of strength because of the wealth of seldom thought about possibilities it introduces into the lives of the bereaved. Possibilities are in themselves hope messages; they bring hope out of the darkness. One reason why mystery is such an integral part of life is that in part it is designed to stretch our sense of the possible. Helpers must strive to collaborate with the mourner in recognizing and exploring the numerous possibilities that exist for finding ways to meet the challenges of change.

HOPE IN THE FUTURE

Writers through the ages have implied that without hope life loses meaning (some psychiatrists say we die without hope). It is also well-known that coping with any loss comes to a standstill when the mourner falls into utter despair filled with feelings of hopelessness because the future looks dim. Furthermore, it is critical to note that hope is anchored in the future as well as the present. What we believe about what the future will bring, whether it is peace of mind, friendship or the ability to go on living, is powerful in how we conduct our grief work. In this vein, extraordinary experiences feature hope—hope in the existence of another dimension of life, hope in reunion and inner peace, hope that one will never be abandoned, hope that the deceased loved one still cares, and hope to face life without his physical presence. These are all critical future-oriented forms of hope. They are the springboard to reaffirming life.

Hope, therefore, is all about dropping the "if onlys" and zeroing in on what can be done in the here and now. What one chooses to hope for is a fundamental consideration. Hope can and should change its focus over time. When a child is critically ill and dies, hope changes from cure to minimal suffering during the illness and finally to hope that the death is not in vain. Thus, it often happens that death is the impetus to change laws, initiate funding for research or alert the public to prevention measures. The motivation that evolves from hope generated by the EE often spreads to every facet of life. Renewed hope is manifested in the lives of those who have experienced the extraordinary by the way they continue to silently do their grief work with confidence grounded in their belief that there is good reason to continue the fight.

The extraordinary experience is also a profound resource for hope since it affects conscious as well as unconscious beliefs by presenting alternative meanings of death. Many people are not aware that unconscious beliefs molded early in life affect life choices, perceptions of death, ways of mourning (for example, weather to cry or not), and daily behavior. With a little work anyone can begin to uncover unconscious beliefs by carefully studying their behavior and asking what thoughts and feelings are behind the actions they take. For example, after automatically responding to a particular situation, ask yourself, "Why did I do this or that?" You will be surprised at what you will come up with in your self-analysis that can be traced to unconscious motivations and convictions that can be useful in building a reservoir of hope.

Many who find meaning in extraordinary experiences trust their conscious and unconscious selves, are open to the beckoning of their mystical nature, and accept the designed necessity of subjective experience. Unknowingly, the unconscious mind has a compelling influence on how a mourner goes about adapting to the changed outer world and reordering her inner world. The good news is that unconscious beliefs are not only identifiable, they can be changed, as we will see shortly, particularly through the deliberate actions we take. And hope is always part of the mix whenever we consistently act with the intention of achieving a positive outcome.

INFLUENCING UNCONSCIOUS BELIEFS ABOUT HOPE

Most of us are not aware of the impact we have on the unconsciously motivated behavior of those we interact with, including their hope for better days to come. Whether support person or mourner, co-worker or best friend, what we say and do and the attitude we convey, touches others at a deep inner unconscious level. The influence can be negative or positive, and subject to change if desired. It has long been accepted that individuals can change their unconscious beliefs and their influence on personal behavior. How? By consciously reprogramming the unconscious through persistent self-suggestion, new insights and experiences, and knowledge that replaces old perceptions. Then repetitive affirming of the new information is implanted through written reminders, continuous verbal suggestions, imagery, and listening to tape recordings as well as repetitive physical experiences.

The relationship between the conscious and the unconscious minds is best illustrated by the "garbage in, garbage out" analogy of the computer world. If you put the wrong data into the computer, it automatically fulfills the directive whether wrong or right. If your conscious mind says, "I can't deal with this," your unconscious mind will do whatever it needs to do to be sure you see obstacle after obstacle to finding peace and comfort. When again and again you insist that, "I can learn to adapt," your unconscious wisdom will provide an untold number of opportunities to aid and abet your belief.

This is the same unconscious that possesses the wisdom to run all of the physiological processes in your body every second in every day—without your conscious awareness. It is behind the amazing functions of your liver when it detoxifies any chemical ingested. It orchestrates the removal of damaged tissue and the beginning of healing functions whenever you are cut. The list is endless and the unconscious never falters, never sleeps, just does what its told. It can be a best friend or a dogged enemy depending on the directives you feed it and the repetitive thoughts you entertain.

Unconscious beliefs are also reprogrammed by the way we interpret our *interactions with those in our support network*. Furthermore, according to Carl Jung, Swiss psychiatrist and founder of analytical psychology, the unconscious is an exceedingly rich source of information for personal growth and wisdom leading us to enhanced well-being. It is not only influenced by those in our social circle, but also by the daily routines we choose to follow in the process of coping with change.

How then can a helper influence the mourner on an unconscious level, bringing hope for survival? One way is when a mourner is open to suggestion, which happens frequently when dealing with the aftermath of loss, and believes strongly in another individual, whether close friend or a professional counselor. In particular, *the manner in which a helper stays involved with the mourner* as she talks, cries, carries out her duties, retells her extraordinary experience, or deals with various emotions leaves an impression deep within the psyche. The quality of the helper's attitudinal presence becomes part of the mourner's inner symbol of hope, the hope of healing, as she senses the way she is accepted in her time of vulnerability.

Being fully present and authentic in the caring role builds the hope relationship. Whenever a mourner is convinced you are *trying to understand the depth of her loss*—the operative word here is *trying*, since no one can fully understand—you are bound to affect unconscious beliefs about herself ("I am valued.") and particularly about her ability to weather her "dark night of the soul." Coupled with her self-image, the mourner's unconscious beliefs about herself are the hidden factors in minimizing unnecessary suffering, making hard choices, conquering self-pity, and starting each day with the will to persevere. Such is the mindset for springing back from any low point in life. It has long been known that coping well always begins with the *will.*

Therefore, part of the strengthening of unconscious beliefs and choices hinge on your ability to communicate nonverbally. Psychologists tell us that 90% of how we communicate with others is by reading their moods, body language, attitude, and emotions. Only 10% of any message comes from the spoken word. We are always communicating simply by our presence. Silence speaks volumes. For example, quietly accepting the mourner's behavior when facing pain helps to normalize what seems to feel abnormal for her. You communicate acceptance by providing security. The simple gesture of opening your arms to beckon or hold the mourner at especially painful times is another indicator. This action says "its okay to feel what you are feeling and here is a safe refuge." Be assured, the mourner is "reading" your nonverbal messages, especially your attitude. In fact, most mourners are astute readers of the nonverbal, and communication without words from the right person keeps hope alive. Many mourners have later reported how much they were helped by a support person who allowed them to simply be themselves in their time of loss and did not pressure them in any way. They found immense strength and hope in silent support.

Just as the significant persons in the life of the mourner affected her unconscious beliefs about hope up to the present time, now you as a helper can reinforce beliefs about hope at this most precarious time. Without a doubt, as corny as it may sound, you are a beacon of hope. And you are there to help the mourner rekindle her hope in a quality life despite her great loss. This comes about by showing that there is an invisible world of caring that surrounds her. How will you show her that it is available? Through your input in her decisions on how the EE can be used and in making suggestions regarding why she has received such a gift. It begins by reminding her that the EE is in itself an act of caring by the deceased, a loving Higher Power or both. It is a signal to further develop her interior life and her orientation toward nonphysical reality. It is broadened by discussing the unexpected synchronous events that have occurred during the course of her grief work, which assist in getting through an anniversary, a first visit to a familiar place without the deceased, or the first day back at work.

In addition, specifically encouraging the mourner to grieve in her own individual style can be influential on an unconscious level. ("Your way is *the* way.") Ultimately, the mourner's behavior will reflect her unconscious beliefs about hope, herself, her ability to cope with her loss, and her view of the future. Her intuitions, dreams, vague stirrings of the heart, and spontaneous imagery—all of which are roads from unconscious inner guidance to conscious awareness—will further influence her, and so will your responses to these experiences.

Finally, be aware that it is difficult for any helper, if not impossible, to assess the specific changes in a mourner's unconscious beliefs about the Self and her ability to persist that give hope in the process of adapting to loss. This is the albatross of trying to influence the unconscious: there is no readily available assessment tool. Yet stay the course in the conviction that you can have a positive affect on the formation of these potent beliefs. Admittedly, it's not easy to do, but changes in behavior are a major clue. The mourner may also express these changes in thoughts about the comfort she has received or the way she feels over time. The unconscious is not easily evaluated and understood, yet we can see the results of conscious and unconscious mental life expressed in the manner in which the bereaved integrates the loss into life and reveres the past as she builds her future.

Here is an example of hope springing from belief in another reality and motivating the care recipient to look ahead to what she can accomplish. In this account the care recipient, who at her request will remain anonymous, reports an extraordinary experience before and after her father dies.

"I HAVE BECOME A KINDER, BETTER, PATIENT PERSON BECAUSE I WANT TO"

This account of my experience is true!!

January 26, 1998 was my parents' 52nd anniversary. My Dad wasn't feeling well, so my husband Tony and I went over to their house and I cooked dinner. He didn't eat a lot. On Monday he started to cough and not eat at all; on Tuesday he was worse. So at 7:00 p.m. we took him to the hospital. My Dad had MS, arthritis, cancer, and was partially paralyzed. He was 86 years old. They kept him and were running tests but something was wrong; he was designated DNR (do not resuscitate if he had a cardiac arrest).

As the weeks passed by he just got worse and eventually came down with pneumonia. All this time he was having respiratory treatments three times a day. After about three weeks he had a breathing tube put in and was transferred to ICU. I was with him most of the time as was my brother, who lives in North Carolina, and my husband. My Mom came down with bronchial pneumonia and couldn't see my Dad for about 2 1/2 weeks. On top of that I had a root canal; there was so much going on but I managed. And my brother went back to North Carolina.

When my father was in ICU he was put in hand restraints because he was pounding the bed. When our family doctor said my Dad's organs were failing one by one—it was so unusual because I received the strength to deal with it. However, my mom said she felt so bad about the breathing machine that she had it removed on February 19th. It was what he wanted. She signed the papers and I asked my husband to take her home and told him that he should go home too. But I was going to stay. Now is when the "I can't believe it" part began. They untied him and they put his hand on top of mine. When I asked him a question he would squeeze my hand for "yes." So it began. I said to him, "Dad, you know what's going to happen?" He squeezed my hand "yes." I told him he would be able to walk, run, swim, jump, and not be in a wheelchair anymore. He would be with his family and be in heaven. He squeezed my hand. I also said he was forgiven for his sins. I told him to go to sleep. He would wake up, look my way, and I would say to him, "I'm still here Daddy." He did this about 10 times.

He slept for about an hour and I asked him if he saw a bright light. He did. I told him to go to the light and not to worry, that I'd take care of mom and not to be afraid, his family was waiting for him. About 1:30 a.m. he saw 3 people. I asked him if he knew them. He said he knew only one. About 2:15 a.m. I felt a hand on my back. I felt the handprint on my back was so intense I thought I was burned, so I checked my back but saw nothing. I stood and saw a golden glow flow about my father. I felt such love and joy that I cried with happiness. I swear God and I had a talk. There were no words out loud, but I remember that no matter what you call Him/Her—God, Allah, Buddha, whatever—it's the same love that comes to you in death. If you are truly sorry for your sins, you do go to heaven. He is so glorious and kind, but it was pure love. I mean a love so vast you cannot measure it. I was like hypnotized. Then, at 2:30 a.m., I left my father; he passed away at 3:33 a.m. His dying wish was that no one be there with him when he died.

I suffer from panic attacks and that night I could not find my way out of the hospital. But something took over me, calmed me down, and got me to my car. I don't really remember driving but the sky was full of lightning. At 4:30 a.m. the nurse at the ICU called to tell me my Dad had passed on.

A few days later I was in Super WalMart, my husband's and Dad's favorite store. I was standing in a long line and at the opposite end of the store I saw my Dad get out of his wheelchair and *walk away. He was in a much healthier condition. I could not believe this. I went to different support groups but they didn't help. I went to the church groups but to no avail, although my one-on-one with the Reverend of our church was helpful. I still have the feeling that my father is with me, at my side!*

These experiences prompted me to start going to bookstores but something was missing. I was in a Books-A-Million trying to find something in a book that could help me confirm that what had happened to me had happened to others. I was getting discouraged and was about to give up; I'd been in the store about an hour. And then it was like someone invisible just guided me. I looked up and I was in a place in the store where I had never been before. I was so flooded with relief that I wanted to cry. I pulled out your book, read the back cover, and bought it.

Everything I have written to you is as true as the grass is green. I have become a kinder, patient, better person, because I want to. I do things for others. I haven't read the book yet but saw the address to write to if you have had any experiences. Well, I am not crazy. I have been blessed and touched by the hand of our God and yes, He is great and loves us. My Dad is deeply missed but when I asked him if he would be there for me when it was "my time to cross over" because I would be scared, he squeezed my hand "yes." I suffer some of the same medical problems my father had but I know I can handle whatever life gives me because he is by my side and so is God and a wonderful husband. I have a mother who needs me and like I promised my Dad, I'll always be there for her and take care of her.

This is the timeless story of being changed by loss, having come through the refining fire to a higher level of consciousness. As frequently happens, hope has been rekindled through people. Staying connected to the significant people in our lives helps us better understand our own suffering. Hope is a product of those living or in spirit who make it clear to another that, "I will always be there for you." The importance of this series of numinous experiences for inspiring hope in life is clear in this daughter's moving story. Her newfound hope was the forerunner in her desire to be a better person. Without it, she would not be thinking of what she wishes to accomplish in the remainder of her life. In attempting to build on the hope she sees springing from her EE's, it would be important to reinforce and encourage discussion of the exchange that took place between the mourner and her father when she asked him if he would be there waiting for her when it was "my time to cross over." In addition, asking how patience and kindness will be demonstrated in her life, will open up many avenues to strengthen hope through what she sees herself doing in the months and years ahead.

QUESTIONS TO BE POSED TO THE DAUGHTER

Here are eleven questions to begin a dialogue for the purpose of recognizing the deeper meaning of our existence, the optimism that spreads through the EE, and to help the mourner maintain hope in her ability to find meaning in all that she does.

1. What is the implication of the glow that surrounded your father in the hospital and your telling him to "go to the light?"
2. Who was it that touched you on your back and what was the message or meaning of being touched?
3. What lessons of hope and determination have you learned from your father when he was alive and since he has died?
4. Why do you think your Dad wanted to be alone when he died? Have you considered that perhaps he wanted to spare you suffering and give you hope to carry on?
5. What do you feel calmed you down and got you to your car for the drive home when you left your Dad at the hospital?
6. What has motivated you to become "a kinder, patient, and better" person?

How will you continue to make this assessment of yourself a permanent part of your lifestyle?

7. Having asked your Dad to be there for you when your time comes, and as you think about your extraordinary experiences, do you feel you will be fearful or hopeful of what lies ahead?

8. Healing has been defined as a subjective, qualitative change in a person and it can come at a time when a person is filled with anguish and sorrow. You have experienced healing. How did hope play a role in that healing?

9. How did the Reverend at your church help you in regard to your EE's? What hope did he generate about your ability to deal with the loss of your Dad?

10. What "gifts" are you reminded of when you think of all your father has given to you?

11. How has the love of your parents influenced the love of yourself, and given you hope for the future?

Depending on the answers given to these questions the time may be ripe to continue with: Where do you think EE's originate? Why do you think you had the experiences? What do you think others could learn about life if they had experiences like you have? Such follow-up helps the mourner add to the meaning associated with her experiences and become more aware of her mission-oriented perspective. That perspective carries with it faith and hope in life and her ability to make her mark. In this regard, the mourner has already redirected her energies in the pursuit of taking care of her mother. This could be highlighted with caution to take time daily for herself as a caregiver who has a mission that could become too demanding given her own health constraints. Her love for her mother should be recognized and praised, and the need for self-care (self-love) made a critical consideration in order to provide continued quality care.

The hope that emanates from having a prayer answered can be one of the most potent sources of strength to be utilized in accepting the death of a loved one and finding meaning. Here is an example from Fred Zimmerman of Lorain, Ohio whose son Eric died unexpectedly in an automobile accident.

"SOMEONE OR SOMETHING WAS SHOWING ME THE ANSWER TO MY QUESTION"

On November 10, 1998 the following event occurred that gave me reassurance my thoughts and prayers were answered from a different dimension.

A friend of mine, John Paine age 56, died of cancer on October 15, 1998. That day was the birthday of our 25 year-old son Eric, who died on December 21, 1997. John Paine had fought cancer for 5 years and it was getting the best of him in the Fall of 1997. He was a friend of the family and knew Eric as we had talked about our families often during golf league and socializing afterward. I was to see John at Eric's funeral in December as he was not even able to finish the golf season because cancer was now throughout his body. John was very weak and sick from chemo, yet he never complained about his situation or even let the constant pain get the best of him. We all knew different but John refused to complain and was a true fighter to the very end.

I told John of the after death visit I had had from Eric, 45 days after Eric's passing, in order to help John in what he faced in the near future—certain death.

I saw John Paine one week before he passed and we spent a couple of hours talking and reminiscing about the good golf shots and life in general. Before I left John's house I said that I was praying and asking Eric, our departed son, to help John in his transition to the other side. John said, "I will be looking for the big fella," as Eric was 6-5 and 260 lbs.—an athlete and a police officer. I asked John to come back and visit me when the time was right.

John passed and was buried and I made a visit to his gravesite on November 10, 1998. I had brought some flowers and stuck them in the ground, as he did not have a headstone yet. I thought of John and talked to him about old times, conversations, golf, and the Pittsburgh Steelers. I then went the 30 feet back to my van to have some pop and chips as this was my lunchtime and lunch hour visit. The day was windy and the leaves were being blown around in the brisk Fall air. I opened my passenger side window about 2 inches to let in some air while doing my computer work for the morning business. I occasionally glanced at John's grave, then back to my computer work. About 12:45 I took a break from work and thought to myself, "I wonder if our son Eric was there to greet John when he passed away." My very next thought was "I wonder if they are together?" I no sooner completed my thought and I heard some-thing moving at the passenger side window. This window was open about 2 inches for air circulation. I heard a slight noise and saw 2 leaves enter the crack in the window! They were parallel to each other, perfectly flat, same type of leaf, and one was larger than the other. They did not float down or fall lazily down, rather they were "guided" side by side and looked like a plane landing on the pas-senger seat! Amazing!!! Neither one was floating or blowing around in the van as one would expect, but came down in perfect unison; they were placed or guided by some force unknown to me and landed within an inch of my hand, which was on the seat.

This was showing me that John and Eric were together on the other side! I presume that symbolically the larger leaf was Eric and the smaller one was John, just as in real life. The fact that they stayed in perfect unison or alignment and "landed" on the seat as if they were twins, still amazes me. For at least one week, the larger leaf was quite warm to the touch as I had many people hold both leaves without saying a word—and to a person each would com-

ment, "This leaf is warm." Go figure that out.

Again, my answer came by way of those 2 leaves immediately and directly after I thought of the question. I could sit there a 100 years in my van and that event could never occur by way of coincidence or some sort of random occurrence. It just would not happen! I did not sense John or Eric being there but to me that was a sure sign they were together on the other side. Someone or something was showing me the answer to my question. It could have been a guardian angel or a spirit guide. I understood the meaning of this truly amazing event. Thanks.

Hope reveals itself in many ways. A friend shares a similar loss with you. Another suggests a way to deal with a particularly depressing day. You listen to a talk radio show that brings a key message into your life. A chance meeting with a stranger ultimately results in the motivation to keep going. A dream gives a light-bulb solution to a disturbing problem. The theme is readily apparent and continuous. Moments of hidden grace are expressed in the form of what we have learned to label coincidence. Where does it all come from? How is it that things seem to fall into place when needed? For Fred, those questions need not even be considered. The answer is obvious. And what about the two leaves that are his marvelous symbols of hope? They have been prominently displayed on the refrigerator in his kitchen.

QUESTIONS TO BE POSED TO FRED

Every day people pray for signs about many things as they seek divine assistance in making decisions with regard to work, family, or any dilemma being faced. Praying for a sign that a loved one is okay, that he be spared additional suffering, or is with God is certainly not uncommon. As Fred indicated early in the description of his experience, he had prayed and now believed his prayers had been answered.

In this regard, the use of prayer can also be introduced when the need for understanding, insight, and wise decision making is apparent, as it so often is when pain seems to be never ending. It was Mohandus Gandhi, the great Indian spiritual and political leader, who said that "Prayer is not an old woman's idle amusement. Properly understood and applied, prayer is the most potent instrument of action." And mourners need to take action, to do something, and prayer is action that unburdens. When appropriate, suggest the possibility of forming or joining a prayer group to emphasize this potent instrument of action. Asking for the strength to endure and the wisdom to make the right decisions in dealing with all the ramifications of a particular loss can be prayer petitions of great value to some mourners and their families. The suggestion of the use of prayer evolves naturally from the telling of the EE.

A helper might begin by asking Fred questions about his beliefs in prayer and how it helps in the process of coping with the death of his son. Then she could proceed to explore the hope-filled insights that accrue from belief in divinity, what it might be like for John and Eric "on the other side," and the help that is often received from deceased loved ones.

1. How has the answer to your prayer given you hope in dealing with your loss?
2. How does prayer fit into your daily life since your extraordinary experience? Have you considered creating a Book of Hours that would lead you through the eight points of the day? (Here a helper would need to find information on the purpose and insights that accrue from the Book of Hours practice.)
3. What usually starts conversations about Eric and John within your family?
4. Do you regularly pray to Eric in the belief that he can hear you and help you?
5. Do you believe that John came back to visit you inasmuch as you asked him to do so before he died? What fuels this belief?

6. What have you learned from suffering the loss of your son?
7. Have you had any skeptical reactions from others? If so, how have you dealt with them? What gives you strength to deal with the skeptics?
8. Do you frequently look back on the experience and use it as a source of consolation? What thoughts fill your mind at this time?
9. Have you had the opportunity to share the experience with John's family?
    What has been their response?
10. What do you think "the other side" is like?
11. Why do you believe your prayer was answered?
12. In what ways has your hope for the future been given a lift?
13. How have you shared your hope and faith that your son lives on?
14. How have friends and relatives who are close to you maintained hope in the face of loss?

Because Fred said, "I understood the meaning of this truly amazing event," it would also prove useful to review and discuss what he interprets as meaningful. Then tie it to its meaning for the rest of his life. What will it spur him to do? Can he involve other family members and John Paine's family in his quest? That he can set goals, contribute his talents to the welfare of the community (he is currently helping others who are coping with the deaths of children), and initiate new projects are strong hope-oriented behaviors that unknowingly facilitate his own grief work.

Whenever the mourner has a strong belief in God (Allah, Krishna, the Universal Mind, the Almighty, the Tao, etc.) and experiences what others would call a coincidence or a series of coincidences it is an excellent opportunity to spur hope and strengthen beliefs in the following way. Speak of how a natural process, the so-called coincidence, can have a spiritual purpose. Specifically, inform the mourner, that his God *can use natural processes to turn a spiritual purpose.* This is so because God is the Lord of all natural processes. The mourner is important and has been given these helpful events to learn from his loss and to know his loved one is with the Creator. He can continue on with the tasks of mourning. He has found meaning and insight to infuse hope. He can give thanks and always place his trust in Divine Providence.

In further exploring avenues for maximizing hope, here is an example of the extraordinary that could be utilized to strengthen hope that a loved one still lives, reinforce the belief that the deceased is still caring, and reassure the mourner so she can deal with his absence. Edith Simm of Mattituck, New York had several experiences that made a major difference in her grief work and motivated her to reach out to others.

"HE'S LOOKING AFTER ME"

My husband had colon and lung cancer that then spread to his pancreas. He died on April 22, 1993. The first few weeks after his death I could not stay in the house without him so I went to stay with my daughter who was so good to me. In May I finally decided to come back home. I was so lost but the dogs helped.

About 9:00 a.m. one day the house was quiet and I heard my husband call me by name. Then he called me again. He twice called me Eadie. I was not hearing things. It was clear and distinct. It made me feel that he was looking after me and he wanted me to know he was near. This is so important to me.

However, the most dramatic thing that occurred took place one evening many months after I was back in the house. That evening I had gone out to visit and upon returning (I had gotten a ride home) I used the garage door opener to get back into the house. Normally, after coming in, I would stop and put the door opener back into the car. But this time as I was about to stop and open the car door I was pushed from the back to go right past the car and into the house. I no sooner closed the door to the kitchen and I heard a loud bang. I was petrified. Immediately, I called my neighbor and told him about the loud sound, thinking there might be someone who had broken into the house. He came right over and began a search. When he went to the garage he knew right away what had happened. A heavy garage door spring had broken. It landed right where I would have been standing if I had stopped to open the car door and put the garage door opener away. Someone, perhaps my husband, or Something was looking out for me. These experiences, and there were others, have strengthened my faith in God. I have no doubts, there's got to be life after death.

I sense his presence when I am worried about something. He's there. I know he's there. That's why I don't want to leave here. All of this has made a better person out of me. I help my friend who has lost her husband or somebody else in need. You've got to help others.

Where Edith once saw nothingness she now sees potential, promise, and self-growth. The hope that is renewed by the EE points to the promise of managing change and enduring the present moment. Inspired by her strong beliefs and the presence of her husband Edith finds purpose in assisting the grief-stricken and those in need while at the same time she is confident that consciousness survives death and her husband is here to help. Reinforcing these themes during conversations with her and in framing questions to clarify how she will reinvest in life will bring valued support as she persists in adapting to her loss. Unknowingly, hope always grows when we become aware once again of the real business of life: to do, to give, to find our individual niche, and give back. It never fails to help the mourner as the unsinkable Edith demonstrates.

QUESTIONS TO BE POSED TO EDITH

Given the motivation that Edith has generated from her experiences and her conviction that her husband is with her, let's consider some questions that would open a dialogue about continued hope for still better things to come.

1. How does the sense of presence of your husband give hope so that you can accept his death?
2. Has the presence of your husband helped you in finding new purpose in life without him? How has his presence helped to suggest taking another direction?
3. Since we are all summoned on a journey where we need to learn new skills, what are you doing for yourself that you never used to do before your husband died?
4. What are the things that you read that inspire and fill you with hope?
5. How have you been transformed by this wrenching change in your life?
6. In what ways would you say that your faith has given you hope in the future and in your ability to deal with life without your husband?
7. How do you deal with your fear of living alone? Of making decisions by yourself?
8. Do you see yourself now in different roles than you had before your husband died?
   Would you describe them?
9. What are the ordeals you face that most often challenge your hopefulness?
10. Since you will have more losses—we all will—how do you think you are better prepared to deal with them?
11. What are the cues that indicate the sense of presence of your husband when you are worried about something? How then do you go about dealing with those worries?
12. Who are the people in your life who have contributed to the hope for resurrection from the losses you have experienced?
13. Do you believe that each of us has a purpose for existing, a plan that is continually unfolding?
14. Having been touched by the extraordinary, how will you remind yourself to use the experience to nurture your interior life in dealing with the trials of aging?

Whenever a mourner indicates that, "You've got to help others," as Edith has, it is an opportunity to inspire hope for the future. Do this by asking how the mourner plans to fulfill her belief. This discussion will normally focus on ways and means and future choices she will have to make in the process. *One of the tasks of every helper is to assist the mourner to see the choices she has before her.* Her planning is hope inspiring. All of this will give direction to her life. At the same time, the feeling of regaining control, of being useful and making a contribution, strengthens the will to adapt.

CONCEPTS TO EXPLORE AND DEVELOP IN REESTABLISHING HOPE

It has been said that hope empowers, opens us to the new, and subtly motivates. Hope receives an assist whenever we accept our loss as part of the chain of losses all must endure. Everyone has to face the task of accepting his or her loss, although not everyone is clearly aware of the importance of doing so. Accepting the death of a loved one or a divorce does not mean you have to like it; it means saying yes to the circumstances of your life and letting hope do its work. To assist you in your hope work, read about the power of your unconscious mind and how to utilize its transforming qualities. Below are some ideas that will help clarify personal tasks and refresh hope along the way. Use these suggestions as the basis for sowing your seeds of hope.

1. A little known and practiced source of profound hope and direction in life is a daily review of how one has given, not given, or rejected love (with the hope it contains). This daily practice can begin just after you retire and are lying in bed or early in the evening when you especially begin to miss your loved one. Ask yourself who or what you rejected or failed to reach out to that day. Then review who or what was an occasion for receiving and feeling loved.

   The practice of reviewing how you have given or not given and how you have received love *each day* will be a positive force in showing what you must do to bring peace into your life. It will also point out where you need to make changes toward specific people or events. If you have rejected love or refused to be more loving to someone during the day, ask yourself how you might be able to avoid that pitfall the next time. Specifically, what will you choose to do differently? Thought must transform into action. What will be *your first thing to change as you begin a new day in which you give and receive love?*

2. Practice the art of distraction. The technique of distraction, long used and extremely effective, involves choosing an activity to divert your attention from anxiety and sadness. Everyone needs to take a break from the demands of grief. Say to yourself, "Enough for now. It's distraction time." Then become fully engaged in your hobby, sending emails, mindful walking, typing the story of your EE, cleaning out the cellar, stringing beads to give to a child, or any other acceptable activity. As you become fully absorbed in your distraction, you will feel your stress level drop and your mood change.

3. Regardless of our age we all need a grand mission in life because it gives meaning to existence. Are you clear on your dreams and your mission now that your loved one is gone, has said he is okay, and wants you to be happy again? What do you wish to accomplish? Cut out a star or a picture of an Eagle and paste your type written mission and dreams on it. Then hang it in a place where you will be reminded of where you are heading. Ask yourself each day what steps you are taking in the pursuit of your dreams. If you need ideas on finding a new mission read *The Wish List* by Barbara Ann Kipfer.

4. In the adversity you are dealing with look for the germinating seed of triumph waiting to be awakened through the extraordinary experience you and your family have had. There is *always* a positive in every negative if you look for it.

Despite your heavy burden, reconsider the positives that have already drifted out of your thoughts and the messages they are sending to give you hope to continue on.

5. Think small in dealing with hassles and irritations. The difference between hope and hopelessness is specifically the way we explain our loss to ourselves. So take small steps in tackling the hassles and irritations of your new surroundings. Patiently take them on one at a time. Weed out the tendency to exaggerate the obstacles to your recovery.

6. Despite your tragic loss, never minimize the fact that *you still bring to humanity something no one else can give because you are the only "you" in the history of the world.* Meditate on the meaning of that belief for examining the potential you have yet to develop and the people you can readily influence by your behavior. Believe you can rediscover your hidden talents or develop new ones that will bring you back to focusing on life and living. Begin by accepting this hope-filled fact: *all things change and anything can happen.* Take the time to dwell on what those beliefs mean for your life now and in the future.

7. Meditate on the beauty in your extraordinary experience. Sister Macrina Wiederkehr wrote that beauty "often appears upon the scene when hope seems gone. It has the power to heal, restore, comfort, and delight that part of you that is overcome with grief." Beauty can also be found in nature, music, fine arts, literature, and architecture as well as the EE. It is soothing and stress reducing, a motivating force. It will soften your transition and speak to the wisdom of your soul.

Gradually increase the time in which you look over the blinders of sorrow for the beauty that surrounds you. It is part of your inner work to nurture your spirit throughout life. Deliberately search for beauty in your surroundings. As the young Anne

Frank so eloquently put it, "I don't think of all the misery, but of all the beauty that still remains."

8. The illusion of safety from living in the past can be replaced by choosing the hope that resides in *breakthrough activities—activities you learn to do by yourself that you would not have normally done in the past all alone.* (For example, go on a short trip, attend a weekend seminar, pump your own gas, attend an Elderhostel, learn to repair a leaky faucet, take a cruise, go to a movie, stage show or a museum.) Once you have such a breakthrough you will discover more hope. You will experience that I-can-do-it-feeling. Start with a carefully measured step you have never taken before, then on to a more challenging breakthrough activity.

9. Happiness has little to do with what happens outside, although that is what the media constantly tells us. Happiness and the hope that infuses it is essentially an inside job, a state of being and doing, a set of *inner skills* that can be developed just as you would develop cooking or athletic skills. And as any athlete will tell you, it takes work, lots of hard work and practice. Of course, in your work it must be recognized that happiness is elusive, sometimes as slippery as a wet kitchen floor. We never fully "own" happiness; it is something we discover and rediscover.

How will you hone the skills of happiness that will inevitably buoy your hopes so that you can live in the now? Here is what many have done as a starter. When dealing with the problems of change, ask yourself one question: Will the action I take bring peace and joy?

All grief work includes much inner work. Do you understand how to go about doing your inner work and what constitutes a strong interior life? Where will you find the answers for cultivating your inner life? Some people use journaling and count their blessings. Others go on retreats or seek solitude. There are spiritual counselors, lots of reading materials, or close friends who can point you in the right direction, if you will only search them out.

10. The EE is believed by many to be a spiritual experience that can be used to reduce worries. Anna Robertson Brown wrote in *What Really Is Worthwhile*, a little book that stayed in print for 67 years, "Worry is spiritual nearsightedness, a fumbling way of looking at things, and of magnifying their value." Everybody worries to some extent. That's good because a little worry is a stimulus for problem solving.

    Chronic worrying is the bane of the mourner and commonly needs to be squarely addressed.

    Decide what worries and fears you have magnified, how they have reduced your hope for dealing with your loss, and how you will reduce their prominence in your life. Worry slowly eats away the foundations of hope. Make a promise: Never worry by yourself. Constant worry reduces your ability to cope. Choose to worry only when you are with someone you can share it with. Read *Worry*, by Edward Hallowell, M.D. who makes it clear that worry is a disease of the imagination.

11. If you prayed for a sign that your loved one was okay and you received your answer through the EE, then start keeping a prayer journal. A prayer journal opens up another avenue for you to honor your relationship with the divine and your loved one. It also provides solace and hope for guidance and strength. Having a record of your inner spiritual life (to count the blessings and chart progress) can be most rewarding in providing inspiration and bolstering faith as you read entries made months ago. This priceless archive will give direction and remind you of the mysterious ways in which prayer is answered, unexpected changes occur, and hope is renewed. Writing is an overlooked tool in rebuilding emotional and spiritual health. Don't fall into the trap of minimizing its importance.

    Begin your journal with a description of the petition that was answered through the extraordinary experience and the hope it spawns through faith. Write at length about the hopes the EE has generated in your life. Then each evening make an entry of thanksgiving and/or petition and explain your feelings in writing. Here is where you can begin to practice giving thanks for the little successes of the day. Also write about your hopes for the days and weeks ahead. The act of recording these events will alert you to become more aware of their presence and meaning in life and to use them with trust that more will follow. As time goes on and you review your notes, notice how many of your prayers have been answered and hopes filled in ways that have been forgotten. There is nothing untoward about praying through your writing for an abundance of hope, for the wisdom and grace needed, for the insight to take advantage of the opportunities that are in the present and the future.

12. Create a pattern of caring. This is hope medicine. Ask yourself what the extraordinary experience has to teach you about caring for yourself and other living things. In planning or *creating something to look forward to each day*—an important technique to use to deal with loneliness—include in your pattern of caring a person, plant, pet, environment, and yourself.

    Human touch is a gateway to hope, cement for the healing process. Touch and be touched. For your grief and your emotional needs reach out to hug and be hugged; it is a powerful anti-depressant and silent communicator of caring. Remember, every act of affection, every word uttered that brings joy, lifts the level of hope for the days ahead. If you show up each day with that mind-set, hope will surely flourish.

13. Everyone carries a burden but not everyone shows it. Look around you for those who are carrying heavy burdens, someone who is mourning as you are, someone who has lost all his earthly possessions, or someone who is dying—yet manages to maintain a sparkle in her eyes, a hopeful outlook. That hope comes from faith in something.

Find out the origin of that hope, what that something is that keeps her going, that keeps her looking forward despite her condition. Ask her what it is that fills her with hope.

THE HEART OF HOPE: A SUMMARY

Vaclav Havel, former president of Czechoslovakia, has had much to say about hope because for years he and his country had to deal with what appeared to be a hopeless situation. He once said, "Hope is an orientation of the heart." That is, it has much to do with the right feelings in one's heart. He goes on to say that without hope "it is impossible to live in dignity and meaning much less find the will for the 'hopeless enterprise' which stands at the beginning of most good things."

Grief often appears as a hopeless enterprise, but if we are open to its transforming insights we begin to change, seeing and doing good things. Willingness to see life and the world in a different light, and trust others in times of loss, are prerequisites to obtaining that inherent wisdom in the transformative power of grief. As Richard Bach, in *Illusions,* wrote, "there is no such thing as a problem without a gift." Every mourner needs to meditate on the meaning of that statement, particularly for the added gifts of hope waiting to be discovered. Ask yourself if you have consciously extracted all that you can from your loss and your EE.

Though always hidden and seemingly unknown, hope is the fuel for dealing with transition in the present and facing inevitable suffering. It is the foundation for unconsciously knowing that you can find freedom from the pain of loss and continue to grow in wisdom and awareness. However, before this can be accomplished, you may have to deal with whatever unfinished business may be impeding the development of hope for the future. This is the subject of the next chapter.

9

Finishing Unfinished Business: Reducing Unnecessary Suffering

We forget that there is no such thing as empty space. All space is full of presence, particularly the presence of those who are now in eternal, invisible form.

John O'Donohue in
Anam Cara

Peace of Mind

My mother died when I was 27, and even though the loss was great, it was also a relief for me because my Dad had severely abused her and was eventually the cause of her death. In my sleep one night, shortly after her death, I was reliving some of the horrible acts she endured and came up out of a deep sleep ready to scream at my Dad to leave her alone. But as I sat up fully awake, trembling and my heart racing, I found Mom sitting on the edge of my bed just as real as my husband sleeping next to me. She said, "It is okay Leora. I am okay and he can't hurt me anymore. Don't worry about me anymore. I love you and will always be with you. Listen for me." I am what I am today because of the daily help from those who love me who couldn't help me while they were still in human form. Because these experiences have been so real and so rewarding, I have found them to be a very substantial part of my life on a daily basis, not that I have these experiences every day, but the effects of them carry me through and enrich every day.

—Leora
On her EE after the death of her mother

∞ ∞ ∞ ∞ ∞ ∞

Grief often seems to be an unforgiving teacher about love, change, and interpersonal relationships. It consistently reminds us of the importance of being open and honest in our relationships, express our love and tell it like it is, so there will be no unfinished business when death intrudes.

Regrettably, despite all the lessons that grief teaches, *unnecessary suffering* is often a central factor in mourning the death of a loved one. While the pain and distress of the death of a family member or friend has to be faced by anyone who chooses to love, unnecessary suffering is essentially an optional choice. Not infrequently, it is engendered by our propensity to jump to unwarranted conclusions, to believe that we have been unfairly chosen to bear such a burden, to think the worst about the Self at our time of sadness, or to assume that we somehow should have miraculously prevented the death.

Sometimes a mourner will hold on to grief or refuse an invitation to dinner thinking that to feel better, to slowly reinvest in life, is to dishonor the deceased. In short, mourners inflict added emotional pain on themselves at a time when their emotional guard is down. They unwittingly isolate themselves physically, socially, and emotionally. However, unnecessary suffering is not heroic, nor does it hasten or reduce grief work. It does not in any way honor the deceased.

Perhaps most painful of all is the unnecessary suffering associated with things unsaid, intentions unfulfilled. The lament "I never took the time to say what was in my heart" or "I said I would be there at the end and I wasn't" are not uncommon themes dotting the landscape of grief. Regardless of the nature of unfinished business, the EE provides a ready vehicle to begin reframing the meaning of the mourner's feelings of inadequacy and dissolving the myth that the relationship with the deceased is badly broken.

FORGIVENESS AND UNNECESSARY SUFFERING

We begin by looking at two principle causes for the continuation of and failure to bring unnecessary suffering to a close: anger and the inability to forgive Self and/or others. Anger, often accompanied by guilt, is a normal and common response to loss despite the cultural ethic dictating against it. This is so because the death of a loved one is often interpreted as an assault on one's sense of respect and importance. More specifically, anger commonly finds its roots in a sense of abandonment, betrayal or loneliness. Furthermore, it may mask the fears of being alone or unable to cope.

Anger may be focused on friends or relatives who the mourner believes were not helpful enough when the deceased was ill, on medical personnel who were negligent, on the funeral director, on the Self for some omission, or on those who did not come to visit during the time of illness. Any time you believe God causes or allows misfortune it can lead to anger. God may be the object of rage for not hearing prayers to spare the loved one. Anger at the deceased may be the result of a sense of having been deserted, thoughts of an unhealthy lifestyle the deceased had engaged in, or negligence that contributed to the death, as may happen in accidents.

Whatever the case, anger strangles the soul (the Greek word for soul is psyche). The release of anger through writing, screaming, talking to a confidant, exercise, confronting the source of anger, imagery or pillow pounding is often critical to the resolution of grief. It may be necessary to burn or simply throw away symbols of anger if there is something in writing, a picture, or some other tangible reminder. Recognizing the implicit actions of the deceased through the EE can also relieve or eliminate it.

Whether the source of resentment and anger lie with the mourner's previous behavior toward the deceased, or the mourner is directing anger and resentment toward something the deceased had done (sometimes there is anger at the deceased for dying), *forgiveness is the first step toward healing.* This especially means forgiving oneself. The history of mourning is replete with examples of persistent anger that resulted in eventually consuming and destroying the mourner by keeping him in the past.

Forgiveness frees up energy and restores strength that is needed in dealing with grief. Any act of forgiveness is a gift one gives to the Self. The negative feelings generated toward others or the deceased, for whatever real or imagined transgressions, do not hurt those to whom they are directed. The deadly toll is paid both physically and emotionally only by the one who refuses to forgive. Anger affects the mind *and* the body regardless of whether it is openly displayed or silently held inside in the form of deep bitterness. But when forgiveness is freely given a new start on the road to loving Self and others begins. Forgiveness reclaims the power given to the object of scorn and anger, opening the way to achieving peace of mind and continuing the work of mourning. Peace of mind does not imply freedom from the stress of mourning, it is a quality of mind that allows rising above the seducing and devious frustrations of coping with change.

Most importantly, forgiving does not mean forgetting; it allows you to shift *how* you remember. Forgiving moves you from thoughts of revenge, low respect, and ill will to being a catalyst for rising above inner conflict and seeing life with eyes of wisdom. It becomes a new point of departure. You can forgive and remember without paying the emotional and physiological price.

If you are wrestling with your inability to forgive yourself and let go of guilt or anger, the simple fact that you received the gift of the extraordinary experience is, in itself, a clear statement of exoneration from the deceased for all transgressions. He has forgiven you or he would not have made the effort to communicate. Having been given a glimpse of something truly revelatory, use it to let go of self-created turmoil. Use it as your reason to make an abrupt change in how you view your mistake or omission, or release the anger directed at yourself. The deceased wants the survivor to be happy and release all painful emotions. The peace of forgiveness is essential in order to find comfort, think clearly, and to live once again. Begin the release from your self-imposed torment by reading about what you can do with your anger. Start with *Forgiveness: How to Make Peace with Your Past and Get On with Your Life* by Simon & Simon. Then take the steps that will release the past and allow you to concentrate on building in the present.

In addition, think about your EE from the perspective that it seeks to provide a two-way route to forgiveness. In the following experiences Michelle comes to the realization that her unfinished business with her father may now be released as she views his contacts as a gift for adapting to her great loss.

"I FEEL THAT SPENDING MORE TIME WITH US IS PROBABLY EXACTLY WHAT HE WOULD HAVE WANTED"

I recently read your book and when I saw the notice to the reader section at the end, I knew I had to write to you. I bought the book because I was looking for some kind of validation of the experiences my mother and I have shared since the death of my father in June of '97. He and I didn't get along very well (because we were so similar) though it was understood that we loved each other very much.

I moved in with my Mom about six months after his death. Shortly thereafter, I came home and my Mom's eyes were huge, her face white. I knew something serious had happened; she told me to listen to the messages on our voice mail. I did but I didn't hear anything out of the ordinary. She told me that when she had checked the messages just a few minutes before, she had heard the song "Cat's in the Cradle" ("my child is just like me, my child is just like me. . .") with no spoken message. She hung up the phone immediately, so it should have been with the new messages. But of course it was gone. Later that night, I went to the grocery store (my father's favorite daily chore) and "Cat's in the Cradle" immediately came on the store's public address system. This was my first clue that my Dad was with us.

My father was Cajun and absolutely loved to cook. For months after his death I smelled chicken fried steak cooking in the kitchen at about the same time every evening. He loved greasy, fatty foods, but because he had been on a diet for the last few years of his life, he hadn't been able to enjoy them. The experience that truly stands out, though, is this: on a Saturday night, I went into the kitchen to get myself a glass of water before going to bed. As I got closer to the kitchen, the smell of boiling shrimp (his favorite) was unmistakable. During his life, he generally cooked Cajun-style seafood only on the weekends and stood in front of the sink eating. We do live in an apartment, but the walls are so thick we never even hear our neighbors, much less smell their cooking. Then, just last weekend, I smelled breakfast sausage cooking in our kitchen.

Something else happened. About a year ago, I bought a little jar of expensive eye cream for myself. On Saturday morning, my mother and I were packing up to go to our lakehouse for the weekend. I showed her the eye cream and then put it in my bag. When we arrived at the lakehouse and I began unpacking, I couldn't find it anywhere. I knew I had put it in my bag, but it just wasn't there. I decided to search our apartment thoroughly upon arriving home, but I didn't find it there either. My mother works out of town and she flies back and forth every week. Because of this constant travel, she keeps a set of clothes, makeup, etc. in her hotel room and another set at home so that she only has to carry her laptop computer with her. When she left town on Monday morning, there was still no sign of the cream. Then, on Wednesday, she called me and said she had just gotten out of bed and gone to brush her teeth—and my eye cream was sitting right there on the counter! I knew my father had chosen to take the cream because he knew I'd miss it immediately.

Under the category of dreams, I've also had an experience. When my Dad died, I was living 1500 miles away from the rest of my family. I came to visit him in the hospital and left just a few days before he died. I chose not to attend the funeral, a decision I regret to this day (I guess it really is better to regret something you have done than to regret something you haven't done!). Anyway, the night after his funeral, I dreamt of him. I was at a family party and I spotted him from across the room. He approached me and I saw he was wearing a yellow print Hawaiian shirt with a matching hat (Dad never wore yellow—he hated it as much as I do). I was so happy that he wasn't dead and I tried to speak to him and couldn't say a word. We walked into the yard and sat down. Instead of talking, I just cried. He sat with me and held me, not saying a word. I remember how badly I wanted to talk with him, just to say good-bye, but I was unable to speak. I also remember sensing that he was just about to say something really important and profound, but of course, I woke up.

This dream was important to me for many reasons. After I hit puberty, my father stopped touching me. I hadn't had a real hug nor any other kind of physical affection from him since I was eleven years old, though I wanted it so badly. Up until puberty, I could do no wrong in his eyes; after puberty, everything I did was *wrong. We argued constantly and he barely looked at me. I believe he came to me in that dream to hold me one last time, to do what he regretted not doing, and to take care of a little unfinished business. That dream gave me a great sense of peace and of being loved by him.*

There were many unresolved issues and much unfinished business between my father and I. Because of an argument, I never told him I loved him during the last six months of his life, and I have been very regretful about it ever since. For a time, I felt guilty for enjoying his visits because I thought they were proof that he wasn't at peace. Now, however, I feel that spending more time with us is probably exactly what he would have wanted. I adore his presence, and I don't see how I could have survived the last two years emotionally intact without them.

Michelle can still tell her father that she loves him both verbally and nonverbally through her dream experience. This can be accomplished by using a version Jung's technique of creative imagination. The imagination is there to help us solve problems in any area of our lives. First, suggest that she go to her special quiet place where she will not be disturbed and can talk to her father just as she would when he was alive. Then tell her to take several deep slow breaths to relax. Once relaxed, then she can go back into her dream. In this case, it can be suggested that she create a dialogue with her father just as she saw him in her dream. She can ask questions and wait for answers. Just listen! She can tell him she is sorry about not saying more during those last six months. She can thank him for that meaningful hug. She can say in her soft and gentle way, "I love you Dad." Again, it would also be appropriate to suggest that our deceased loved ones no longer pursue unfinished business as we would here, for they are in a loving environment where such things are of no consequence to them.

QUESTIONS TO BE POSED TO MICHELLE

It is obvious that Michelle's extraordinary experiences have been immensely helpful in mourning the loss of her father. Specifically, she interprets the contacts as a healing of the relationship. What is needed at this time is someone to validate the love her father has for her, to emphasize that his visits are love inspired, and that love never dies.

1. Please tell me more about the song "Cat's in the Cradle" and it's meaning to you and your mother.
2. What specific message do you feel your father is sending through the lyrics of the song? What understandings?
3. From your Dad's contacts with you what is obvious and supportive of the belief that you always loved him and he has absolutely no ill feelings that you didn't say so during the last six months of his life?
4. Why do you think both you and your father were unable to converse with each other in your dream? What is the symbolism here?
5. What significance do you attach to the yellow shirt that your dad was wearing in the dream? What does the color suggest?
6. How do you interpret the many sense of smell experiences that have occurred in your kitchen? What was the message of forgiveness?
7. Having been held by your Dad in the dream, having your eye cream suddenly appear on the counter top in your mother's room, and realizing you and your Dad have similar dispositions, what are the implications for you to see that no other unfinished business will hamper any of your other relationships? What will you do, how will you act, to prevent situations that lead to unfinished business?
8. How will you use your extraordinary experiences in coping with the physical absence of your father?
9. How have you and your mother chosen to remember your Dad on the anniversary of his death, his birthday and significant holidays?
10. Do you talk to your mother about your extraordinary experiences? How does she respond?

11. Is it possible that through all of your experiences your Dad is saying, "I'm okay and you can be okay too?"
12. Would you like to find a way to tell your dad you are sorry and that you love him so much? What are your options for reaching out in this way?
13. Is there one lesson you have learned that you would like to share with young adults to help prevent the pain you have experienced?
14. Have you asked anyone you deeply trust how they would finish their unfinished business with a loved one?
15. What was different about the way your father looked in your dream and his appearance during the last few months of his life?

If Michelle is not interested in using the creative imagination approach, after the discussion of the above questions, it would be appropriate to ask her if she might consider talking out loud to her dad to tell him she was sorry about her actions. There is nothing morbid or strange about talking to a deceased loved one. Many people do it without directions from a counselor. And in therapy, many counselors use a therapeutic tool called, The Empty Chair Technique, where it is recommended that the mourner talk to the deceased for the purpose of resolving conflicts and to say goodbye or whatever is needed in order to deal with emotional turmoil.

It could be suggested that Michelle go to a place she honors, put a picture of her father across from her in a chair and sit quietly for a few minutes thinking of good times she had with him as she was growing up. She can then let her thoughts drift to the disagreements and, with her heart leading the way, reflect on what she would like to say to him. Using her imagination in this manner could allow her to let go of her sadness over not being more demonstrative about her love for her father when he was alive. Encourage her to tell him how she feels and that he will hear her words.

Another example of unfinished business comes in the form of neurotic guilt, what one caregiver called the gift that keeps on giving. This is an emotion that frequently has to be dealt with during the grief process. Neurotic guilt is commonly defined as guilt in which the effect (the way one feels) is way out of proportion in relation to the cause. That is, guilt is exaggerated and not truly warranted under the circumstances. Sometimes guilt is maximized and mixed with fear due to the extraordinary experience of another family member. Take for instance the plight of Lori whose husband committed suicide.

"I ASKED HER IF THIS APPARITION FRIGHTENED HER"

My eight-year old daughter's father died of suicide on August 3, 1997. He struggled lifelong with depression and memories of an abusive childhood and little love. Approximately six weeks ago my daughter, following a presentation of "Nanny's Goats Gruff" at her summer school, told me that she had "seen daddy this morning." As we walked from the school to the car I questioned her further, assuming she had seen him in a dream. She told me, "I was sleeping and woke up when I felt someone was watching me. I rolled over and daddy was sitting on my desk chair, next to my bed, watching me." I asked her to give me more details. What did he say? What did you do? What was he wearing? She continued, "Daddy looked real foggy. He was wearing a T-shirt and jeans, and he didn't say anything. When I saw him I was too surprised to say anything, and then he just slowly faded away." She said he had no apparent expression, he was just sitting watching her, as he often did when he was alive. He was in a constant state of wonder and pride when it came to her. They were extremely close and couldn't spend enough time together. She was the only person who could make him smile and undoubtedly made his brief thirty-seven years well worth the extra effort he always seemed to place in "kicking" his depression.

I asked her if this apparition frightened her and she readily said, "No." Apart from this "miracle" for her to remember always, and perceiving as a loving, caring father who is constantly watching his little girl, the aftermath of this has been different for me. I have become jumpy, frightened and am always looking into rooms and turning corners expecting to see him, and never do. I would like to see him to know he is okay and at peace—at last. However, I was angry with him prior to his death and am scared that he is blaming me for his state of mind at the time of his death (as I blame myself endlessly), and that should he appear to me he will be vicious and vengeful. Or perhaps he has shown himself to Graci out of love and is purposely not communicating to me out of spite for his demise. I loved Steve more than anything. His suicide has left me an emotional shipwreck and I would give anything to go back to that day and tell him I loved him one last time.

There are few things more devastating to the natural progression of grief work than dwelling on the "if onlys." But it happens frequently and is essentially self-defeating. You can only point out how unfair it is to the mourner and the deceased loved one, as well as the unnecessary suffering it inflicts, when such a course of action is taken. Can Lori still tell her deceased husband she loves him? Of course she can. She can even use her daughter's experience as a tool for talking to her husband. A support person can use Lori's belief in her daughter's apparition to suggest that Steve can hear her and it is not too late to express those feelings.

Recommend that she find a quiet place in her home where she can sit and relax. Then imagine the scene of her husband visiting her daughter and expressing his loving concern. Emphasize that Steve's state of mind in his new life is not the same as when he was on earth. He understands the turmoil Lori is dealing with and the anxiety that is creating such disorganization and fear in the present. He recognizes now that his own condition was very difficult for Lori to deal with. Suggest that Lori tell

Steve of her love, fear, and sorrow. Give her permission to let go of her guilt. Tell her she did the best she could at the time. That is all anyone can do. Remind her that she and her daughter will always have a place in their hearts for Steve. Restate that Steve is much more knowledgeable and understanding of the situation now than he ever could be when he was with them. They can use the EE as part of their living memorial to Steve and a way of assisting Graci to deal with the loss of her father.

It would also be very supportive of Lori for a helper to openly recognize her wisdom in accepting her daughter's extraordinary experience and assisting her daughter to accept it as a normal part of life. Many parents would dismiss a child's report of a deceased loved one. Lori can be encouraged to use it to teach her daughter about love, giving, trust, and the beauty of mystery that is a part of every life and the world in which we live. This is a golden opportunity to balance the societal emphasis on physical reality with nonphysical reality and strengthen her daughter's interior life.

Furthermore, major emphasis should be placed on the fact that *an apparition occurring to one family member is a message of love for all family members* since it is coming from a place in which love reigns supreme. There is no malice or hate where Steve resides; he is a loving, caring father as well as a loving, caring husband sharing his love from the other side through the gift of an apparition. Loved ones do not come back to induce fear and blame others for their state of mind at the time of death. They come back out of concern and care. It is a normal part of desire for mutually comforting relationships. We are now more than ever, still family.

QUESTIONS TO BE POSED TO LORI

Certainly there are some instances where true cause and effect guilt are part of dealing with one's grief work. Thus some form of reparation or amends is essential. However, the vast majority of mourners experience neurotic guilt. In fact, it is nearly impossible to live with and love someone and not experience pangs of neurotic guilt over something that occurred prior to, during the illness or before a sudden death. Most neurotic guilt is built on an exaggerated sense of responsibility for everything that happens in a relationship or the mourner has long entertained unrealistic expectations and rigid standards of behavior. No one is perfect, yet most mourners are talking and thinking perfection—an omnipotent awareness of the situation, the expectation of flawless relationships, and faultless insight—when they talk about what they should have done. For any helper, gently testing that perfectionistic attitude ("Do you really think you could have seen this or that so far in advance?") and planting seed ideas for later review by the mourner, is an ongoing job demanding wisdom in when to speak about guilt feelings and when to listen, when to point out the normalcy of human error and the application of unrealistic standards. Do not think you can explain away guilt or tell the mourner she should not feel guilty. But you can provide perspective and food for thought.

In the final analysis, the mourner can purge herself of much neurotic guilt after constant review and being allowed to express it without interruption. Once more, the eventual realization that we are imperfect beings, living in an imperfect world that combines to spawn ambivalent relationships and neurotic guilt, will lessen its impact. Here are some questions I would pose to Lorie to assist in the task of resolution.

1. What would you need to happen in order to forgive yourself?

2. Is it not quite possible that Steve came to your daughter because he knew that both of you needed support? Could it be that Steve realizes you have assumed responsibility for his behavior when only he could be in charge?

3. Since love is the motivation behind the extraordinary visit, why not assume that Steve, knowing that Graci would share her experience with you, wants you to share in his loving gesture? Isn't it possible that Steve could only come through to Graci?

4. In what ways might your high expectations of yourself be a significant factor in your feelings of guilt? Why not consider that Steve is saying that because he is in a different place now he sees things much differently and perhaps you might look at them from a different perspective as well?

5. What feelings has Graci expressed about her father's visit?

6. What would you need in order to give up your fear and believe that Steve wishes both you and your daughter a good life?

7. Steve knows his daughter is also your daughter and she is in your care. Why not assume that Steve knows that in hurting you he would be hurting his daughter? Isn't he really in a position to realize that now?

8. Have you considered asking for a personal sign that Steve is okay and is now whole and happy? You could ask him or God for a sign.

9. In what ways have you tapped the wisdom of others who deal with guilt? Have you talked about Graci's extraordinary experience with a friend, counselor or clergy person, and shared your feelings? Have you asked them how they might deal with guilt in a situation like yours? Is it possible that your guilt is not true cause and effect guilt but a common form of neurotic guilt?

10. In what ways has anger and fear surfaced in the situation that you are now facing? Do you know that guilt often masks two underlying emotions: fear and anger and that women tend to readily assume guilt due to cultural conditioning?

11. In what ways might your strong sense of responsibility for everything be a part of your guilt feelings? What would allow you to realize that Steve does not hold a grudge and that he wishes both you and your daughter find happiness?

12. How have you reinforced for Graci the belief that her father will always love her? How will you periodically remind her?

13. In what ways do you think you can still tell Steve you love him one last time and be confident that he will hear you? Have you focused on all the good things you did for Steve while he was alive?
14. Have you considered that Steve may have only been given the opportunity to visit Graci and no one else?
15. What will you do on key anniversary dates, birthdays, and graduations to help your daughter perpetuate her belief that her father loves her as you do?

In summary, because Lori said she "loved Steve more than anything" it should be suggested that Steve now fully understands this and would not come back to "be vicious and vengeful." Her perceptions are based on a false premise: that Steve, in a higher state of consciousness, free of depression, wants to inflict pain. This is an irrational premise that should be gently but firmly challenged. This challenge could also make inroads on her guilt over Steve's state of mind at the time of his death.

In the final extraordinary experience in this chapter, let us turn to how we might help mend relationships in a situation where family members could not openly mourn the deceased loved one through funeral ritual. The circumstance of no ritual after the death of a loved one can be especially hurtful and a major source of lingering sadness for years since there is no opportunity to say goodbye or make amends. Jennie Ratajczyk did not enjoy a consistently positive relationship with her ex-husband, but his death brought much sadness to her and her family, and eventually an enduring awareness of another reality and much to talk about to diffuse the pain of unfinished business.

"I FEEL BAD THAT MY CHILDREN WERE NOT NOTIFIED OF THEIR FATHER'S DEATH"

My first husband and I were married in 1957 and we had three children. My husband had some serious problems and things weren't working out so I divorced him in 1963. During the years we were married, whenever he was not at home and in some kind of trouble, I would dream of him. A few years later I remarried him and we had another child. Shortly after our son's birth my husband got into some trouble and was sentenced to prison. I again divorced him and got on with my life with my children. He never remarried and we always had some kind of contact all the following years.

He served all his time, finally decided he'd had enough of living his life in prison, found a place to live in Detroit and filed for Social Security. The last time we all saw him was in the Fall of 1995 after a family wedding. I had a brief marriage at the time and our children were not interested in his company because of his lifestyle, nonsupport of them, and his lack of interest in their lives.

He mainly came down on a bus to see our oldest daughter, who lives in Colorado, because they got along well and she had been here for the wedding. About a year ago, I had a dream about him and told our son about the dream and the fact that I only dreamed about his father when he was in some sort of trouble. I remember saying, "I hope nothing is wrong and that he is all right." After that I forgot about the dream. My son didn't. He has a computer and around the end of August of this year he decided to look up the Social Security Death Index and found his father's name. He had died the previous year, July 1997. We were never notified of his death and it was quite a shock to all of us. My daughters took it especially hard.

A few weeks later some strange things began to happen. I came home from work one day to find what I thought was a hatpin lying on my front porch in front of my door. I thought it kind of odd, but picked it up, brought it into the house and laid it on my kitchen counter. It was either later that day or the next day when I was in the basement washing a few sweaters in the washing machine. As I was removing them I heard a noise from inside the machine so I looked in to see what it was, and lying there was another hatpin. I *live alone. No one had been over to visit and I do not carry hatpins in my pockets. I had not seen one since the wedding in 1995. I brought it upstairs and laid it next to the other one.*

A couple of days later, I was carrying a small amount of clothing across my arm upstairs to my bedroom from the basement. There is a small section of my room that has a hardwood floor when you first walk in and I heard something drop on the floor. I laid the clothes down on my bed and turned around to see what I had heard—and their lying on the floor was another hatpin! I finally decided to tell someone about what had happened and we all got chills wondering what was going on. The pins were actually corsage pins, all the same size, pearlized round heads except one that was oval shaped. Three pins in one week. (I would also like to mention that any corsage pins I had were kept in a closed tin along with thread, needles, safety pins etc., but I had thrown most of them away some time ago. I can assure you that I thought of every possible explanation carefully before I even mentioned this to anyone, after I found the third pin.) Almost a week went by with no further incidents until October 1.

I was again down in the basement washing a few clothes and again, while taking them out, I heard a click, looked in, and saw another pin. I ran up the stairs and called my daughter to tell her. She promptly informed me my son had called her and said that the night before as he and his wife were preparing for bed about 11:00 p.m., the doorbell (that didn't work!) rang. He went and looked out but no one was there except their cat. My son tried the bell and it did not work. His wife said the same thing happened the next day at approximately the same time.

I called my daughter in Colorado a few days later and asked her if anyone had told her about what had happened. She said no, so I began to tell her about the pins, when suddenly she remembered something that happened to her that was unusual. She works for *the Post Office in Denver. As a government office their year ends on October 1st and she was changing her calendar. When she came across December of 1997, the 19th was circled. She said she thought to herself, "That's dad's birthday." She also said she did not remember ever circling the date, and why would she? She wasn't going to send him a card. She didn't even know his address. And why would she do it on a calendar at work? As she was telling me this, it was dawning on her and she said she was getting chills, thinking her father may have been contacting her, and she said she felt comforted by the thought.*

Three things happened on October 1st to three family members. I still could not figure out the significance of the four pins I found: three in one week, and then the fourth one a week later. My third daughter said, "Mom, you and dad had four children, three from the first marriage and then there was a break before you had Vic, your fourth child." She was right! After that we have not had any other contact. Our two other children do not recall anything unusual happening to them.

I feel bad that my children were not notified of their father's death and that they cannot have the closure of a funeral. However, we did find out how and why he died, where he is buried, and we have been out to the cemetery to see his grave.

Honoring a member of the family, regardless of his past history, can have long term effects on family life. In particular, it can provide a way to let go of those painful memories in order to find peace and embrace life. Jennie's EE's can be the basis for healing old wounds as she sets an example for her children by allowing forgiveness to work its healing power. It can also create a spiritual legacy to be passed on to her children and grandchildren. The helper could focus discussions on the EE's as signs suggesting that her ex husband is searching for forgiveness as well as the opportunity to draw attention to and eliminate ill feelings and the resultant stress that had been present over the years within the family.

QUESTIONS TO BE POSED TO JENNIE

The failure of notification of the family of the death of a father brought much sadness to the mother as well as the children. Now that they know the cause of death and the place of burial, their extraordinary experiences can be used to soothe the wounds of estrangement and work toward bringing peace of mind. The overall goal of the questions would be to point out possible reasons why these contacts were made—out of a wonderful sense of reparation and concern. In a conversation with Jennie I suggested that her ex-husband is in a position to see life and death from a much different perspective. He seeks forgiveness, he is sorry for his behavior, and it will be healthy for the family to acknowledge that need for themselves as well as for the deceased. It can also be suggested that he wishes to bring his family peace and solidarity in a way that he was unable to do when he was alive.

1. Why do you think your ex-husband (or?) made these contacts?
2. What do you think is the overall message your ex-husband (and father) is sending in his efforts to make a statement to those he realizes he has hurt?
3. What are the kinds of things you can tell your children that your ex-husband (or the Absolute) is trying to do through his contacts?
4. How would you like to use your experiences to bring peace of mind to yourself and possibly to some family members?
5. Did you ever sense your ex-husband's presence at any time when you had the pin experiences?
6. What dreams have you had about him since you learned that he died?
7. Why do you think you would dream about your ex-husband "when he was in some sort of trouble?"
8. How has your oldest daughter felt about her father in view of these extraordinary experiences?

9. What is the meaning of "getting chills" when discussing these unusual experiences with family members? What does it suggest?

10. How has your son responded to the series of extraordinary experiences the family has had?

11. Would you like to use one or more of the EE's as a way to remember your ex-husband on special days or to help your children better cope with his death and their feelings? In what ways could you establish a meaningful remembrance?

12. Have you thought of having an informal memorial service where only the family comes together and can talk about their father? What is one story from your life together that you would like to share with them?

13. Have your family or friends encouraged you to express your feelings about the death of your ex-husband and your EE's?

14. What emotion or feeling would you like to express to your husband that still lingers in your thoughts about him?

CONCEPTS TO EXPLORE AND DEVELOP ABOUT UNFINISHED BUSINESS

Because unfinished business is energy-depleting, anxiety provoking, and may eventually lead to bouts of depression, it is critical to find ways for expressing the feelings involved that will lead to peace with the deceased. Otherwise, your ability to focus on the tasks of mourning will be limited at best. Therefore, taking care of unfinished business has to be among your highest priorities. Here are some possibilities for releasing the past in order to focus on the tasks of rebuilding your life.

1. An effective way to assuage neurotic or illegitimate guilt is to dwell on all the good things you have done over the years in the relationship with your loved one, up to the time of his death. The tendency when mourning is to narrowly focus on the few negatives, often highly questionable negatives, and blow them all out of proportion to the overall relationship. This especially happens when there

has been a long illness preceding the death. Think of all the times you sacrificed in your devotion to your relationship and your care for the loved one: the sleepless nights, the long trips, the special meals, giving medication, and the refusal to leave his bedside. If you think of all you have done, your few supposed transgressions will pale in significance. The whole is so much greater than the small part you are giving undue attention.

Constantly dwell on all you have done. You are only human.

2. Find the most personally meaningful avenue of communication to forgive the deceased or yourself. Do not let the fact that you cannot be face to face with your loved one cause you to think your act of forgiveness will be any less effective. Your loved one *will* hear you. Forgiveness may be initiated through gift giving (a visual expression of love), a silent prayer, inner dialogues, a ritual, open dialogue when alone in a natural setting or through the creative arts. It can come through something only you and no one else feel is appropriate: A symbolic offering or a simple gesture of restoration in his name at the opportune time. Learn to vent, to let off steam, in order to save your health. A support group, crisis hotline, a counselor or a member of the clergy could provide you with the information and outlet you need.

   It may be appropriate for you to write a letter of forgiveness. Tell him/her that you are sorry for whatever happened and what you wished you had done or said before he died. Tell him you are using the EE as an instrument of forgiveness and as a sign of consent and mutual agreement that you must begin living again.

3. Some counselors believe that to forgive "is the ultimate act of self-love." Ponder the implications of that statement applied to your unfinished business. Forgiveness is more a positive act for the Self. It is also a positive act for all of the people you interact with because you will have a more positive outlook and be a pleasure to be around. It is the first step to healing as it eliminates self-punishment. Give

away forgiveness by remembering Rousseau's observation: "When man dies, he carries in his clenched hands only that which he has given away."

4. The extraordinary experience highlights togetherness and can be viewed as another means through which relationships are restored despite previous conflict. No one can ever be forgotten where there have been close emotional ties. Those in the spirit seek reparation and peace. Connectedness is an inherent quality of all spiritual beings, living or deceased. Society teaches us to be separate, to do our own thing, when in fact we are seamlessly tied to each other more than we realize. The EE is a forgotten opportunity to build a permanent bond with loved ones. Use it as a new bonding vehicle of your own choosing. Decide how you will take advantage of the new beginning you have been offered to eliminate conflict and bring joy.

5. Recognize that anger toward the deceased or family members can hide behind sarcasm and words like annoyed, disappointed, irritated, or sick and tired. Be honest in your inner search for anger. You may have missed the message of your extraordinary experience to let go of your anger because it has been hidden. Refuse to live in the past. Carefully review your feelings to determine if anger is hiding behind your speech or your actions.

6. Think for a moment about intent, the intent you had throughout the illness of your loved one to do all that you could to ease his pain and suffering. Did you ever have intent to do a slipshod job of caring? Of course not. Intent is critical in analyzing any of the causes of the emotions you are dealing with in your unfinished business. Now focus on the intent of your EE. Put your intent of caring and comfort in the same category as the intent of your EE— and release your unfinished business.

7. By letting go of anger you will be able to reduce the associated bouts of depression that often follow. Depression keeps you

immobile and away from the light of a new day. Ask yourself what is the message that anger/depression is carrying for you? There is always a message in emotions if you will look for it. What does it say about your behavior? What must you give up or accept in this period of change? These are critical decisions to be made in your release from the grip of depression. To persist with your anger or depression is to continue to give away your power when it is needed in adapting to the changes which must be faced.

8. Being a perfectionist is often a root of depression just as it is linked to guilt and anger toward the Self. We are spiritual beings who have bouts with imperfect interpretations of the way we think things should be. Are you aware of and will you change the beliefs that support your brand of perfectionism?

9. Psychiatrist M. Scott Peck in *The Road Less Traveled* says that depression is our inability to give up the old for the new. Yet giving up the old for the new is the perpetual calling of life. The spontaneous extraordinary experience is the new in lieu of the old and can be used as a tool to manage reactive depression and remove blocks to reinvesting in life. What is old that must be released and what is new that you are resisting?

10. Grief is stressful and it is necessary to develop an instant stress reducer. It is not unusual to have trouble unwinding, reducing tension or getting off to sleep because of hanging on to unfinished business. The most ancient yet practical stress reducer guaranteed to work is any one of a number of breathing exercises. Try this one: Breathe in through the nose slowly counting to 5. Hold the breath for a three count. Then exhale through the mouth to the count of 6. Repeat at least ten times. Concentrate on the sound and feelings of the air entering and leaving your body. You will relax.

11. Depression, anger, and guilt are all natural emotions with specific purposes. They always suggest taking another path in order to smooth out our relationships with ourselves or our loved ones.

But they are also a signal for change just as the EE is a signal for change. What path is suggested and what changes are demanded are the issues to be addressed. It's what one does with persistent emotions that counts. Here is a way to deal with them: First own them by admitting their presence; then recognize them for what they are saying about redirecting life; most importantly find a way to let them go; and then refuse to let them back into your life. The only alternative is unnecessary suffering.

12. Practice lifelong learning. The world of loss and change cries out for understanding because our death and loss denying culture is primarily open to the pleasure principle. Unnecessary pain and suffering always emanates from our worldview. Thus there is no reason why we cannot keep learning and growing in a variety of areas other than loss, and in the process develop the wisdom to see unfinished business and the experience of loss as the teachers they are meant to be. More than that, the ongoing commitment to learn consistently generates choices for living life more fully and leaving a legacy of example for our children to follow. Here is a little-known bonus: Any continuing education encourages the growth of synapses and dendrites (connections and branches in the brain) for healthy brain function as we age.

MEMORIES AND UNFINISHED BUSINESS

One effective way of dealing with the aftermath of unfinished business, once the mourner recognize the futility of hanging on to neurotic guilt or other emotions, is to deliberately flood the mind with important memories of the immediate past that point to progress. There is a time to look back. In fact, it is important to look back to see how far we have come. This perspective is commonly overlooked as a source of comfort and satisfaction. The mourner can compare her disposition now with her condition early in her grief work. She may need reminders to see how far she has come in her journey. The helper can assist the recall by "remember when" comments and by stressing significant changes now obvious in her behavior. Remind the mourner that now she goes places that she did not go to a few months ago. Tell that she is watching TV again. Perhaps she is visiting relatives more and reaching out. She has not forgotten the beloved in her movement forward. She has begun the process of integrating her loss into her changed conditions.

Grief is also about endurance, sometimes having to endure a whole succession of unfamiliar feelings associated with unfinished business. Although the mourner may not think so now, in the end, her endurance traits will provide her with invaluable skills, if she will take the time to look back and recognize them. Suggest that she ask herself how she has been able to endure up to this time? What has she done to get this far that can now be used to deal with any unfinished business? Champion her endurance and talk to her about its importance as reflected in her progress.

On the other hand, there are many other happy memories of the deceased loved one that form the backbone for stepping into a world devoid of some of the familiar surroundings that gave security and encouragement in the past. In the final chapter we examine the power of memories, especially memories associated with the extraordinary experience, to heal, motivate and empower.

10

Maintaining Positive Memories: Bridges From The Past To The Future

Memory nourishes the heart, and grief abates.
Marcel Proust
French Novelist

A Forever Memory

What an experience, what a joy, what a gift—I got to visit with Mom with her newly restored body. She had made it to her eternal home for sure! Until we meet again and are joined together again as a family— we love you Mom and miss you.

-Paulette F.
On her EE after the death of her mother

∞　　∞　　∞　　∞　　∞　　∞

Comforting memories are to the coping process as breathing is to health and well being. Not only mourners, but everyone has a need for positive memories because of the simple fact they are conducive to good emotional health and the reduction of stress in its variety of forms. Fantasy or not, positive memories induce welcome physiological changes, since when recalled, they reproduce the same effects internally as when originally experienced. The problem with the development and maintenance of positive memories is that most people give very little importance to the role memory plays in the good life, especially in dealing with massive change.

To be sure, nobody goes around thinking, "I'm going to savor this moment and focus on all the detail so I can recall it later," unless they have been instructed to do so by a counselor for a specific purpose. However, the conscious formation of memories to use as safeguards and sources of comfort is something we can all capitalize on for its power to heal and change outlook. Thankfully, the resources and experiences from which rich and meaningful memories can be fashioned are an inherent part of every life. Experiences with people, places and things are full of selective items for recall that either agitate every cell in the body or bring repose, solace, and joy. Loved ones especially are highly influential sources of memory to lead us out of the self-traps we create and back into the world of opportunity. And we have a brain, wired to facilitate recall, with all of the powerful negative or positive results to boot.

How powerful are memories? Just consider the available research linking persistent anger with heart and circulatory disease. People who anger easily and refuse to let go of anger on a long-term basis consistently have to use memory in the recall of events that trigger their damaging response. When a person recalls an event that precipitated anger long after it occurred, the process of memory recall is the pathway to creating all of the same physiological responses in the body—the so-called fight or flight response—that, when persistently activated, is extremely damaging over time. This is a potent negative force and incalculable inhibitor of good thinking when under pressure.

On the other hand, that same memory recall process, focused on a pleasing exchange that took place between a mourner and a deceased loved one prior to death, can be a source of immense pride, comfort, and satisfaction with corresponding physiological benefits. The importance of positive thoughts on immune system functioning should not be minimized in this regard.

In the "El Molleh Rachamim," the Jewish memorial prayer for all of the departed, the last sentence asks: "Grant that their memories ever inspire us to noble and consecrated living." Memories of living and deceased loved ones are not merely critical grieving tools for all concerned, they are also the springboard to changing behavior and finding new ways to enhance the lives of others. Because most extraordinary experiences involving a deceased loved one bring peace and comfort, they are particularly potent forces for creating positive memories for use in the coping process as well as for savoring as the years go on. The deceased remains an influential part of the inner life of the survivor whenever his memory has taken the best of the relationship and incorporated those characteristics into his life. Memory allows the most exalted of tributes to the deceased to occur. In this way memories are secretly nurturing and life-affirming.

Memories are also strong motivators we can use to enhance the quality of life. The recollection of a single memory can inspire and change the course of negative thoughts or feelings. In my own life, whenever I start to feel sorry for myself, I recall Senator Max Cleland, (D) Georgia. Thirty-two years ago he was a husky 6 foot 2 inch 215 pound marine serving in Vietnam. When a grenade exploded he lost both legs and his right arm. Today he rises at 6:00 a.m. to be at his office by 9:00 a.m. He takes three hours to dress himself and get ready for work—without any help. He refuses help. Here is a man who is thankful for his life everyday. He seeks no special attention and worked his way up to one of the highest offices in the country—an amazing feat with only one limb. *Having seen his scars*, all I have to do is recall Max and it is an immediate inspiration for me to change my current thinking pattern.

A single memory can be equally compelling for one who is mourning the death of a loved one. It can help the mourner take the next step, choose the next goal, or let go of a feeling or emotion that is dragging him down. And the source for that memory can be the extraordinary experience, a specific part of the experience, or the specific message of the deceased urging the mourner to carry on. Because the brain is constantly arranging and rearranging memories, anyone can pick out bits and pieces of memories to be preserved and fit them together in a pattern that is deeply personal, comforting and consistently useful. They don't wear out. Thus a mourner or helper can build a stash of bright memories to use in grief work or whenever life takes a turn and dark clouds seem to fill the horizon. But we all need to be educated about the process of gathering and living with memory.

HOW TO RETAIN MEMORIES

The key to memory retention, as it is with so many of our other faculties, is repetition or practice. Practice will make any memory your own and imbed it permanently in your memory bank. So we have to use this faculty in a deliberate, organized way. It includes choosing the best memories, repeated, planned recall, and the use of word or picture triggers. All will lead to strengthening that memory pathway in the brain.

When assisting the bereaved in using memories to cope with loss and change, discuss ways to choose and recall memories at specific times. Talk about how to initiate recall with little reminders placed in convenient locations where they can't be missed. Most people need constant reminders placed all over the house and in the car because of the tendency to dwell on sadness and negative memories. A photograph of a happy scene, with or without the deceased, can jolt the mourner out of a destructive mind-set. Any object holding personal meaning can do the same. What I am suggesting is something about which most of us give little thought: a deliberate plan to choose and build healthy memories with external visual triggers. Placed in the right locations these visual reminders will bring an immediate change in mood and a shift in direction to change a day that may be spiraling out of control. Lest we forget, visual reminders that feed the "mind's eye" bring refreshing messages to change a train of thought.

Planning for the creation of comforting or motivating memories begins with a simple suggestion to the mourner when thinking about a ritual or observing an anniversary. The suggestion can also come when discussing how to use the extraordinary experience. Any meaningful event that it is considered by the mourner to be a memorable occasion is one she may want to use in the future. By taking in all the detail and grandeur of that occasion and savoring the feelings of love and beauty it arouses, it will be a wonderful way to remember the loved one. Whenever an occasion arises involving discussion of the deceased that the mourner shares with you—and takes great pleasure in the telling— remind her of the importance of it as a comforting memory. Ask for details and further descriptions. Emphasize why it is important and how it can be used. By generating awareness of the use of memories you can help in the process of building a memory bank that heals and assists in allowing the mourner to move on with respect for the past. You may even suggest associating a particular memory with another that is traditionally recalled and already firmly entrenched within the family. Or you may want to remark after an event that, "This something we will always remember."

For people of faith, any extraordinary experience involving a vision of an angel or what is believed to be a Supreme Being is especially useful in imprinting memories that bring powerful results in daily life. Positive emotions and feelings are conducive to forming and utilizing specific memories. Thus talking about the message and what it means adds to retention and recall. In this vein, there have been a number of Christ encounters experienced that have resulted in complete turnabouts in the lives of recipients and have left inspiring memories for later use. Take, for example, the experiences of Lisa and her grandson, and what happened over a seven week span after the death of her father, and as her brother lay dying from AIDS. Her EE's led to changes in behavior based on memories that will remain strong for the rest of her life.

"HIS BRILLIANT SMILE AT THE END SAID IT ALL"

It's been one year since my father and then my youngest brother died at age 37. I can't tell you all the questions I've gone over and over, time after time, about these signs which I know now were Our Lord's way of helping me help my brother. I realize now He allowed my Dad to show these numerous signs.

I've tried to write down in order the sequence of events for you, but they became so long and detailed I don't know where to begin or end. Most of these encounters were witnessed by me, but three were in the presence of other family members. The most emotional of all was the visual experience my grandson, James, had of my father with Jesus on the night of my father's wake. I believe Jesus allowed this so I could help my brother Tom who was dying of AIDS. Tom was one of the kindest and most gentle persons I've known and he needed help to cross a spiritual bridge. You see, all of his adult life, he stated that he believed there was no God and that when life ended that was it.

After my father died, my brother, who was in Los Angeles, decided to fly out for the burial. I began very slowly to tell him about the signs (tactile and symbolic ADC's) I had experienced. I did this due to the fact he had so much burden dealing with my father's death—and his own that he knew was coming quickly. He was not receptive and just said, "The last time I believed in God I was nine years old. Drop it."

My four-year old grandson was concerned about me and stuck by me all the time. That night after the wake my grandson got in bed with my daughter and he kept saying, "Grandpa didn't say goodbye. Why did they close the lid on my grandpa? Why didn't he say goodbye?" Suddenly he looked up toward the ceiling and said, "Mom look, its grandpa. He's waving to us." My grandson is waving back and he says, "Goodbye Grandpa Pops." Then he says, "Mom look, it's Jesus." He then immediately said, with such sorrow, "Poor Jesus, he has 'owees' (his word for wounds) on his feet, hands, and tummy." The intensity in his face was beyond description and his eyes were tracking as though following someone. He said, "I love that man. Wave to Grandpa Pops and Jesus." He was thrilled because, "He's in heaven now." I have to emphasize, my grandson never had imaginary friends.

The next day he said to me, "Grandma, we have to go to the store today. We have to get a book about Jesus." Then he said, "Grandma, why did Jesus have "owees?" (He was referring to the wounds he saw.) He held his ribs and then he touched his palms and feet. I was amazed. We don't go to church. He had been once. "Don't be sad anymore," he said, "because Grandpa is happy in heaven." Then he showed me my Dad's signature wave. How could he do that? He wouldn't be questioning me if he knew all of this beforehand.

On the day of the funeral, Tom went to the cemetery for the burial. I didn't want to see him break down. It was so difficult for him. However, he got through it and decided to stay with me longer to see my nephew graduate from college. He didn't look good and on the way coming out of the graduation ceremonies he collapsed. He said to me, "Lisa, I think I'm dying." We got him into the car and he looked like he had died. All of a sudden he blinked his eyes and we got him to the emergency room in record time. He stayed at the hospital for four days.

The Doctor said he didn't think we could get him well enough to get him back to California. But in a few days he regained some strength and wanted to go back to Pat, a friend who had been caring for him, and who paid for his fare back to L.A. and Cedars Sinai Hospital. In the meantime, I told Pat about all of the ADC's and she said I should start telling Tom. So I did and this time he did not tell me to stop like before. Four days before the flight to San Francisco, Tom said to me, "Lisa a miracle has happened. Yesterday I prayed the Our Father when they were wheeling me in for the tests. When I came back to the room I saw Jesus. It wasn't a dream. I went up to Him and said 'Are you God?' His response was, 'I've always been with you and you've been a good boy.' His excitement when he called to tell me of his encounter with Jesus was overwhelming. He then went over in detail all the ADC's I had told him about, but now with the intense belief of truth. Finally, the Doctor in L.A. said he could get on another plane to go back home to San Francisco.

They got him to San Francisco and he died six days later. His peace, contentment, and calm those last ten days before his death was something to behold. I prayed he would not be afraid. Pat said he was contented and died in his sleep. His brilliant smile at the end said it all.

That was not the end of the story. Four months after I had received this report from Lisa and had interviewed her, she telephoned me. I sensed she was tense about making the call. After identifying herself she began with:

You know when we spoke on the phone back in July and you asked me about my grandson and his vision of Jesus? Well, you had asked if during the vision Jesus had said anything. I said no at the time. I did that because I didn't want what I am going to tell you to get out and I was afraid he would be inundated by people and telephone calls.

However, I have prayed a lot about this and decided I should tell you. As I said before, my grandson said Jesus smiled and waved. After all of this was told to me my grandson's last statement was, "Grandma, Jesus said He's coming down soon! What does that mean?" When he first told me this I thought it meant that Jesus was coming to take my grandson and I was scared. Then I spoke to a friend who reads the Bible a lot and goes to church and I told her about it. She said she thought it referred to the Second Coming where Jesus would return at the end of the world.

I reassured Lisa that I would protect her and her grandson's anonymity and would not reveal their real names or the part of the country in which they lived. I also told her that what she had just told me was thought provoking and something I would be thinking about a great deal. She said that because of her and her grandson's experience she was "paying more attention to the Bible and I have returned to church." In a follow-up letter she closed with the following statement. "Again, I find the magnitude of these events more than I can understand or comprehend. So I find myself relying on sheer faith because no other answer is possibly plausible. These explanations you may find useful for your understanding to change or not. I'll leave that to you, Doctor. I'll sign off for now. Thank you so much." Need I say that Lisa's and her grandson's experiences were thought provoking at the very least?

QUESTIONS TO BE POSED TO LISA

An important consideration in using memories of an extraordinary experience in the coping process is to pair emotion with a specific scene. Experiences where emotion is strong are usually much easier to recall and can have significant effects on changing behavior. So ask about emotions associated with the messages and the circumstances in which the experience took place. Emphasize asking the mourner to describe her feelings during and after the experience and how she feels when she looks back on what happened. Inquire about detail, color, environment and messages. Allow, even encourage, repetition of descriptions, as it will strengthen specific memories. Help decide what part of the experience brought great emotion that the mourner wishes to recall in the future.

How the mourner interprets the message of the extraordinary experience often dramatically determines the direction and intensity of grief work, including accepting the death and reconstructing one's shattered life. Much good can come from clarifying the message of the experience in the mind of the mourner and what it means to him. Ask for specifics ("When you think of the message of your experience what picture comes into your mind? What feeling is most gratifying?"). One effective approach, therefore, is to sharpen your skills in encouraging the mourner to repeat the telling of significant parts of the experience and the feelings that accompanied them. Questions like, "What did it feel like when this was happening," or "What was going through your mind when you heard that," are appropriate in this regard. Here are some questions for Lisa to help draw out memories that can be highlighted and ultimately chosen by her to use in building her bridge to the future while retaining a link to the past.

1. What pictures of your experiences do you hold in your mind that convince you that you will be able to deal with your loss and go on with your life? What memories motivate you to deal with your pain?

2. As you review all that has happened, what stands out in your thoughts as the most significant events that can be used to teach your grandson about life, love, and death?

3. When you think of your brother and father what scenes immediately come to mind? A place? Their faces? Something they did or said?

4. What person, other than yourself, was most helpful to your brother during his life? What was done? What memories do you cherish?

5. What were the circumstances surrounding the first two extraordinary experiences that you had? The time? Place? Your feelings just

before each event? And what do you continually remember about the feeling *after* it was over?

6. Who has been most helpful to you as you mourn the death of your brother? What will you always remember about how he/she treated you?

7. When you talk about your EE's with others, describe what happens to you as you talk about them? Are there physical as well as emotional changes taking place within?

8. Would you describe how your grandson looked and responded when you talked to him about his encounters?

9. What emotions where most obvious in your grandson's behavior when he talked about his grandfather?

10. How will you celebrate life and love in your family in remembrance of your brother and the Christ encounter of your grandson?

11. In what ways have your experiences affected the feelings you have about your faith and your early childhood beliefs?

12. What is the meaning and memory for you of "His brilliant smile at the end said it all?"

13. What is the most frequent trigger of a positive memory of your brother?

14. What possessions of your brother's do you have that bring back pleasant memories? If you have none, would you like to obtain something of his for this purpose or something that is symbolic of the Christ encounters?

15. What visual reminders of positive memories of your father do you have in your home? Do you use them as a visual feast to brighten your day?

MEMORIES GUIDE BEHAVIOR

We all tend to forget that memories, coupled with beliefs, are behind whatever we decide to do or wherever we decide to go. It is memory we rely on when we take a bike ride, head out to our favorite nature spot, or make the cake or special dish at holiday time. What is indelibly imprinted in our memories from the moment we are born to the present tells us how we feel about ourselves, how we presently deal with a loss we are coping with, and even how our mental and physical health is affected. Certainly, the way a mourner is presently coping with her loss is a function of the memories of how she has coped with other "little deaths" and big deaths in her life, either consciously or unconsciously. And these memories could be helpful or could hinder her present situation depending on how they were chosen and why they were retained.

We are literally bundles of powerful memories. Importantly, we have the ability to alter those memories and supplant them with new ones that can assist in making the changes and adaptations essential in coping with the death of a loved one. The relationships we establish with our deceased loved ones must be based on solid memories in order to sustain us in creating a new life without the deceased and to reinvest our emotional energy in life-giving pursuits.

As we have witnessed, the dramatic nature of extraordinary phenomena, the meaning it conveys, and the choices it provides is ideal for laying down new memory pathways and finding ways to honor the deceased. Selective choosing of memories to retain and others to let go are critical processes in the course of grief work.

Memories, therefore, are not merely critical coping tools; they hold the power to give the mourner freedom to choose new roads to travel and mould a life without the departed loved one. *Remember, memories are highly suggestible and mood altering.* Therefore, the choice and quality of memories deliberately retained and used is highly significant. How should they be chosen? With patience, over time, and with the goals of the mourner clearly spelled out: what is most cherished and how the mourner wishes to picture those prized moments. What are the criteria for choosing? Review the mourner's life with the loved one, including the EE's, and the descriptions of actions recalled. What was the situation (event or reason for being together) and location (physical surroundings) of the incidents recalled? Focus on the acts of compassion and caring described and what they mean to the mourner. Compassionate responses often carry special meaning as we think about our loved ones. Consider examples of compassion associated with the EE's. The above are crucial topics that can be addressed and discussed with the mourner at various times.

MEMORIES OF CHILDREN

Memories of our deceased children are especially helpful in keeping them in our perpetual care as fathers and mothers are wont to do. In the next account, Janet Nokes, who lives in Vermont, has memories of her son, Ben who reminded her that he was near, that he cared deeply for her, and wanted to make sure she was okay. These insights were a result of two sense of presence experiences, the experience of touch, and a dream visitation. Her son took his own life at an early age. The memories of her experiences as a child, coupled with her special intuitive ability and her EE's, have been added gifts in forming loving memories of her son and his love for her.

"I FELT HIS RIGHT ARM LYING ACROSS MY SHOULDER"

I have always been afflicted with precognizance and thought that I was just a little crazy, but it happened so often, coincidence couldn't explain it away. So I tried to ignore it—until one day I felt and saw a brilliant explosion in my head. Underneath it I saw "Ben at 24." Ben is my son and he was eight at the time. I tried to forget about it, but every once in a while I'd get the explosion without the words as a reminder. Ben grew up, went to college, then joined the army. When he told me that he was volunteering for the bomb squad, I thought, "Well, here it is." I tried to dissuade him, but it turned out there were no slots for additional personnel, so he never got into that unit.

A year after he got home from the service we were talking in the family room. I looked at him and thought how strong, happy and handsome he looked, and that he only had five months until his 25th birthday. Three weeks later I felt the explosion again, but this time it was so violent that it physically made me stagger. I thought, "WHAT was that?" then tried to brush it off. Two days later, they came to get me at work to tell me that Ben had shot himself sometime during the weekend. Now I knew what the explosion was.

A week after he died, I was standing in the family room where we had spent so much time. I suddenly felt him standing directly behind me. I could feel warmth all along my back. I could feel what he was feeling. It was regret, such great regret.

A week after that, some friends were over to keep me company for a while and we were sitting again in the family room. Suddenly we heard a crash, like glass breaking. We looked all over the house until I went upstairs into Ben's bathroom. The glass on the sink had fallen into the bowl and shattered into hundreds of pieces. It seemed as if he was telling me he was still there, but he wasn't happy.

I was in the habit of going outside at night before I retired to look up at the stars and sing him a lullaby. One night soon after the previous incident, I felt his right arm lying across my shoulders, giving me a hug. It only lasted for an instant, but I had no doubt of what had happened. A few days later I was out walking the dog thinking of Ben. I looked up to see a very large crow sitting on a branch a few feet above me. The crow began to caw very loudly, and not only cawed but also made staccato sounds I have never heard coming from a crow. I knew immediately that it was Ben. He was scolding me for being so heartbroken. I spoke to the bird and it spoke back in its own way for about five minutes. Then we were both quiet and it simply flew away with one final loud caw. Later, I remembered the time Ben told me he wanted to come back as a crow. One of his favorite movies was "The Crow."

A few nights after that, he stood by me on the patio and I could feel his agitation and ambivalence. He wanted to make sure I was *okay but also wanted to be on his way. I told him, "Go Ben. It's all right now—you can go." He moved a few yards away and then I felt this incredible rushing sensation of traveling at unimaginable speed in a sort of twilight. He was gone. That was the last time I 'saw' him.*

*About a year later I was very hurt by a crude, insensitive joke that someone had made regarding suicide. I went to sleep very depressed. During the night, for the first time, a picture came while I was asleep. I was looking into a room filled with a soft warm golden yellow light, and there was Ben sitting on the arm of a chair, smiling and talking to my husband, who stood across from him in a very relaxed way. I was filled with the most incredible joy that I have ever felt, and it seemed to last for a long time. I did **not** want to wake up. I wanted to stay with them, but knew I couldn't. My husband will precede me in death but I will see both him and Ben again.*

*Now when I encounter people who have lost a child or a spouse I try to encourage them to believe they **will** see their loved one again. This fact acts as a reminder to stay strong and continue on this journey, no matter how painful. Maybe this story will help someone else who is wondering or doubting.*

The death of a child is always a most gut wrenching experience. The need to look back on the child's life and be reinforced in the closeness of the relationship enjoyed is especially helpful in order to counter the natural tendency to blame oneself in some way as being responsible for the death. The mourner can always find something she could have done better and link it to a litany of possible reasons why his life ended prematurely. These are the very memories that need to be allowed to drift away. But it is the same recall of life with the child that can spawn some of the most exciting and comforting memories. Here is where the support person can ask questions about the child's favorite places, interests, and avocations as a source of rich memories that also included Janet. Of course, the memory Janet will forever have of Ben sitting in the chair in a room filled with a soft golden yellow light, and her incredible feeling of joy, can be an important memory for her to recall at any time.

QUESTIONS TO BE POSED TO JANET

Keep in mind as we consider Janet's stories that she has been gifted with precognition or as she puts it "I have always been afflicted with precognizance and thought I was just a little crazy." Her intuitive gifts add power to her beliefs about her experiences and the meaning she can draw from them. Here are some questions to begin the dialogue for eventual memory building.

1. In what way was your gift of precognizance helpful to *your acceptance* of Ben's death? What specific memory accompanies your answer to this question?

2. Have you had other experiences in which precognizance played a role and resulted in happy memories you continue to recall? What is the most common memory that you recall when you think about your precognition experiences?

3. Were you surprised the first time you sensed Ben's presence in the family room? What was the feeling like? What will you never forget about it?

4. In what way was the sense of Ben's presence helpful in your coping with his death? How has he helped you to go on?

5. What is the symbolic meaning for you of the Crow you encountered when you were out walking the dog? What memories do you recall when you think of the Crow experience?

6. What visual reminders do you have of the generosity and joy that Ben brought into your life?

7. How will you use the beautiful memory of Ben sitting in the chair in your dream? Have you captured all the details of the scene?

8. What has Ben taught you in the nearly twenty-five years that you knew him?

9. Why do you think you have been the recipient of these contact experiences?

10. What is the most important message you have received from your experiences that you can recall to enhance your life?

11. What memories of Ben's life do you most cherish? How would you describe the relationship you now have with Ben?

12. How have you and your husband chosen to remember Ben on his birthday?

13. What is most symbolic of Ben's love for you? Was it expressed in your extraordinary experiences? What do you believe are Ben's wishes for you?

Again, emphasize through discussion those memories, with accompanying emotions, in which both mother and child were involved and brought much happiness to both. This could include early family get togethers around holidays or family reunions as well as memories of the extraordinary experience. Ask questions in order to give opportunities to repeat parts of the story and refresh specific details in the mind of the mourner. Janet's real-life story of love for her son and a son's love for his mother is indicative of the stronger bond that can evolve from the extraordinary. The conviction that she will see Ben again, coupled with the importance of her helping others realize that death is not an end but another beginning, will be sustaining forces as she continues to adapt to his death.

In the final extraordinary experience to be examined for the purpose of creating positive memories, we look at the death of an infant girl who died in a drowning accident.

"I HOPE I WILL HAVE CONTACT WITH HER SOMEDAY"

On Mother's Day, May 10, 1998, my daughter Jamie, age 14 1/2 months, was involved in an accidental drowning. We live on a 70-foot yacht in Alameda, California. The three older children grew up living on a boat. On Mother's Day I went to work as a registered nurse. My husband took care of the four children on the boat. He forgot to close a door. Jamie was moving around, going from one end of the boat to see the other kids and then to see my husband at the opposite end. My husband lay down on the couch to take a short nap. Jamie lay next to him for a few seconds, then gave him a kiss on the cheek, and waved her hand. That was the last time he saw her.

About 10 minutes later he was looking around for her all over the boat and on the dock. She was nowhere to be found. Two brothers saw a piece of rag floating in the water next to the boat. It was Jamie floating upside down. My husband did CPR until the paramedics came and took her to Alameda Hospital. He then called me from Alameda Hospital emergency room. The emergency team was doing CPR when I arrived. They were able to start her heart beating after one hour of CPR. She was then transferred to Children's Hospital in Oakland and was put on a ventilator. The doctor who was the Chief of the Medical Staff gave us a poor prognosis on her condition. We decided to terminate any life support on May 12 at 11:20 a.m. She died peacefully in my arms.

My three other children, Jennifer, age 10 1/2, Johnny, age 9, and Jacqueline, age 6 1/2, were in school at the time we decided to terminate life support. After we picked up the children from school and gave them the bad news, my son John stated that Jamie appeared to him at the same time she died at 11:20 a.m. He was walking down the hallway to the cafeteria for lunch when Jamie appeared to him. She was holding his hand and smiling up to him. John stated she looked kind of foggy like an apparition. She was gone when he was getting his lunch money out of his pocket. My older daughter Jennifer states that while she was sitting down in class, she felt Jamie hugging her leg. When she looked down under the desk she saw an indentation on her pant leg.

When Jamie was in Children's Hospital being worked on, my mom heard her calling out to her. She said Jamie would say, "Mom, Mom, Mom." That was the only word she could say at that time of her short life. My mother did not know at that time that Jamie had drowned and was in the hospital in a coma.

I feel I have been blessed with Jamie coming into our lives for a short period of time and to appear to my son at the time she expired. I always ask my son when he saw Jamie last: he always says the same thing that she appeared to him in school at the time that she was taken off the ventilator. It makes me feel good that there is life after death. Unfortunately, my husband does not believe in spirituality and life after death. He has tremendous guilt that she died under his care and states that he will never forgive himself. The surviving children are doing well mentally. I hope I will have contact with her someday.

Belief reborn. Belief in spirit life and a world of spirits comes in a variety of packages and is a highly functional resource for spurring memory formation in order to cope with the losses and changes in life. In particular, it helps promote acceptance of the loss and brings meaning to address why the loss happened. Although this mother did not directly experience the EE's, they have clearly impacted her grief work. Because spirituality is expressed in a multitude of ways, a helper must learn about this mother's views about the after life, spirits, and the continuation of consciousness after death. What does she believe about mystery and the Unknown? Her brand of spirituality must be highly respected if suggestions and validation of memories is to occur. The helper will also need to discover what is most important in her value system. This will be useful in asking questions as this mother searches for the joyful memories from Jamie's short life.

The EE's in this situation, are special causes for one to step above the material to the spiritual essence of the events and the person being mourned. In this instance, Jamie's mother's belief in life after death should be legitimized whenever she introduces the subject into discussion or when inferring that her daughter lives on in another existence. Her images of the after life and Jamie's presence there will be one source from which memories can be formed. Another will be her son's telling of his contact with Jamie at school and then coming home with the news. Of course, all of this must be done with sensitivity to her husband's feelings and an awareness of the great burden of guilt he is carrying.

It would also be appropriate to suggest she find a chapter of the Compassionate Friends, a self-help group for parents who are mourning the death of a child, where the presence of others mourning their children can more easily allow her to express her feelings. Invariably, the discussion of extraordinary experiences will arise during one of the meetings as many parents report similar experiences. Additional encouragement and normalization will occur and a source of solace will be found. She may also find suggestions on how to help her husband deal with his guilt if he refuses to attend meetings with her. Pursuing help for her husband will also lead to increased understanding of her ambivalent feelings.

There is a carryover effect in the discussion of esoteric subjects: mourners come to realize that everything that happens is not a result of their action or inaction; so much is beyond their control. Something else is at work. This insight causes a refocusing from the Self to something outside of the Self. It can be a welcome relief for the mourner to have reason to get outside of herself and think about the source of the unexpected. Often a spiritually meaningful context in which one finds strength in dealing with a loss is further developed and expanded to other areas of life. One begins to listen more to "the still small voice within" than what is outside—and to act on it.

QUESTIONS TO BE POSED TO JAMIE'S MOTHER

In assisting Jamie's mother to establish positive memories, it would be helpful to begin by asking about the day her daughter was born, how she responded in those early hours, and what kind of a baby she was during those middle-of-the night feedings. Then a support person could move to when Jamie began to walk and gradually build a solid framework of early memories. Follow this with a recall of the most important parts of the EE's her family experienced and how they have helped her in her mourning. Here are some questions to begin the life review.

1. What photograph of Jamie is your favorite? What emotion does it stir?

2. Where was the picture taken and what was the occasion for taking pictures on that particular day?

3. What did you feel when your son John told you that Jamie appeared to him as he was waking down the hallway to the cafeteria?

4. How does the scene of Jamie's apparition as described by John help you in coping with her death?

5. What would need to happen for your husband to forgive himself? Have you forgiven him? How? Did it involve your use of the extraordinary experience?

6. How has John interpreted the meaning of his sister's visit to him?

7. How does your Mom explain Jamie's auditory contact with her?

8. Is there a global or universal message that you receive or think about when you consider all the contacts involving Jamie that took place within your family? It seems that you have received multiple gifts and a message for your husband.

9. What memories of Jamie do you openly share with your children?

10. When you have a thought of Jamie or when someone mentions her name, what picture pops into your mind? What feeling do you experience?

11. Where do you talk out loud to Jamie when you are alone and thinking about her? What do you say to her?

12. Have you and your husband considered putting something special in your home to remind you of all the extraordinary experiences that your family has had to tell you that Jamie is okay where she is? Can you use it as a reminder?

13. What is different about the way you look at life and death after all you have been through?

14. How can you use the words "Mom, Mom, Mom" that Jamie spoke?

15. Who will you talk to in order to refresh positive memories of Jamie and learn of their remembrances of her? Who is most open to listening to you?

Helping a mourner review the positive memories of a deceased loved one, and tactfully asking her to describe them in detail, is an art as well as an essential strategy for all helpers. In this session, tactfully ask the following questions: (1) "Where do you believe Jamie is now?" (2) "Will you see her again some day?" (3) "Why were your children given these gifts?" and (4) "How can you and the children build on and use them through the years?" Jamie can be a source of growth for all in the family.

Encouraging the recollection of memories (have a family "remember when" session some evening) and emphasizing to the children who are mourning that they can talk about the deceased at any time, will create an openness that will facilitate the imprinting of positive memories for lifetime remembrance. The children's memories of Jamie could also be of use to Jamie's mother. Adult behaviors, in this instance the openness and willingness to talk about the deceased and the unseen, will provide the needed example from which many memories can be recalled. As a family, this session may naturally be resisted by Jamie's father because it is too painful.*

DEFUSING PAINFUL MEMORIES

The extraordinary can also be a resource in dispelling fearful or negative memories that cause pain and confusion. This can be accomplished by simply substituting a positive EE memory for a painful one that surfaces. Learn to use the simple tried and true Stop Technique. It involves challenging the negative memory by saying out loud, "Stop" when the negative memory comes into conscious awareness. It is best if you can say it out loud in a strong voice, as you pound your open palm down on a table. Or make a fist and pound it into the open palm of your hand. Some people put a rubber band around their wrists and when the unwanted thought comes into their mind yell out "STOP" and snap the rubber band. It's a nice sharp wake-up call. Then you can slip in a beautiful memory (or the message that was part of the EE) in place of the stressful one and/or walk away from where you were standing when the painful memory flashed into your mind. Combine thought with action.

Or you may wish to use a similar technique that a woman in a support group I was conducting shared during a discussion of how to deal with unwanted thoughts. She dubbed it the "Toilet Technique." "When I get overwhelmed with bothersome thoughts," she said "I walk into my bathroom, pretend to take the thoughts out of my head and into my hand, pitch them in the toilet and flush them down. Then I walk away." This is mentally healthy inasmuch as one is employing positive action along with mental commitment. Another widow used the Windshield Wiper

---

* Because of the circumstances surrounding Jamie's death and the great burden her father carries, it would be wise for any support person who is not a certified counselor to seek advice on how to assist the father. In particular, asking advice on how Jamie's mother's way of coping could negatively affect her husband would be essential information in order to prevent further pain for both mother and father.

Approach. When the painful thoughts persisted, she would bring her arm and hand up vertically in front of her face and keeping the elbow at chest level, move her arm back and forth like a windshield wiper.

Most approaches to defusing painful memories will work—if you will work at it. But they are not a panacea. Painful memories do not magically disappear. But as the days go by, you will be surprised that you have reduced the intensity, frequency, and the length of time unwanted memories remain in conscious awareness. Keep in mind that for each success in limiting the attention given to the painful memory you have also reduced the time of repetition that helps keep the memory alive. You can reduce the frequency of the pain experienced by choosing to *reduce the intensity of your reaction* to those memories when they appear. In short, allow the unwanted memory to pass out of your thoughts just as it came in.

CONCEPTS TO EXPLORE AND DEVELOP FOR MAINTAINING POSITIVE MEMORIES

How not to forget is something most people would like to master, especially as they get older. Not surprisingly, an inadequate diet, stress, anxiety, sleep deprivation, and constantly keeping busy are factors in poor memory recall. Many mourners experience all of the above. Significantly, those factors can be reversed.

Below are some additional considerations for building your memory bank as you move from the past and build a memory bridge into your new life.

1. Take a favorite keepsake that belonged to the deceased and at a special time of your liking give it to a family member or close friend. Discuss the significance of the object, how it was used in the loved one's life, and build on the memories that the recipient of your gift shares with you. Each time you see the person you will be reminded of your gift and the beautiful memories it brings forth.

2. One of the most therapeutic and comforting memories is to think of a time when you felt especially loved by the deceased when he was alive. Dwell on the impact it had on you and your life. Recreate that time and the meaning it carries especially in moments when you give thanks for all you have received. This could become part of a daily ritual at the close of each day as well as a reminder of the love received on that day.

3. Review your extraordinary experience and draw from it one or two key elements that are most characteristic of the deceased and his love for you. Create these scenes in your mind in detail to include all of the color, sounds, and feelings you experienced at the time. Use these memory scenes as joyous reminders of the importance of your invisible relationship.

4. Search for a memory from the life of your loved one or from your extraordinary experience and consider how you might be able to bring it alive in your life by helping others *as you remember your loved one helping you*. In this way, your loved one will live on not only in memory but in something you say and do. Your actions will also strengthen your self-concept through the satisfaction of giving.

5. Choose a specific memory to be used when you feel especially stressed that will help you relax as well as bring comfort. Don't forget that emotion is rekindled with memory when you decide on a specific memory to recall as your safety valve. Thus choose a memory that brings release, inner peace, and tranquility.

6. Choose a specific time each day that you label as "Memory Time" where you devote your full attention to creating and savoring memories for use as you go about your daily duties. This can be part of your daily stress break that mourners and helpers alike should schedule into their routines. Find a place to relax where you can get off your feet to begin the "Memory Time" period of reconstruction. This daily infusion of joyful memories can include family and friends as well as the deceased. Include beautiful places

in your planned memory recall. Look at "Memory Time" as taking a daily vacation.

7. Combine memories of your extraordinary experience with memories drawn from notes on sympathy cards or letters received from friends and relatives about how your deceased loved one influenced their lives.

8. Memorize passages from the Bible, Koran, Talmud, or from any other inspirational sources that are reminders of the way your loved one conducted her life. Use them to remind yourself of what you should continue to work on. For example, if the deceased was very understanding and patient, you might memorize this Biblical quote: "Give to your servant an understanding heart."

9. Here are some more suggestions and things to do to enhance the formation of warm and useful memories.

* When an important memory is lacking in detail, if possible, go back to the place where it occurred in order to refresh your thoughts, or ask others about it who were there and shared that time with you. Relive the memory on site (an excellent way to refresh it and imprint it within). Immerse yourself in the environment for the express purpose of recall at a later time and to give you joy and appreciation for all that you possess. Use as many of your senses as possible in your experience: sight, touch, smell, taste, hearing. Reinforce the memory with a physical cue: a smile, a wave of the hand, a slap on the thigh or clap your hands. This is called anchoring your memory as you put thought, emotion and a physical cue together.

* Write on 3 by 5 cards descriptive cues from your extraordinary experience to use at times when sadness becomes too encompassing. For example, use something that was said, a description of a smile or other facial expression, a symbol of the experience, the location where it occurred, an object in the experience or a particular insight that was received.

Place the cards in a convenient place, easily accessed, so you can get them when needed. By flipping through the cards you will stimulate further recall.

* Write a song or a letter to your loved one about your fondest memory of him and what it means to you. Place it in a letter file on your desk to be read as a source of inspiration, comfort, or as a reminder to give thanks for the experience. On holidays read it as a special tribute to him.

* Think of a value or characteristic of the deceased that you would like to pass on to your children. Create a symbol (acronym, original design, sign, etc.) that represents that value or characteristic. Place the symbol on the dashboard of your car or in a significant place in your home as a reminder to *live and demonstrate* the value or characteristic to your children. This symbol can also become a symbol of hope or an expression of a desire or goal for the future.

* Listen to a song like *My Heart Will Go On* by Celene Dion. Use it to remind you of specific memories of your loved one, of your extraordinary experience, and of love that death can never destroy.

* To trigger a pleasant memory place a favorite flower of the deceased next to his picture.

* Ask yourself the question, "How am I better off for having known her?" What memory of your loved one came to mind when answering the question? Take it and build it into your memory bank to be used specifically to counter the sadness that revisits during the "year of the firsts."

* Take an object belonging to the deceased that may or may not be associated with your extraordinary experience (ring, watch, dog tags, medal, gold chain, special hat, souvenir, something you saw in your experience, etc.) Have it made or reshape it yourself into a piece of jewelry, a lapel pin or something you

can wear as a reminder of your loved one, or of a particular loving memory.

* When you are alone, you may want to hum or sing the deceased's favorite song or a song whose lyrics have special meaning and will serve as a way to imprint a specific memory of your years together . Incidentally, singing is not only good for memory retention; it is considered a very healthy activity for optimal brain function. You may also wish to consider reciting a poem or other inspirational message that was written by the deceased, or that he liked to read, that gives you comfort and recollection of cherished memories.

* Plan an event for the sole reason of its memory potential, so that you can use at a time when you are alone or feeling low.

One final note: It is never too late to create peaceful memories, scented memories, even memories that will come unbidden and create good feelings within. All it takes is intent, a little imagination, and the conviction that memories have a distinct purpose: using the past to make a better future. This means always honoring what you had, but realizing you must continue on with life "until we meet again."

Our life stories are constant works-in-progress and it is certain that we will all continue to meet the extraordinary and the unexpected experience in ways we never thought possible. Let's stay alert for and *expect* these opportunities to present themselves as we continue to honor the sea of mystery and change that is a part of every life.

Do not weep, for I shall be more useful to you after my death
And I shall help you then more effectively than during my life.
The remarks of the dying
St. Dominic to his brothers

Author's Request

I am continually searching for accounts of extraordinary and unexpected experiences from anyone who at the time of the experience was mourning the death of a loved one. In particular, I would appreciate hearing from anyone who has had an experience and how it was used to cope with the loss of your loved one. This information could be helpful to others who have had similar experiences. Please send this information to:

Louis E. LaGrand
Loss Education Associates
450 Fairway Isles Drive
Venice, Florida 34292
E-mail: BL450@aol.com

If you have a child who has had an extraordinary experience please also consider sending the account along with how it helped the child deal with the loss of the loved one.

Suggested Readings

The following readings are offered to give the reader a variety of choices in examining extraordinary experiences. Inclusion of a specific title does not necessarily imply that I endorse the book in whole or in part. This reading list will hopefully provide you with the opportunity to appreciate the great diversity of situations in which the experience unfolds, insight into the people who have been gifted with the experience, and an awareness of differences of opinion on the subject among authors and researchers.

Anderson, Joan Wester. WHERE MIRACLES HAPPEN. Brooklyn, NY: Brett Books, Inc., 1994.

Anderson, Ken. COINCIDENCES: ACCIDENT OR DESIGN. Sidney: Collins, Angus & Robertson, 1991.

Barbato, Michael, et al. "Parapsychological Phenomena Near the Time of Death." JOURNAL OF PALLIATIVE CARE. (Summer 1999), 15, 30-37.

Bosco, A. "White Bird." GUIDEPOSTS. (September, 1966).

Bramblett, J. WHEN GOODBYE IS FOREVER: LEARNING TO LIVE AGAIN AFTER THE LOSS OF A CHILD. New York: Ballantine Books, 1991. (See Pages 147-157.)

Canfield, J. & Hansen, M. CHICKEN SOUP FOR THE SOUL. Deerfield Beach, FL: Health Communications, Inc., 1993. (See pages 5-7.)

Chance, S. STRONGER THAN DEATH: When Suicide Touches Your Life. New York: W.W. Norton, 1992. (See pages 114-116.)

Cosgrove, J. "Our Consoling Visitor." VENTURE INWARD. (January/ February, 1994).

Cox-Chapman, M. THE CASE FOR HEAVEN. New York: G.P. Putnam, 1995. (See pages 33-34, 39.)

Currie, I. YOU CANNOT DIE. Rockport, MA: Element Books, 1995. (See pages 19-20.)

Devers, Edie. "Experiencing the Deceased." FLORIDA NURSING REVIEW 2 (January 1988): 7-13.

Devers, Edie. GOODBYE AGAIN: EXPERIENCES WITH DEPARTED LOVED ONES. Kansas City: Andrews & McMeel, 1997.

Durkee, C. & Cooper, J. "The Bee Gees Search for Life After Disco." PEOPLE. (August 7, 1989).

Eliach, Yaffa. HASIDIC TALES OF THE HOLOCAUST. New York: Oxford University Press, 1982. (See pages 39-41, 169-172.)

Finley, Mitch. WHISPERS OF LOVE: Encounters with Deceased Relatives and Friends. New York: Crossroads, 1995.

Flammarion, Camille. THE UNKNOWN. London, 1900.

Freeman, E. TOUCHED BY ANGELS. New York: Warner Books, 1993. (See pages 1-9.)

Garfield, P. THE DREAM MESSENGER. New York: Simon & Schuster, 1997.

Gean, C. "Awakened by an Angel." BEREAVEMENT MAGAZINE (July/August, 1994).

Gottlieb, A. "How Your Dreams Can Heal You." McCALL'S (July 1994): 84, 86-89, 138.

Greeley, Andrew. "The Paranormal is Normal: A Sociologist Looks at Parapsychology." THE JOURNAL OF THE AMERICAN SOCIETY FOR PSYCHICAL RESEARCH 85 (1991): 367-374.

Greeley, Andrew. RELIGION AS POETRY. Transaction Publications, 1995. (See Chapter 12.)

Greeley, Andrew. THE SOCIOLOGY OF THE PARANORMAL. Beverley Hills, CA: Sage Publications, 1975.

Green, M. & Mathison, D. "The Drama Behind Mask." PEOPLE. (March 18, 1985).

Guggenheim, W. & Guggenheim, J. HELLO FROM HEAVEN. New York: Bantam, 1996.

Halberstam, Yitta & Leventhal, Judith. SMALL MIRACLES. Holbrook, MA: Adams Media Corporation, 1997. (See pages 143-144.)

Halberstram, Yitta & Leventhal, Judith. SMALL MIRACLES OF LOVE AND FRIENDSHIP. Holbrook, MA: Adams Media Corporation, 1999.

Haraldson, Erlendur. "Survey of Claimed Encounters with the Dead." OMEGA 19 (1988-89): 103-113.

Haraldsson, Erlendur. "The Iyengar-Kirti Case: An Apparitional Case of the Bystander Type," JOURNAL OF THE SOCIETY FOR PSYCHICAL RESEARCH (1987): 54, No. 806.

Harlow, S. R. A LIFE AFTER DEATH. New York: Doubleday, 1961. (See Chapters 3 and 4.)

Hart, H. "Six Theories about Apparitions," PROCEEDINGS OF THE SOCIETY FOR PSYCHICAL RESEARCH (1956): 50, 153-239.

Heckler, Richard. CROSSINGS: Everyday People, Unexpected Events, and Life-Affirming Change. New York: Harcourt Brace, 1998.

Hopcke, Robert. THERE ARE NO ACCIDENTS. New York: Riverhead Books, 1997.

Hull, J. & M. HEAVEN-WHY DOUBT? The Wynstay Press, 1997, 21 Wynstay Rd., Wirral, Merseyside, England, L47 5AR.

Hurley, Tom. "Dwelling with the Mystery of Death." NOETIC SCIENCES REVIEW (Spring 1994): 6-7.

Inglis, Brian. COINCIDENCES: A MATTER OF CHANCE—OR SYNCHRONICITY? London: Hutchinson, 1990.

Jung, Carl. MEMORIES, DREAMS, REFLECTIONS. New York: Vintage Books, 1965. (See pages 312-314.)

Jung, Carl. SYNCHRONICITY. Princeton, NJ: Princeton University Press, 1960.

Kalish, Richard and David Reynolds, "Phenomenological Reality and Post-Death Contact," JOURNAL FOR THE SCIENTIFIC STUDY OF RELIGION, 12, 2 (June 1973), 209-221

Kastenbaum, Robert. IS THERE LIFE AFTER DEATH? London: Multimedia Books Limited, 1995. (See pages 90-96.)

Kelsey, Morton. DREAMS: A WAY TO LISTEN TO GOD. New York: Paulist Press, 1978.

Kelsey, Morton. AFTERLIFE:The Other Side of Dying. New York: Crossroad, 1982. (See pages 95-102.)

Klass, D., Silverman, P., & Nickman, S. (eds.), CONTINUING BONDS. Philadelphia: Taylor & Francis, 1996.

Kubler-Ross, E. DEATH IS OF VITAL IMPORTANCE. Barrytown, NY: Station Hill Press, 1995. (See pages 95-98.)

LaGrand, Louis. MESSAGES AND MIRACLES: EXTRAORDINARY EXPERIENCES OF THE BEREAVED. St. Paul, MN: Llewellyn Publications, 1999.

LaGrand, Louis. AFTER-DEATH COMMUNICATION: FINAL FAREWELLS. St. Paul, MN: Llewellyn Publications, 1997.

LaGrand, Louis. "Are We Missing Opportunities to Help the Bereaved?" THE FORUM NEWSLETTER, Vol. 23 (September/October 1997): 5.

LaGrand, Louis. "Extraordinary Experiences of the Bereaved." THE PSI RESEARCHER (November 1996) No. 23:8-11.

Lawson, Lee. "Love Letters from the Infinite." IONS NOETIC SCIENCES REVIEW (September-November 2000) No. 53:29-31.

Lewis, C.S. A GRIEF OBSERVED. New York: Bantam, 1980. (See pages 85-87.)

LIFE BEYOND DEATH. Pleasantville, NY: The Reader's Digest Association, Inc. 1992. (See pages 90-92, 98-99.)

Lightner, Candy. GIVING SORROW WORDS. New York:Warner Books, 1990. (See pages 212-214.)

Linn, E. PREMONITIONS, VISITATIONS AND DREAMS. The Publisher's Mark, P.O. Box 6939, Incline Village, Nevada, 89450, 1991.

Lord, J. "This May Sound Crazy..." MADDVOCATE. (Spring, 1991- Published by Mothers Against Drunk Driving).

Martin, J. & Romanowski, P. LOVE BEYOND LIFE. New York: HarperCollins, 1997.

Mackenzie, Andrew. HAUNTINGS AND APPARITIONS. London: Grenada, 1983.

Mackenzie, Andrew. THE SEEN AND THE UNSEEN. London: Grenada, 1989.

Matott, J. MY GARDEN VISITS. New York: Ballantine Books, 1996.

McCarthy, D. "One Gold Angel." CATHOLIC DIGEST (August 1992).

Morrell, D. FIREFLIES. New York: E.P. Dutton, 1988. (See pages 33-47.)

Morse, M. PARTING VISIONS. New York: Villard Books, 1994.

Morsilli, R. "I Still See Him Everywhere." READER'S DIGEST (July 1984).

Myers, F.W.H. HUMAN PERSONALITY AND ITS SURVIVAL OF BODILY DEATH. New Hyde Park, New York: University Books, 1961.

Oliveira, Jacquelyn. THE CASE FOR LIFE BEYOND DEATH. Elm Grove, Wisconsin: William Laughton Publishers, 2000. (See Chapter 10.)

Olsen, P., Suddeth, J., Peterson, P. & Egelhoff, C. "Hallucinations of Widowhood." JOURNAL OF THE AMERICAN GERIATRICS SOCIETY 33 (1985): 543-547.

Owens, N. "My Gift From God." SHARING & HEALING. (April/ June, 1994).

Peale, Norman V. THE TRUE JOY OF POSITIVE LIVING. New York: Morrow, 1984. (See pages 293-298.)

Phillips, J.B. THE RING OF TRUTH. New York: Macmillan, 1967.

Radin, Dean. THE UNCONSCIOUS UNIVERSE: THE SCIENTIFIC TRUTH OF PSYCHIC PHENOMENA. San Francisco: Harper Edge, 1997.

Rees, W. "The Hallucinations of Widowhood." BRITISH MEDICAL JOURNAL 4 (1971): 37-41.

Richo, David. UNEXPECTED MIRACLES. New York: Crossroad, 1998.

Rogo, D. "Spontaneous Contact with the Dead: Perspectives from Grief Counseling, Sociology, and Parapsychology." In Doore, G. WHAT SURVIVES? Los Angeles: Jeremy P. Tarcher, 1990. (See pages 76-91.)

Sechrist, Elsie. DEATH DOES NOT PART US. Virginia Beach, A.R.E. Press, 1992.

Seymour, S. & Neligan, H. TRUE IRISH GHOST STORIES. New York: Causeway Books, 1974. (See pages 146-174.)

Spangler, Ann. DREAMS: True Stories of Remarkable Encounters with God. Grand Rapids, MI: Zondervan Publishing House, 1997.

Sparrow, Scott. I AM WITH YOU ALWAYS: True Stories of Encounters with Jesus. New York: Bantam, 1995.

Treece, Patricia. MESSENGERS: After-Death Appearances of Saints and Mystics. Huntington, IN:Our Sunday Visitor Publishing Division, 1995.

von Franz, Marie-Louise. ON DREAMS AND DEATH. Boston: Shambala, 1986. (See pages xv, 111-114, 133.)

Wakefield, Dan. EXPECT A MIRACLE: The Miraculous Things That Happen To Ordinary People. San Francisco: HarperSanFrancisco, 1995. (See Chapter 8.)

Walker, P.R. EVERY DAY'S A MIRACLE. New York: Avon Books, 1995. (See pages 85-87.)

Williams, O. TEMPTATIONS: New York: G.P. Putnam, 1988. (See page 163.)

Winter, W. THE LIFE OF DAVID BELASCO. New York: Benjamin Bloom, Inc., 1972 (See pages 466-468.)

Wiitala, G. HEATHER'S RETURN. Virginia Beach, VA: A.R.E. Press, 1996.

Woods, Kay Witmer. VISIONS OF THE BEREAVED. Pittsburgh: Sterling House Publisher, 1998.

Wright, Sylvia Hart. "Paranormal Contact with the Dying: 14 Contemporary Death Coincidences." JOURNAL OF THE SOCIETY FOR PSYCHICAL RESEARCH. 63 (October 1999): 258-267.

Wright, Sylvia Hart. "Experiences of Spontaneous Psychokinesis After Bereavement." JOURNAL OF THE SOCIETY FOR PSYCHICAL RESEARCH. 62 (July 1998): 385-395.

Zinsser, W. (ed.) SPIRITUAL QUESTS: The Art and Craft of Religious Writing. Boston: Houghton Mifflin, 1988. (See pages 105-106.)

Books On Grief

The books listed below are but a fraction of the many good books dealing with grief and mourning. I have found these to be useful. It is recommended that before purchasing any book check with your local library or bookstore and page through it to be sure it is what you are looking for.

Attig, Thomas. HOW WE GRIEVE: RELEARNING THE WORLD. New York: Oxford University Press, 1996.

Boss, Pauline. AMBIGUOUS LOSS. Cambridge, MA: Harvard University Press, 1999.

Davidson, Joyce and Doka, Kenneth. LIVING WITH GRIEF AT WORK, AT SCHOOL, AT WORSHIP. Levittown, PA: Brunner/Mazel, 1999.

Dietz, Bob. LIFE AFTER LOSS. Tucson, AZ: Fisher Books, 1988.

Doka, Kenneth. (ed.) DISENFRANCHISED GRIEF. Lexington, MA: Lexington Books, 1989.

Doka, Kenneth. (ed.) LIVING WITH GRIEF: CHILDREN, ADO-LESCENTS, AND LOSS. Washington, DC: Hospice Foundation of America, 2000.

Fitzgerald, Helen. THE GRIEVING CHILD. New York: Simon & Schuster, 1992.

Fitzgerald, Helen. THE MOURNING HANDBOOK. New York: Simon & Schuster, *1994.*

Hickman, Martha Whitmore. HEALING AFTER LOSS. New York: Avon, 1994.

Jackson, Edgar. UNDERSTANDING GRIEF. Nashville, TN: Abingdon, 1957.

Kelley, Patricia. COMPANION TO GRIEF: FINDING CONSOLATION WHEN SOMEONE YOU LOVE HAS DIED. New York: Simon & Schuster, 1997.

LaGrand, Louis. COPING WITH SEPARATION AND LOSS AS A YOUNG ADULT. Springfield, IL: Charles C. Thomas, 1986.

Sanders, Catherine. SURVIVING GRIEF AND LEARNING TO LIVE AGAIN. New York: John Wiley, 1992.

Staudacher, Carol. BEYOND GRIEF. Oakland, CA: New Harbinger, 1988.

Welshons, John. AWAKENING FROM GRIEF. Little Falls, NJ: Open Heart Publications, 2000.

Westberg, Granger. GOOD GRIEF. Philadelphia: Fortress Press, 1971.

Bibliography

Allen, James. AS A MAN THINKETH. Harrington Park, NJ: R.H. Sommer, 1987.

Brown, Anna Robertson. WHAT IS WORTHWHILE? Cutchogue, NY: Buccaneer Books, 1996.

Bucholz, Esther Schaler. THE CALL OF SOLITUDE. New York: Simon & Schuster, 1997.

Frankl, Viktor. MAN'S SEARCH FOR MEANING. New York: Washington Square Press, 1963.

Frankl, Viktor. MAN'S SEARCH FOR ULTIMATE MEANING. New York: Plenum, 1997, 34.

Harman, Willis & Rheingold, Howard. HIGHER CREATIVITY: Liberating the Unconscious for Breakthrough Insights. Los Angeles: Tarcher, 1984.

Havel, Vaclav. DISTURBING THE PEACE. New York: Knopf, 1990, 181-183.

Jung, Carl. MEMORIES, DREAMS, REFLECTIONS. New York: Pantheon, 1961, 340.

Kinkade, Thomas. LIGHTPOSTS FOR LIVING. New York: Warner, 1999, 219.

Kipfer, Barbara Ann. THE WISH LIST. New York: Workman Publishing, 1997.

Nouwen, Henri. THE INNER VOICE OF LOVE. New York: Doubleday, 1996.

O'Donohue, John. ANAM CARA. New York: HarperCollins, 1997.

O'Donohue, John. ETERNAL ECHOES. New York: HarperCollins, 1999.

Pavlat, Eric. "Godincidence." NEW COVENANT. (January 1999), 31.

Raymo, Chet. SKEPTICS AND TRUE BELIEVERS. New York: Walker, 1998.

Reynolds, John. THE HALO EFFECT: How Volunteering Can Lead to a More Fulfilling Life—A Better Career. New York: Golden Books, 1998.

Schuler, Robert. POWER THOUGHTS. New York: HarperCollins, 1993.

Shallis, Michael. ON TIME. Penguin, Harmondsworth, 1982, 140.

Siegel, Bernard. PEACE, LOVE, AND HEALING. New York: Harper & Row, 1989.

Wiederkehr, Sister Macrina. SEASONS OF YOUR HEART: PRAYERS AND REFLECTIONS. San Francisco: HarperSanFrancisco, 1991.

Zeller, Max. THE DREAM: VISION OF THE NIGHT. Boston: Sigo Press, 1990.

Index

9 780595 178698